SEX THERAPY WITH EROTICALLY MARGINALIZED CLIENTS

Sex Therapy with Erotically Marginalized Clients: Nine Principles of Clinical Support provides a clinical guide to relational sex therapy with individuals, partnerships, polyships, and alternative family structures where one or more of the clients are erotically marginalized. This term refers to people who are at risk of being pathologized and oppressed both outside and inside the clinical setting due to their gender identities, sexual orientations, or sexual practices.

The book outlines nine principles for therapeutic practice which meet the needs of erotically marginalized clients, whose forms of sexuality and desire are rarely spoken about and for whom there is a dearth of language in therapeutic contexts. Each principle concludes with a series of "key points" and then followed by illustrative clinical case studies, contributed by sex therapists and clinicians who self-identify as erotically marginalized and who also work with erotically marginalized clients. The book also provides a full glossary, "Defining Erotically Marginalized Identities."

The authors and case contributors use a radical and affirming lens to examine erotically marginalized identities that are often neglected. The book bridges gaps between the past, present, and future in the field of sex therapy and greatly expands the diversity of experiences and identities within the field, particularly the experience of multiple oppressions.

The book marks a valuable contribution not only to sex therapists but to the wider clinical and therapeutic community.

Damon M. Constantinides, PhD, LCSW, is an individual, relationship, and sex therapist in Philadelphia, PA. He is also adjunct faculty in the Human Sexuality Program at Widener University.

Shannon L. Sennott, LICSW, is the co-founder of Translate Gender, Inc. and The Center for Psychotherapy and Social Justice in Northampton, MA, as well as, adjunct Faculty at the Smith School for Social Work.

Davis Chandler, LICSW, is an individual, family, relationship, and group therapist in Western MA. They utilize a social justice framework focusing on gender diversity and erotically marginalized clients.

"This is a game-changing book for sex therapists and other practitioners working across gender, sex, and relationship diversity. It provides a clear framework for working affirmatively with erotically marginalized clients, illustrated by a powerful range of case contributions which highlight the impact of intersecting oppressions and the diversity of client experiences. Principles are helpfully divided into sections focusing on foundations, practice, and systems, which help the reader to explore how they might work ethically and with integrity, for example by naming systemic oppressions, by challenging binary thinking, by emphasizing clients' own narratives, and by practising active allyship within wider communities. An essential addition to any practitioner's reading list. Highly recommended."

Meg-John Barker, PhD, author of *Queer: A Graphic History, Life Isn't Binary, Mindfulness in Sex and Relationship Therapy* and the British Association for Counseling and Psychotherapy resource on gender, sexual, and relationship diversity.

"This is a clinically sophisticated yet highly accessible text. This book explores, in an engaging and in-depth manner, the experiences of and therapeutic principles for working with erotically marginalized clients. A unique and indispensable component of the text is the use of powerful and detailed clinical vignettes, which not only describe clients but also illuminate the therapists' own process. Practical advice is provided throughout the book—yet this advice is far from a set of simplified steps of 'what to do.' Rather, the authors engage the reader in the gritty realness of working as real people with real clients, and their advice is informed by and reflects that realness, in all its messy and complex glory. The contributors are diverse in their intersectional identities and personal and professional experiences, and the style and content of the chapters mirror that diversity. The result is an eclectic collection of perspectives and content, whereby a reader does not necessarily have to read the entire book in order or in its entirety to effectively use and benefit from it. Careful explanation of key terms, and the inclusion of user-friendly clinical resources and forms, are also key features of the book. In sum, this is a rich and interesting resource that clinicians and other professionals will surely find of great interest."

Abbie Goldberg, PhD, professor of psychology and Director, Women's and Gender Studies Program, Clark University

"As a psychotherapist and trainer, I am beyond excited that this book is now a resource for our communities. The information is clear, thoughtfully laid out, and fills a much-needed gap in the field. Case examples beautifully demonstrate the nine principles that clinicians can use to better serve erotically marginalized clients, and this is done very skilfully and grounded in an intersectional, social justice framework. I recommend it to anyone who works with clients on topics related to gender and sexuality. Well done!"

Sand Chang, PhD, licenced psychologist and author of *A Clinician's Guide to Gender-Affirming Care*

SEX THERAPY WITH EROTICALLY MARGINALIZED CLIENTS

Nine Principles of Clinical Support

Damon M. Constantinides,
Shannon L. Sennott, and
Davis Chandler

Routledge
Taylor & Francis Group
NEW YORK AND LONDON

First published 2019
by Routledge
2 Park Square, Milton Park, Abingdon, Oxon OX14 4RN

and by Routledge
52 Vanderbilt Avenue, New York, NY 10017

Routledge is an imprint of the Taylor & Francis Group, an informa business

British Library Cataloguing-in-Publication Data
A catalogue record for this book is available from the British Library

Library of Congress Cataloging-in-Publication Data
Names: Constantinides, Damon M., author. | Sennott, Shannon L., author. | Chandler, Davis, author.
Title: Sex therapy with erotically marginalized clients / Damon M. Constantinides, Shannon L. Sennott and Davis Chandler.
Description: Milton Park, Abingdon, Oxon ; New York, NY : Routledge, 2019. | Includes index.
Identifiers: LCCN 2018054127 (print) | LCCN 2018055131 (ebook) | ISBN 9781315616780 (Master eBook) | ISBN 9781138671805 (hardback) | ISBN 9781138671812 (pbk.) | ISBN 9781315616780 (ebk)
Subjects: LCSH: Sex addiction—Treatment.
Classification: LCC RC560.S43 (ebook) | LCC RC560.S43 C66 2019 (print) | DDC 616.85/833—dc23
LC record available at https://lccn.loc.gov/2018054127

ISBN: 978-1-138-67180-5 (hbk)
ISBN: 978-1-138-67181-2 (pbk)
ISBN: 978-1-315-61678-0 (ebk)

Typeset in Minion
by Swales & Willis Ltd, Exeter, Devon, UK

CONTENTS

FIGURES AND TABLES

Figures

Tables

AUTHOR BIOGRAPHIES

Damon M. Constantinides, PhD, LCSW, provides individual, relationship, and sex therapy in Philadelphia, PA. He is a trans and queer identified therapist who has the privilege to work with trans and queer adults and teens. He works towards a world that makes space for people of all genders, identities, and bodies to heal and find joy both in their lives, including their sexual selves. Dr. Constantinides is a trainer and supervisor for the Advanced Program in Transgender Mental Health at Widener University where he is also adjunct faculty in the Human Sexuality Program. Damon provides consultation and supervision through his private practice (www.drdamonc.com) and at Relationship and Sex Therapy Collective and is especially interested in supporting queer and trans therapists, social workers, and clinicians.

Shannon L. Sennott, LICSW, CST, is the co-founder of Translate Gender, Inc. and the Center for Psychotherapy and Social Justice, she was clinically trained at the Smith School for Social Work and the Eastern Group Psychotherapy Society in New York City, and is an AASECT certified sex therapist. Shannon is a faculty member at the Smith School for Social Work, teaching family theory and sex theory, as well as maintaining a full time private practice at the Center for Psychotherapy and Social Justice in Northampton, Massachusetts. Shannon utilizes a transfeminist therapeutic approach in her work with individuals, adolescents, and families, her interests extend to working with couples, consensually non-monogamous and polyamorous relationships, and groups, and she especially enjoys working with those in alternative family structures. Her clinical orientation is influenced by both narrative therapy and dialogic practice traditions. Shannon's published paper in *Women and Therapy Journal*, introduces her transfeminist therapeutic approach, 'Gender Disorder as Gender Oppression: A Transfeminist Approach to Rethinking the Pathologization of

Gender Non-Conformity'. More recently, Shannon delivered the keynote for the Ackerman Institute for the Family annual conference in 2018 and she is enjoying clinically supervising and training other clinicians, institutions, and organizations in their work with erotically marginalized people.

Davis Chandler, LICSW graduated from the Smith College School for Social Work. They live in Western Massachusetts and are the co-director of Translate Gender, Inc. where they currently co-lead therapy groups for trans and gender nonconforming young people, families and couples, as well as offer education, training and advocacy work related to gender, sexual orientation, sexual practices, power, oppression and privilege. They also maintain a private practice with the Center for Psychotherapy and Social Justice working with individuals, relationships and families. Additionally, they work at a small nonprofit serving adults experiencing extreme states of mind and/or major life disruptions. Prior they worked as a family therapist with children and their families in a community mental health setting. Davis self-identifies as queer and nonbinary/trans.

CONTRIBUTOR BIOGRAPHIES

Amy Basford-Pequet, LICSW CGP is the Clinical Director of Northampton Sex Therapy Associates, LLC and the Program Director of The Center for All Men and Sexual Health, both housed in Florence, MA. Amy identifies as a white, queer, fat, cis, femme of working class descent with many privileges related to whiteness, functional ability, mobility, current class status, citizenship status, and education. Amy believes in the power of systemic change through exploration, understanding, and shifting within the personal, intrapsychic, and embodied sense of self and self as a sexual being. She holds the importance of personal accountability, radical vulnerability, and grief processes as foundational parts of change. Amy's clinical work draws on trauma, relational, queer, feminist, systems, and group theories and is also informed by principles of sexual health, intersectionality and sociopolitical positioning and (de)construction, harm reduction, and motivational interviewing.

Jaycelle Basford-Pequet, LICSW is the Director and Founder of The Institute for Emerging Adulthood, Inc. a group private practice in Western Massachusetts which compassionately engages people of color and LGBTQ identified adults within an anti-oppression framework providing psychotherapy for being and becoming in changing terrain. They are the Associate Director of Field Education and Adjunct Assistant Professor at Smith College School for Social Work. They teach and present about queerness, race, and clinical practice with a particular interest in queer of color critique, Sensorimotor Psychotherapy and embodied experience. They have presented at the National Council on Family Relations, the American Group Psychotherapy Association, and the American Psychiatric Association.

Eve N. Bogdanove, LICSW is a sex & gender feminist therapist working with children, youth, families, partners and polycules through an anti-oppression lens in the small New England town of Greenfield, MA. She currently facilitates three long standing groups: Partners of Survivors, Anger Management for young adult queers, and queers who use non-consensual power & control in intimate relationships. Eve earned her MSW from Hunter College OYR Program in January 1997 after working in the field as a paraprofessional since 1988. Eve trained in feminist and psychodynamic therapy and, along with her years of activism in the LGBTQ, pro-feminist male, AIDS and women's health movements, Eve came upon the field of sex therapy after observing the deficit of kink competent therapists within her own communities and sought out mentors and trainers who could teach her what she needed to know. Eve especially appreciates the work of Esther Perel, Terry Real, John Gottman, Margie Nichols, Charles Moser, Peggy Kleinplatz, David Ortman and Joseph Winn.

Dr. Lexx Brown-James (She|Her|Doctor) is a licensed marriage and family therapist and certified human sexuality educator. Dr. Lexx is a keynote speaker, trainer of helping professionals and graduate level educator who provides comprehensive, medically accurate, inclusive and justice-oriented sexuality education and services. She is the owner of The Institute for Sexuality & Intimacy, LLC in St. Louis, Mo where she works on healing for those who need support. Dr. Lexx is currently completing two manuscripts, including a children's book. In her therapeutic practice, Dr. Lexx uses EMDR, Emotion Focused Therapy, and Contextual Therapy to help her clients resolve past trauma, increase self-esteem, gain intimacy, and move forward in their lives with positivity.

Dr. Erika Evans-Weaver (she/her/they) holds a PhD in Human Sexuality Studies from Widener University, in addition to Masters' Degrees in Human Sexuality Education (Widener University) and Marriage and Family Therapy (La Salle University). She holds a License in Marriage and Family Therapy. Dr. Evans-Weaver maintains a boutique private practice called L.I.F.E (Lessons in Freedom and Empowerment). Erika sees therapy as an opportunity to help people gain a deeper understanding of the lessons they've accrued in their life journey, exploring how emotional and relational wellness is defined personally which results in them feeling more empowered to live life freely and authentically. It's an individualized approach because each person and accompanying narrative is unique. Dr. Evans-Weaver is a Clinical Assistant Professor in the Center for Human Sexuality Studies Graduate program at Widener University and continues to support the development of burgeoning Marriage and Family Therapists at La Salle University.

Lourdes Dolores Follins earned her M.S.W. and PhD in Social Work from New York University. As a Black queer femme psychotherapist, a behavioral scientist, and an organizational consultant, Lourdes has worked with and for adolescents and adults of color who are marginalized because of their racial, gender and/or sexual identities for over 25 years. Her clinical and research interests are resilience and resistance in LGBTQI people in the African diaspora; decision making in young gay men of color; female and femme sex workers' resilience and resistance; using EMDR to liberate people of color; and health disparities faced by LGBTQI people of color. Lourdes has published several academic articles and book chapters about the factors that impact and enhance the health of LGBTQI people of color, as well as an award-winning book on *Black LGBT Health in the United States.*

Anastasia Fujii, LCSW, is a psychotherapist in private practice, as well as an LGBTQ+ cultural humility consultant and trainer. Anastasia decided to pursue psychotherapy professionally after personally struggling to find care services that resonated with their life experience as a chronically ill, queer, mixed race, person of color. Anastasia works primarily with QTPOC individuals, partnerships, and families, with a clinical focus on identity, family dynamics, trauma, chronic illness and disability. Anastasia's approach to psychotherapy is relational and social justice oriented; recognizing and integrating the biological, psychological, and social aspects of experience, as well as the individual, institutional, and cultural roots of issues as they arise. As a consultant and trainer, Anastasia supports organizations and academic institutions working to increase LGBTQ+ cultural humility practices through education and policy change. Anastasia lives in Philadelphia, PA with their family.

Laura A. Jacobs, LCSW-R, is a Trans and GenderQueer-identified psychotherapist, activist, author, and public speaker in the New York City area working with transgender and gender-nonbinary, LGBTQ+, and alternate lifestyle communities of BDSM, nonmonogamy, and sexwork. They serve as Chair of the Board of Directors for the Callen-Lorde Community Health Center in NYC, have been featured in television, radio, and print media, and have presented at countless community and healthcare conferences, professional associations, medical schools, and other organizations. Laura is the recipient of a 2018 Gay City News Impact Award as well as the 2017 Dorothy Kartashovich Award by the Community Health Center Association of New York State. As Lawrence Jacobs, they worked as a musician, composer, photographer, and less glamorous corporate middle management. www.LauraAJacobs.com.

Rachel Keller is a clinical social worker and sex therapist in practice in Northampton, Massachusetts. She works with individuals, people in relationships, and families, and really enjoys working with people in varied relationship structures. Her work often uses narrative, feminist, disability rights, social justice, and attachment theory approaches. She is particularly interested in the intersections of sex and disability, and feels there is great value in creating clinical practices that hold all people in its frameworks.

Ellie Lipton is a queer identified social worker and psychotherapist, passionate about deconstructing systems of oppression and ideas of "normalcy." Ellie works with erotically marginalized children, families, and adults through a small private practice at the Center for Psychotherapy and Social Justice, as well as with adults experiencing extreme mind and mood states at a nonprofit mental health organization in Northampton, MA. Ellie's work is rooted in critical race studies, queer theory, psychodynamic theories, and holistic approaches to health and wellness.

Dr. AndreAs Neumann-Mascis is a clinical psychologist with areas of specialty that include gender variance, trauma, and physical and psychiatric disability. Dr. Neumann-Mascis has worked as a provider, educator, advocate and activist across communities and has had access to working with complex people in a wide range of settings. Dr. Neumann-Mascis founded and developed The Meeting Point, a collaboration of independent healthcare providers in Jamaica Plain, MA. The Meeting Point serves intersecting communities including the LGBTQ community, survivors of trauma, and disability communities. The Meeting Point is founded in the knowledge that social justice heals, and is growing to meet the unique strengths and needs of people through community activity, personalized approaches to well-ness, and physical and mental health care that is responsive to the needs of complex bodies and identities.
www.themeetingpoint.org.

Dulcinea Alex Pitagora holds an MA in Psychology from the New School for Social Research, an MSW from New York University, a MEd in human sexuality and PhD in clinical sexology from Widener University, and a CST from AASECT. Pitagora has a psychotherapy and sex therapy practice in Manhattan working with individuals, couples/multi-partner relationships, and poly/leather families. Pitagora's practice is holistic and integrative, person-centered and strengths-based, and is informed by personal involvement in the kink/BDSM, poly/CNM, queer/non-straight, trans/GNC, and sex work communities. Pitagora conducts research, lectures, and seminars; has published in peer-reviewed journals; and has presented at conferences on topics related to gender, sexuality, and relationship diversity. Pitagora is an adjunct professor of sexual health at New York University; is the founder of ManhattanAlternative.com, a sex-positive provider listing; and is a co-founder of the AltSex NYC Conference. Pitagora is Kink Doctor in the Web series by the same name.

Dr. Thomas Wood is a Pennsylvania licensed clinical social worker and certified sex therapist with the American Association of Sex Educators, Counselors, and Therapists (AASECT). He has his doctorate in Human Sexuality. Dr. Wood co-founded the Relationship and Sex Therapy Collective in Philadelphia and is adjunct faculty through the Human Sexuality Education Department at Widener University and the Department of Psychiatry at Temple University. In addition to his treatment of general psychological concerns, Dr. Wood is trained in the treatment of sexual and relationship problems. He specializes in male sexual concerns, disability, sexual identity, orientation, compulsive behaviors, trauma, and the impacts of spiritual abuse. Dr. Wood has presented on relationship and sexual topics on both a state and national level and has been recognized for his contributions to the field of sexuality.

PREFACE

Our Process

We, the authors of this book, met and got to know each other through different networks of therapists and at conferences. We had heard of each other, had attended each other's presentations, and over time we began to talk, connect and collaborate. The connection was organic and slow while also being intentional and purposeful. This project grew out of a presentation that two of the authors prepared for the 2015 AASECT conference, when one author was unable to attend and participate because of a death in their community the third of us stepped in and provided a supporting role. From the presentation came a meeting with a publisher, a book proposal and then this book.

During the writing of this book, between the three of us, we have lost a parent and became parents while living through a traumatizing political moment in our national history and the ensuing fear, heartbreak and outrage. We have had one of our two-year-old children break their femur and be confined in a Spica cast for five weeks. We have witnessed through our screens the shooting at the Pulse Nightclub in Orlando, we have heard of countless deaths and murders of people of color in our country, young black men and trans women of color. We have gotten involved, been overwhelmed, spoken up in our families and communities, felt empowered and helpless. We have experienced periods of blissful joy and of devastating heartbreak. We have done all this and also lived our lives, worked in our private practices and agency settings, and while not being in the same physical location we have gone through it all together, we could not have completed this process without a deep connection to one another both professionally and especially personally.

Writing this book has been arduous and intensive, inspiring and exciting. We met at least one Sunday a month for three hours and had many all-day writing retreats both in person and remotely. We began every meeting, regardless of length of time, with a personal check in, an update on the goings on of each other's lives. We kept in touch in the interim through witnessing each other's lives on social media and through email and text, but always carve out some face to face time, even if it required technology, to attend to the fabric of our connections to one another. During our longer retreats we met from 8am–6pm. We worked for the therapist 50-minute hour, leaving ourselves 10 minutes at the end of every hour to check in, ask questions, get snacks and be available to one another.

Each one of us has experienced erotic marginalization and have felt profoundly isolated at times in our lives. We continue to feel isolated and marginalized in our professional lives, for our own identity statuses, for focusing our clinical work on serving erotically marginalized clients and for writing this book. Being connected to one another and collaborating on this project has been the antidote to a sense of isolation, our relationships and commitment to the work make it all feel possible.

Despite our deep connections to one another and because of our commitment to this project, around a year into writing we all were struck by a discomfort underlying our work. We are all parts of communities of colleagues that are working with erotically marginalized clients, but we, three white, middle class sex therapists, were the sole authors of this book. We felt the call of our final principle, to build a community of colleagues and to work to center the voices of marginalized clinicians, especially therapists of color. We needed to expand our authorship and utilize our vibrant and diverse networks of colleagues to elicit new voices to weave into the fabric of this work. The dream of the case contributions was born and the work was fundamentally changed. Inviting in new voices brought a renewed enthusiasm, deepened the conversations, complicated our narratives and created something much bigger than we had ever imagined. We are profoundly grateful to our case contributors for putting their skilled clinical experiences into words, with authenticity, vulnerability, and transparency. This book became what it is because of our contributors, they are our community of erotically marginalized clinicians and sex therapists, and we are all each other's accomplices and colleagues.

ACKNOWLEDGMENTS

Working on this project has been a privilege. I would like to first thank my co-authors who have taught me so much about resilience, friendship, and clinical practice. For me this project was born out of need, a need to connect to other erotically marginalized clinicians, to feel mirrored and seen, and during a dark time to move our world slowly towards a place where all of us are seen and valued. I would like to thank the contributors both for their brilliant case studies and the work that they do on a daily basis supporting erotically marginalized clients. Thank you Linda Hawkins for your ongoing support of me and my work and Thomas Wood whose perspective has been invaluable throughout this project. It feels deeply important to acknowledge all of the trans and queer folks who have walked this road ahead of me and made it possible for me to be an out queer and trans therapist. And lastly, thank you Beth Pulcinella for working and loving at my side to create magic together and for believing so deeply in my work and Jacobia Constantinides for showing me all that is possible by being your fierce and loving self.

Damon Constantinides

Co-creating this work with Damon and Davis has been one of the most rewarding experiences of my life. I am honored to have been chosen by them to bring this work to life on the page. Similarly, I feel that my womantours have woven the most sturdy and buoyant network of guidance and support imaginable for me. Mary Olson, Jassy Timberlake, Arlene Lev, and Abbie Goldberg – you have been my beacons throughout this process, but also, and always, throughout my career and life. I want to acknowledge our contributors and all that they offered to this project. They did this while living their own radical and magical lives, they created case studies that have never been seen in print before. Our contributors are trailblazers, they too are my teachers, each one. I want to thank my parents, Lee Sennott-Miller and Jerry Miller. Jerry did not live to see this book to print but both of their love and adoration over a lifetime made me the kind of person who thought this project was possible, and they were by my side from the inception. Lastly, I want to thank my partner, Davis Chandler, for believing in this project and deciding to work with Damon and me on it, it has been an incredible journey of co-learning and co-living and I feel deep gratitude to you.

Shannon L. Sennott

There are countless people I could thank for supporting me in the completion of this project. First and foremost, I would like to thank my co-author/editors Damon and Shannon, for birthing the idea for this book and the original principles, for inviting me in, believing in me and trusting me to help make their visions a tangible reality. I would also like to thank the case contributors for coming into this process enthusiastically and thoughtfully, bringing a depth of insight and razor-sharp intellect to this project. They have all contributed hours upon hours of unpaid labor for which we are all endlessly grateful. I also could not have done this without the mentorship and guidance of Shannon Sennott, Phoebe Walker, and Mary Tibbetts who have helped me find my voice in this field and made space for me to take my seat. My family - of origin, queer, and chosen have all had my back and loved me endlessly through all ups and downs the journey of the last few years has included. My partner, Shannon, it's no coincidence this is your third mention, I would not be the person I am professionally, personally or relationally without your wisdom, love and spaciousness. Lastly, I would like to thank all of the multitudes of people who have come before me, the therapists, activists, thinkers, the queers, the gender complex creatures, the wild hearts and radical spirits who have lived their lives as fully as possible so that I could be here today living mine.

Davis Chandler

INTRODUCTION

Sex Therapy with Erotically Marginalized Clients: Nine Principles of Clinical Support

In the field of sex therapy there is a dearth of resources available to work with clients who are marginalized, fetishized, or discriminated against based on their sexual identity or sexual behavior. We developed nine principles of clinical support with accompanying case studies written by a diverse group of contributors, to be used as a tool by sex therapists working with erotically marginalized clients. Our aim is to provide a framework to address privilege and power in sex therapy practice and it is our hope that this book is the beginning of a much larger conversation as we continue to work to offer sex therapy that is accessible and competent to erotically marginalized clients.

It is ethically essential that therapists be able to recognize and name the intersections of identities related to sexuality and oppression. The term *erotically marginalized* describes people who are at risk of being pathologized and oppressed both outside and inside the clinical setting due to their sexual identities, orientations and practices. Erotically marginalized people can include those who identify as lesbian, gay, bisexual, pansexual, asexual, demisexual, queer, trans and gender nonconforming, nonbinary, intersex, polyamorous, consensually non-monogamous, kinky, BDSM practitioners, or who have alternative relational and sexual structures in general. This list is not exhaustive, nor is it meant to be. New language to describe the experiences of erotically marginalized people is constantly being developed. Erotically marginalized clients face stigma and discrimination in their lives and in clinical settings their identities and experiences are often overlooked and lack mirroring.

For many clients these marginalized identities or behaviors remain obscured and unnamed; the ability to give language to these subtle and nuanced experiences is at the cutting edge within the field of sex therapy. Thus far, the scope of therapeutic inquiry often ends at the point of coming out or walking a client through an identity development model until they experience integration. Over the last ten years there has been an expansion in the narrative of sexual practices, intimacy, and desire for erotically marginalized clients.

We address a gap in the field of sex therapy by building upon the tools currently available to work with marginalized clients. Using the term *erotically marginalized* we are able to focus on the shared experience of living with a marginalized sexual or gender identity and the ways that can affect desire and sexual behavior. Working from an intersectional perspective we make visible the complicated experience of navigating sexual practices and desire for people with multiple marginalized identities. These nine principles create a therapeutic structure for therapists to better meet the complex needs of clients.

We use the terms *clinician, therapist*, and *sex therapist* interchangeably throughout the book because these principles are relevant to the work of a larger body of providers than sex therapists alone. It is our belief that all clinical providers are in a unique position to begin to deepen their understanding of the needs of erotically marginalized clients in clinical settings in general, and in sex therapy settings specifically. For example, sex therapy models rooted in the binary gender system may not be able to properly affirm and support clients whose lived experience lies outside of that binary.

In this book we present a new approach to working with individuals, partnerships, polyships, and alternative family structures that is framed as a nine principle model for best practices in sex therapy. These nine principles include: (1) Maintain transparency and name systemic and individual oppressions, (2) Challenge binary thinking and its constrictions, (3) Support willingness to experience the anxiety of uncertainty, (4) Practice a relational and dialogic approach to sex therapy, (5) Emphasize clients' own words, knowledge and narratives, (6) Locate oneself and respond to clients' meta-communication, (7) Support participation of family and communities, (8) Practice active allyship, and (9) Build a community of colleagues. The nine principles provide tools for work with clients who are not just negotiating changes in their sexuality, gender, or relationship structure but are looking to deepen the intimacy of their sexual practices through creating language for the liminal unspoken awareness that lie between touch and how one feels desired by another when they are truly and authentically *seen* by a sexual partner.

The principles are divided into three sections that include foundational concepts, clinical practice tools, and larger system approaches. Each chapter will include a discussion of a principle using vignettes and examples from us, the editors, Damon Constantinides, Shannon Sennott, and Davis Chandler, followed by case studies written by clinical contributors who self-identify themselves as erotically marginalized. These case studies provide a glimpse into the way that the nine principles can be applied in practice. As we developed the principles based on our own experiences in our therapy and sex therapy practices we realized the necessity of including more voices than our own. In a parallel process, our ninth principle called on us to build a community of colleagues. We hope to diminish isolation in our work and that this book itself acts as a network of connected and committed therapists working to support each other, our clients, and communities.

Who We Are

There are three of us authoring and editing this book; we are all licensed clinical social workers and sex therapists who inhabit identities that are erotically marginalized. Principle One, maintain transparency and name systemic and individual oppressions, and Principle Six, locate oneself and respond to clients' meta-communication, provides an opportunity for us as therapists to identify our social location when we work with clients. In much the same way that we use social location to provide a context for our clients and model bringing our whole selves into the room, we feel it is important to do the same as authors.

Damon Constantinides

I hold many identities both from my current and past life experiences. Right now I am deeply connected to being a dad, a role that gives me joy and also feels echoed in my work as a therapist. I am white and a trans man with a middle class background who has had access to both undergraduate and graduate education. When I walk down the street I am usually seen as a white man and move through the world with white and often male privilege. I also identity strongly as queer and before transitioning actively identified as a dyke and a lesbian. My participation in lesbian, dyke, gay, queer, and trans communities both supports and roots me professionally and personally. I work in a private practice and at Relationship and Sex Therapy Collective in Philadelphia, PA supporting clients through individual or relationship psychotherapy. My clinical work has been greatly influenced by social work and sexuality education and I take inspiration from social justice, transfeminist, narrative, and mindfulness modalities. I also identify as a teacher and began my sexuality career as a Sexuality Educator at Planned Parenthood. Since then I've had the opportunity to teach human sexuality and sex therapy at both the undergraduate and graduate levels. Supporting other therapists to provide the highest quality services to marginalized clients drives my teaching, training, and writing projects. Inspired by my work with clients I've also helped organize therapists who want to provide low-fee services to Black Lives Matter Activists in Philadelphia and other major cities through the Healing for Activists project (www.healingforactivists.com). My roles as a dad, partner, child, community member, activist, artist, therapist, writer, teacher, and mentor feel intertwined and anchored by a worldview that sees the work of connecting to joy and healing ourselves and our world from pain, violence, and oppression as multifaceted and structural.

Shannon L. Sennott

I identify as a white queer femme cis woman. "Cis" in Latin means "in line with," my gender is in line with what was socially expected of my designated sex at birth as female. I identify as a person of size and have experienced marginalization within my family and larger social contexts throughout my life as a person of size. I was raised middle class and have educational privilege. I identify as a gender justice activist and educator, and am the co-founder of the advocacy and education organization, Translate Gender, Inc. Through activism and education, I work towards the liberation of all people from the gender binary system. I am an AASECT certified sex therapist and a LGBTQAI couples and family therapist at the Center for Psychotherapy and Social Justice in Northampton, Massachusetts. I am a pediatric gender specialist, and work with young people from ages 3–18. I utilize a transfeminist therapeutic approach in working with all erotically marginalized adolescents, individuals, and families. My clinical experience extends to working with people who identify as part of the kink and BDSM community, polyamorous relationships (polyships), and psychotherapeutic groups related to sexuality and gender. I was clinically trained at the Smith School for Social Work and the Eastern Group Psychotherapy Society in New York City. I currently reside and practice in the River Valley of Massachusetts, however, I lived in New York City for over a decade and during that time worked exclusively in queer and lesbian owned bars and clubs. This experience was a critical part of my identity development as an activist and queer person in the world. Over the last decade I have developed a broad range of specializations having completed clinical trainings in anxiety disorders, depressive and mood disorders, dual diagnosis, sexuality and gender identity concerns, grief and loss, and trauma.

Davis Chandler

I am a queer, white, nonbinary, trans-identified person. I use the pronouns they/them/theirs. Over the course of writing this book I also became a gestational parent and have navigated medical systems and the larger world as a nonbinary pregnant person. I was raised with significant class privilege for most of my younger life and am currently comfortably middle class. I experience unearned privilege based on my race and my class background. I was born and raised in the South in Atlanta, Georgia and spent my twenties living in San Francisco, and attended the Smith School for Social Work program while living in California. I currently reside in Western Massachusetts and am employed at a small nonprofit mental health organization working with adults with extreme mind states and major life disruptions. I am the co-director of Translate Gender, Inc., where I co-lead two therapy groups, one for trans and gender nonconforming young people and their families and the other for trans and gender nonconforming adults and their partners. Through Translate Gender, I also offer trainings and workshops and maintain a private practice with the Center for Psychotherapy and Social Justice. In all areas of my work, I believe that people are medicine, that through attentive, attuned, transparent, and authentic relationships, people can heal from the wounds caused by systemic oppression and marginalization, isolation and distressing mind states. I draw on narrative, transfeminist, relational, mindfulness, and open dialogue therapeutic lenses in my clinical work. Social justice is at the core of my work, it is my mission to resist white supremacy, patriarchy, cissexism, ableism, heterosexism, fatphobia, and all systems of oppression.

We all have both privileged and marginalized identities. The experience of living with these identities influences the lens through which we see the world and our work. Throughout this book we hope to remain transparent about marginalized and privileged identities, to de-center whiteness, and to center voices of people of color. It is our belief that if a therapist can self-identify their own privileged and marginalized identities, it will aid them in being able to support clients in doing the same. We may not share all of these identities with all of our clients, but having our own language to talk about them allows our identities to become dialogic tools of disclosure in the therapeutic context.

Influences and Frames

We developed these nine principles of clinical support for sex therapy with erotically marginalized clients by creating a web of clinical questions and then identifying influences and frames that helped us answer our questions. Dialogic Principles, Narrative Therapy, the Freedom Paradigm, and Intersectionality came up again and again in our conversations about how we approach our clinical work. Our approach is also influenced strongly by the ideas of Transfeminism and Queer Theory.

Dialogic principles, created by Mary Olson and Jaakko Seikkula, are based on the key elements of Open Dialogue and became our inspiration for the use of principles instead of a model that might run the risk of feeling rigid and prescriptive. The heart of dialogic clinical practice is a therapeutic setting that requires "presence, an attention to the living moment without a preconceived hypothesis or specific agenda" (Olson, Seikkula, & Ziedonis, 2014, p.5). Olson and Seikkula believe that there is a co-existence of multiple, separate and equally valid "voices," or points of view in any clinical interaction. This concept is inspired by what Bakhtin calls "polyphony." As described by Olson and Seikkula:

> *Within a "polyphonic conversation", there is space for each voice, thus reducing the gap between the so-called "sick" and "well". The collaborative exchange among all the different voices weaves new, more shared understandings to which everyone contributes an important thread. This results in a common experience which Bakhtin describes as "without rank".*
> *(Olson, Seikkula, & Ziedonis, 2014, p. 6).*

Narrative approach to therapy is designed to unravel the double binds within family systems and to address the oppression of marginalized identities within a larger societal context. Michael White's book *Re-authoring Lives* (1995) is an explicit expression of the theoretical foundation of narrative therapy. Narrative theory proposes that human beings are interpreting beings and that it is not possible to interpret human experience without access to some frame of intelligibility that will provide a context for understanding. The stories that are created and expressed in a therapeutic setting are believed to constitute this frame of intelligibility in the narrative approach. A narrative approach to therapy works on the assumption that there is a dominant *story* in western culture that pictures what it means to be person of moral worth in society. This dominant story emphasizes self-possession, self-containment, and self-actualization. We suggest in this book that another emphasis in the dominant westernized storyline is gender and sexual conformity. The autonomous, independent, and gender (and sexuality) conforming individual is the preferred cultural construction of being in western society. These stories of what a life should look like if it was lived "right" requires certain operations on our lives, much of which are gender and sexuality specific. These operations allow us to govern our thoughts, our relationship to others, our relationship to ourselves, and our relationship to our body.

These governing operations all serve to assist in the reproduction of the "privileged form" or dominant way of being in western culture. The narrative approach attempts to provide a therapeutic climate that thickens the plots of the subordinate storylines of life by exploring other ways of living and thinking. By facilitating the expression of lived experiences that have previously been neglected, alternative frames of intelligibility are able to surface within the life story of a person. Theoretically this approach opens the door to working with erotically marginalized clients because this encompasses any person who could be marginalized, fetishized, or oppressed based on their sexual identities or sexual practices.

The Freedom Paradigm, created by Fred J. Hanna is an overarching paradigm that encourages therapists to create a relationship between their counseling techniques and notions and ideologies of freedom. In his article, *Freedom: Toward an Integration of the Counseling Profession*, Hanna describes the incorporation of four modalities of freedom: freedom *from*, freedom *to*, freedom *with*, and freedom *for*. Hanna proposes that we incorporate freedom into ideas of "agency, self-determination, metacognition, mindfulness, and often unexamined therapeutic techniques from yoga and Buddhism" (Hanna, 2011, p. 365). Hanna makes it clear that the freedom paradigm is not a model, but is meant to generate and be a resource for new approaches to therapy. As we were developing our nine principles the idea of freedom attached to notions of agency and self-determination felt like an ideal way to describe the work we are doing with people who are erotically marginalized. Freedom *from* refers to symptom relief, this includes the alleviation of anxiety and depression, or addictions. It also encompasses a freedom from external situations, including bullying, racism, transphobia, and negative self-beliefs (Hanna, 2011). Freedom *to* describes the ability of a person to view the world freely and to act without "enslavement or entrenchment" when evaluating the circumstances of one's life, and allowing freedom to be integral, rational, and authentic. Freedom *with*, as we understand it for our principles, points to the importance of community and network connections of freedom, both for clients and for therapists. Freedom with allows one to be free without engaging in competition, privilege, status, or exclusivity, and human beings are not truly free until all are free (Hanna, 2011). Freedom *for* is also linked to community building and therapeutic support of clients, it entails providing knowledge and service that results in the freedom of others (Hanna, 2011). That is what we are hoping to accomplish in our book, with these nine principles.

The term Intersectionality was developed by Kimberle Crenshaw (1989) as a way to discuss black women's experience of both sexism and racism. The notion of intersectionality highlights the fact that the combination of these two oppressions is different from experiencing just one or the other. Intersectionality is frequently talked about in the fields of counseling and social work to talk about the intersections of identities. However, the term was designed not to talk about the intersection of identities, but to talk about the intersection of multiple oppressions. The experience of multiple oppressions has been salient for us in our work. Crenshaw's language and concept has been influential in how we have been able to understand our clients' experiences.

Our nine principles of sex therapy with erotically marginalized clients are directly influenced by the transfeminist approach (Sennott, 2011) and Queer Theory. The transfeminist approach to therapy, was written about by Shannon Sennott, in the article, "Gender disorder as gender oppression: A transfeminist approach to rethinking the pathologization of gender non-conformity." The transfeminist therapeutic approach is an alternative therapeutic reconceptualization of feminist therapy based on the weaving together of feminist thought, social justice frameworks, and principles of allyship:

> *The foundational principles of the transfeminist approach are: 1) There does not exist a hierarchy of authentic lived experience for women; 2) To privilege one* type *of womanhood or femaleness over another is inherently anti-feminist; 3) No one individual, group, or type of woman is permitted to define what it means to* be *a woman; and 4) Most trans and/or gender non-conforming individuals have had lived experience, either past or present, as a girl or a woman and have suffered the direct repercussions of socially condoned misogyny and systemic gender based oppression.*
>
> *(Sennott, 2011, p.102).*

We believe that an understanding of this approach is critical to competent sex therapy with erotically marginalized clients because it requires that the clinician acknowledge and give language to the matrix of intersecting identities of marginalization that a client may present with in therapy.

For this same reason, a focus on the intersection of identities of both privilege and marginalization, Queer Theory is one of our overarching theoretical lens for sex therapy with erotically marginalized clients. In the book *Feeling queer or queer feelings: Radical approaches to counseling sex, sexualities, and genders*, edited by Lyndsey Moon (2008), we found great inspiration as they pulled together a resource that challenged current ideas of sexuality and gender in psychotherapy. In chapter 2, *Queer dilemmas: The problem of power in psychotherapeutic and counseling practice*, Ian Hodges beautifully and clearly defines queer theory as it relates to a therapeutic context:

> *Queer Theory is fundamentally about power, politics and activism. In particular, it focuses on the ways in which our most private understandings of who we are, who we desire, and who and how we love, of acceptance and rejection, sameness and difference, are shaped, molded and regulated by relations of language, power and authority. In short, Queer Theory focuses upon the ways in which power gets inside our bodies, our "hearts" and our heads. It is above all oppositional – opposing all forms of oppression including the ways that seemingly liberatory categories, especially "lesbian", "gay", "bisexual" and "trans", may themselves become tied to (oppressive) regulatory regimes and practices.*
>
> *(Hodges, 2008, p. 8).*

Queer theory, along with Intersectionality, are the underpinning of our therapeutic orientations and though it is difficult to describe in the context of sex therapy we will show that it is invaluable for the health of a therapeutic alliance when working with erotically marginalized clients. What is critical to understand about Queer Theory is that a sex therapist does not need to identify as queer to be able to utilize the concepts and standards of care that arise from it, when working with erotically marginalized clients.

Conclusion

This book is a clinical guide that focuses on individual and relational sex therapy with people who are erotically marginalized. We offer affirming examinations of erotically marginalized identities that are often overlooked in discussions of sex therapy including but not limited to, asexuality, demisexuality, pansexuality, trans, gender nonconforming, and nonbinary identities, sexuality intersecting with BDSM practices, kink, and non-monogamous orientations. In our discussion we strive to decenter whiteness, cisgender experience, heterosexuality, and monogamy; and shift from the affirmation of socially sanctioned experiences towards socially sanctioning *all consensual experiences*. We attend to the intersections of both marginalized and privileged identities within the therapeutic relationship. These nine principles for affirming therapeutic practice aim to aid clinicians in better meeting the needs of erotically marginalized clients in the face of a sexuality and desire landscape that is rarely spoken about and for which there is little language in therapeutic settings.

References

Crenshaw, K. (1989). Demarginalizing the intersection of race and sex: A blac feminist critique of antidiscrimination doctrine, feminist theory and antiracist politics. *University of Chicago Legal Forum*, Vol. 1989: Iss. 1, Article 8.

Moon, L. (Ed.). (2008). *Feeling queer or queer feelings? Radical approaches to counselling sex, sexualities and gender*. New York: Routledge.

Olson, M., Seikkula, J., & Ziedonis, D. (2014). The key elements of dialogic practice in open dialogue. The University of Massachusetts Medical School. Worcester, MA.

Hanna, F. J. (2011). Freedom: Toward an integration of the counseling profession. *Counselor Education and Supervision, 50*, 362–385.

Hodges, I. (2008). Queer dilemmas: The problem of power in psychotherapeutic and counselling practice. In L. Moon (Ed.), *Feeling queer or queer feelings?: Radical approaches to counselling sex, sexualities, and gender* (pp. 7–22). New York: Routledge.

Sennott, S. L. (2011). Gender disorder as gender oppression: A transfeminist approach to rethinking the pathologization of gender non-conformity. *Women & Therapy, 34*, 93–113.

White, M. & Epston, D. (1990). *Narrative means to therapeutic ends*. New York: W.W. Norton & Company.

PART I
Foundations

Principle One

MAINTAIN TRANSPARENCY AND NAME SYSTEMIC AND INDIVIDUAL OPPRESSIONS

Introduction

We believe that sex therapists have the power to create radical spaces in which all people can work towards being free from oppression and are able to access their erotic selves. Power is inherent and implicit in the relation between therapist and client(s); the therapist has enormous power in the room. Attending to this dynamic and the ways in which the therapist can unknowingly recreate systematic oppression is a vital component of the relationship. Erotic marginalization is sometimes very clear, and sometimes very subtle. Different clients have different levels of awareness of how the experience of erotic marginalization is affecting them. Sex therapists have the potential, and responsibility, to see and name power dynamics related to erotic marginalization both inside and outside of the therapy room. How we do this is, as always, a complicated clinical decision based on the therapist and client(s).

Vignette

Raina, a 32-year-old mixed race Korean and white straight identified cisgender woman and her husband Sam, a 38-year-old white straight identified cisgender man have seen me for couple's therapy for three years. They originally came to treatment because they wanted to responsibly and thoughtfully open their relationship. Sam has identified as polyamorous for many years and told Raina at the start of their relationship that he would want to open their relationship at some point,

(continued)

(continued)

which she agreed to even though she has historically only been in monogamous relationships. They negotiated opening their relationship beautifully even though it felt complicated and fraught for both of them for a variety of reasons. Eleven months ago, they experienced a miscarriage and have been attending a bimonthly support group at a local health center and have felt incredibly supported by the other group members and the facilitator. After a year and a half of treatment they had dropped from weekly therapy down to every other week because they were feeling very positive about their connection with each other and with the folks they were choosing to date. After their miscarriage a year ago, they increased back up to every week until they found the support group. At that point they moved to every month therapy because Raina felt like she was "getting over therapized." They called their monthly sessions "tune ups" and used the time to primarily discuss their relationship structure.

In a recent meeting following the support group, Raina and Sam came to a tune up session seeming obviously distressed. I checked in with them and asked what was happening. Raina quickly replied, "nothing, it's not a big deal, I think I am just being too sensitive." I pressed a bit and Sam chimed in, "Raina, can I share?" He launched into a story about the last group in which one of the newer members shared about friends of hers who had lost a pregnancy and subsequently decided to open their marriage. The member described their decision as "immature and irresponsible," she felt like they just opened their relationship to escape the pain and sadness of losing a pregnancy. Raina and Sam had never shared their polyamorous identity with the group – primarily because it had never come up but also because they were nervous about the reactions of the group. "See?!" exclaimed Raina in session, "they think that polyamorous people are insatiable or avoiding their relationship, if they only knew how much work and conversation goes into our relationship!!"

I stopped the conversation and shared that I was feeling upset and very protective of them, that their invisible marginalized identity had been injured in what was supposed to be a space of healing. They initially both seemed surprised at how emphatically I was speaking, but they came to see that I was responding in a way that they both didn't feel that they could in the moment because they are both the target of the oppression and also have a personal relationship with the group member who made the comments. We worked out how they could best support themselves and each other in this experience and possibly discuss what had happened with the group member. Raina decided that it felt best to her to bring it up in the next group without outing themselves as polyamorous. That way she could feel out their reactions to them talking about feeling upset that this person had judged another couple's relationship decisions. We also explored how they both had to work to build up awareness of how they are oppressed so that they could ask for support around it.

In this example Raina and Sam experience erotic marginalization based on their relationship structure, an aspect of their relationship that was invisible to the other support group members. Naming and acknowledging this experience of oppression interrupts the process of internalization. Raina and Sam can see that their experience wasn't about them, who they are, or their self-worth. Instead their feelings of frustration can be clarified as a reaction to the enactment of someone else's prejudice. We hope that these nine principles provide guidance for sex therapists to see and support clients like Raina and Sam. Principle One starts us off with establishing a social justice foundation for our clinical sex therapy work.

Foundations

Principle One is built on the foundations of social justice, the Freedom Paradigm, and Preemptive Radical Inclusion. These three concepts interconnect to form a grounded beginning from which we can practice sex therapy with erotically marginalized clients.

Social Justice

Social justice is at the root of all of the sex therapy we do within and outside of the therapy office. We bring a social justice perspective in our sex therapy from the field of Social Work. The National Association of Social Workers (NASW) Code of Ethics (The National Association of Social Workers, 2017) lists the second ethical value as Social Justice, with the ethical principle as "Social workers challenge social injustice." It goes on to say that "social workers pursue social change, particularly with and on behalf of vulnerable and oppressed individuals and groups of people." For us, social justice is the bedrock on which our sex therapy work is built.

Raina and Sam experienced marginalization in their support group based on their polyamorous relationship structure. In this case, as with many examples of erotic marginalization, we lack a coherent language to describe the experience of this kind of oppression. When clients don't have the words that they need it can be difficult for them to name their experience and identify their feelings. In this example the clinician named a possible experience and allowed the couple to decide how well that fit and how they wanted to move forward. A sex therapist might also be interested in how this experience of marginalization affects both Raina's and Sam's sexual experience as a couple and with other partners.

Freedom Paradigm

The Freedom Paradigm, conceptualized by Fred J. Hanna and Betty Cardona (2013), provides a way for us to re-envision our sex therapy work with erotically marginalized clients by framing the therapy goal in a strengths-based and holistic way. Hanna and Cardona proposed that, "the purpose of virtually all counseling endeavors, at some level and to some degree, is to set people free" (363). Hanna and Cardona's concept of freedom in regards to counseling is described as, "a psychological state wherein a person is not bound by psychological inhibitions or restrictions, including symptoms such as anxiety, depression, emotional pain, obsessive thoughts, or compulsions" (365). The application of the Freedom Paradigm to sex therapy allows for a deeper understanding of sexual desire and sexual contentment. Sexual desire and behavior is often seen as an individual experience, and therefore when clients experience problems with their sexual desire or behavior, it is often experienced as a personal failing or fault. The Freedom Paradigm's emphasis as psychological symptoms being caused by the lack of the experience of true freedom (including freedom from oppression) broadens this picture to include external experiences that clients internalize. Our culture sends many explicit and implicit messages about sex and sexuality that are both controlling and damaging. These messages include what your body should look like, how much sex you should have, how you should have it, how long it should take you, who you should have it with, and what it should mean to you (to name a few). When clients show up in our office seeking help for a sexual issue, they carry in all of these internalized messages. And these messages get in the way of experiencing and understanding their sexualities.

Preemptive Radical Inclusion

What if we always assumed that the person we just met was someone who was experiencing oppression and marginalization? Cindy Beal developed a framework, Preemptive Radical Inclusion (PRI) (Beal, 2018), that moves us toward creating a space that is truly inclusive. When we practice PRI in our work, we are intentionally making an assumption that we are sitting with someone who experiences marginalization, whether we can see it or not. This practice allows us to notice and name our own privileges and to be aware of how they are showing up in our clinical work. It is a way of decentering our own experiences in order to make space for our clients.

Practicing PRI means that we are not assuming a client's gender identity, sexual orientation, sexual identity, race, ethnicity, religion, or any other part of their experience. It means specifying that you're talking about a cisgender man instead of just using "man" and "transgender man." Or clarifying client's relationship structures and being curious about the language that they use and what it means to them (Can you tell me what marriage means to the two of you?). By practicing PRI in our sex therapy office and in our lives we are making space not only for people's whole lived experience, but a space in which no part of themselves needs to be left behind. Cindy Beal states,

"Preemptive Radical Inclusion lives at the intersection of trauma-aware and anti-oppression practices." The stance of PRI is critical to working ethically with erotically marginalized clients because the clinician does not wait for a client to bring a need and *then* meet the need, instead, the clinician creates a therapeutic environment that preemptively supports a client's multiple intersecting erotically marginalized identities.

Systemic and Individual Oppression

It is typical for sex therapists to receive training to work with specific populations. For example, transgender clients, kinky clients, polyamorous clients, and lesbian, gay, and bisexual clients (LGB) all have specific concerns and experiences that an untrained clinician needs to learn about. And, one thing that they all have in common, is the experience of oppression. The development of the term "erotically marginalized" came from conversations that we had together about the sex therapy work we were doing. Erotically marginalized clients all experience oppression in some way that is related to their sexual self. The field of sex therapy is built on behavioral research that focused on cisgender and heterosexual people and their individual experiences that is not always pertinent or appropriate for erotically marginalized clients.

Oppression and Sexuality

The experience of oppression is, "prejudice and discrimination as a result of being a member of a group that has historically been marginalized (e.g., women, people of color, immigrants, or LGBTQQ individuals)" (Singh & Harper, 2012, p. 284). The history of the field of sexuality is full of experiences of sexual oppression from Kraft-Ebbing who in 1886 believed that sexual desire was only for procreation and all other sexual behavior was deviant (Bullough, 1995; Califia, 2003) to Magnus Hirschfeld whose Institute for Sexual Research was destroyed by the Nazis in 1933 (Stryker, 2008). Sexologists have historically been both the oppressor and the oppressed and that is also true in our current practice of sex therapy; privilege and oppression "operate together as two sides of the same coin" (Singh & Harper, 2012, p. 285). Sex therapists who have an awareness and understand of their own identities including their experiences or privilege or oppression are more able to constructively address privilege and oppression in the therapy room (Singh & Salazar, 2010).

Intersectionality, Intersecting Oppressions

The roots of what is today described as intersectionality come from the work of black and brown women. The Combahee River Collective, a Black lesbian feminist organization, created a statement in response to the multiple positions of marginalization within the white feminist movement of the 1970s (Combahee River Collective, 1977). The statement they released was revolutionary and in it they developed the concept of "identity politics." Before intersectionality was a recognized term, they argued for an intersectional approach to working towards justice and liberation. They believed that "the liberation of all oppressed peoples necessitates the destruction of the political-economic systems of capitalism and imperialism as well as patriarchy" (Combahee River Collective, 1977). Additionally, they asserted that "if Black women were free, it would mean that everyone else would have to be free since our freedom would necessitate the destruction of all the systems of oppression." Their statement reveals that all systems of oppression are interwoven and inextricably linked, in order for any true liberation to occur, everyone must be set free.

Kimberle Crenshaw (1989) popularized the term intersectionality in her article *Demarginalizing the Intersection of Race and Sex: A Black Feminist Critique of Antidiscrimination Theory and Antiracist Politics.* She explores the experience of Black women as a way of emphasizing the importance of an intersectional frame, showing that examining race or gender in isolation would not adequately account for a Black woman's lived experience. She argues that "Black women are sometimes excluded from feminist theory and antiracist policy discourse because both are predicated on a discrete set of experiences that does not accurately reflect the interaction of race and gender" (140). Intersectionality holds that while individuals are marginalized or oppressed based on specific group membership, every person is a member of many groups, both privileged and marginalized, and all of these identities and experiences work simultaneously and inextricably.

As anti-racist and transfeminist clinicians, we believe that work with marginalized clients needs to include an understanding of the ways in which intersecting oppressions operate. This is both foundational to our therapeutic frame and to our clinical work. The systemic piece, that "Intersectional paradigms remind us that oppression cannot be reduced to one fundamental type, and that oppressions work together in producing injustice" (Collins, p. 21) fuels our commitment to help marginalized clients experience freedom from oppression both as therapists and outside of the office. We also believe that is in the responsibility of sex therapists to have an awareness of the ways that they experience marginalization and the ways that they have access to privilege in order to minimize reenacting systems of oppression in the therapeutic relationship.

Microaggressions

In practice, microaggressions describe the small experiences of disinterest, disinvestment, and thoughtlessness that are the result of living in a culture that

Table 1.1 Example of Microaggressions Directed Towards Erotically Marginalized Clients

Form	Theme	Microaggression	Message
Microassault	Pathologizing	"How could you hurt someone you love?" "Were you abused as a child?"	You are sick. Only a traumatized person could be involved in kink, be poly identified, be trans.
Microassault	Pathologizing	"What about the kids"	Your identity isn't ok for children to be around, you could never be a good parent
Microassault	Centering normative relationship structures	"I could never date more than one person; it just doesn't feel like the way it's supposed to be"	Your relationship is not okay, and there must be something wrong with you to think it is okay.
Microinsult	Assumption of authority	"Oh wow, I would never have known you are trans!"	I have a right to judge you.
Microinvalidation	Denial of personal bias	"I have a good friend who is into kink!" "I get it, I sometimes wish I could be a man, just to know how it feels"	My personal connection to your lifestyle makes me immune to bias. I think I know who you feel and therefore I don't need to be responsible for my actions.
Microassault	Sexualization	"You must have *lots* of sex"	You are insatiable, or your identity only has to do with sex.
Microassault	Minimizing	"Why do you have to talk about your identity all the time?"	Living with your identity is not that difficult and there must be something wrong with you if you think it is.

privileges some experiences and marginalizes others. Sue, Capodilupo, Torino, Bucceri, Holder, Nadal, and Esquilin (2007) define them as:

> *The everyday verbal, nonverbal and environmental slights, snubs or insults, whether intentional or unintentional which communicate hostile, derogatory or negative messages to target persons based solely upon their marginalized group membership. In many cases these hidden messages may invalidate the group identities or experiential reality of target persons, demean them on a personal or group level, communicate they are lesser human beings, suggest they do not belong with the majority group, or relegate them to inferior status and treatment.*
>
> *(Sue et al., 2007)*

The term microaggressions was popularized by Derald Sue Wing, writing specifically about racial microaggressions, however any marginalized or oppressed individual or group can experience them. He believes that no individual is immune to unknowingly or unintentionally using microaggressive speech or behaviors.

Wing identifies three forms of microaggressions which we have found is a helpful way for us to talk with clients about their experiences. The forms he identified are microassaults, microinsults and microinvalidations (see Table 1.1) (Sue et al., 2007). Microassaults are overt and purposeful demeaning speech or behavior, they are often the easiest to detect and are potentially the easiest to name and combat because of their inescapability (Sue et al., 2007). Microinsults are often subtle and unintentional – they can even come in the form of a thinly veiled compliment (Sue et al., 2007). Microinvalidations are also very often unconscious and have the effect of erasing someone's identity and/or experience (Sue et al., 2007).

Clients who are erotically marginalized experience microaggressions consistently and may not have awareness or language to understand and express the impact on their sense of self, identity and mental health. Additionally, sex therapists can sometimes unknowingly use microaggressions towards erotically marginalized clients. For example, a therapist might assume that a client who is an erotically marginalized is coming to therapy explicitly for support around their identity or sexual practices, when in reality they might need support around anxiety or something that many people struggle with in their lives (this would be an example of a microinsult).

Vignette

Billy is a 28-year-old genderqueer, white, and assigned female at birth person who uses they/them pronouns. They identified as transmasculine in their early 20s, had top surgery, never took hormones, but recently realized that they don't identify as female but they don't identify as male either. We have been working together for the past two years, working some with their gender identity, but mostly centering our work on their social anxiety especially as it affects their ability to form and maintain relationships, a frustrating experience for them. An issue that came to my awareness was that talking on the phone, including making phone calls to set up appointments, make reservations, or to call new friends, was extremely challenging for them. I made an assumption that their aversion to making phone calls was understandably due to their anxiety. However, through some thoughtful questioning, it became clear to me that the phone was challenging for them was because of their gender. They described a recent call they made to a doctor's office where the receptionist called them ma'am, then when they learned their name was Billy, they quickly corrected themself, apologizing, calling them sir. They shared this story in session, seeming upset, but resigned.

Through our work I was able to help them see the inherent microaggressions at being gendered at all, we pondered why anyone needs to use ma'am or sir on the phone at all. We then delved deeper and discussed how as a nonbinary person there is even less space for their feelings or experience. A cisgender person would likely not notice being gendered on the phone. A trans person might have feelings that are more clear, being properly gendered or misgendered. For Billy, being gendered on the phone was a reminder of their experience, that they feel like they don't fit in the world, like there isn't a place for them.

Transparency

Maintaining transparency in a therapeutic context is arguably always valuable, but it feels imperative when working with marginalized and oppressed populations. We don't want to burden or overwhelm our clients with naming everything that is happening all the time, but we feel that it is our job to attend to and track what happens in the room, between ourselves and the clients.

The first step in working towards transparency is establishing a culture of openness and honesty from the beginning of the therapeutic relationship. A first appointment or assessment can be a good opportunity to lay the groundwork with clients that you are going to practice transparency and name systemic and individual oppressions. At some point in the first session with every client we include brief statement of our commitment, included in our explanation of how we work and our services. We might say something like,

> *As a therapist who is committed to social justice and a relational therapeutic orientation, I share with all new clients in the first couple of sessions that I work very hard to create open space to discuss all identities, included target identities – such as, but not limited to – race, ethnicity, gender identity and expression, sexual practices, ability, size, citizenship, religion, and age.*

We name at the outset that it is our intention to make patterns of oppression and discrimination visible and minimize reenacting them within a therapeutic context. We also invite clients to help us notice if we have used oppressive discourse or thinking in session if it feels safe for them to do so. It feels important to note that this invitation does abdicate our responsibility to hold a safe space for our clients.

A second step that we feel is crucial in maintaining transparency as a form of resisting oppression is for the therapist to locate oneself within the therapeutic context as is relevant and potentially useful to the client. Dee Watts-Jones describes location of self as starting a conversation with a client(s) about, "similarities and differences in their key identities, such as race, ethnicity, gender, class, sexual orientation, and religion, and how they may potentially influence the therapy process" (2010, p. 405). Location of self requires the therapist to disclose information about themselves that makes visible possible power dynamics in the room. Each of us use self-disclosure and transparency slightly differently in our practices. We encourage therapists to decide for themselves what their own comfort level is around use of self clinically. Location of self is a good starting point for therapists to begin to explore their own identities and have an awareness of what privileged identities they are bringing into the room and what marginalized identities they are bringing into the room. Naming the therapist's own social location models that this is a safe space to talk about power, privilege, and identities.

We try to enact this principle throughout this text. For example, in the introduction we each identify our social location. We've also asked contributors to identify and discuss their social locations as part of their case formulations. Sometimes the most critical moment for a therapist to locate themself is if a client has a marginalized identity that the therapist doesn't share. For example, a therapist who has physique privilege working with a client of size might state clearly that they have different experiences around this particular identity and while the therapist cannot understand the client's position firsthand, they can be an ally to their client. Another moment in which a therapist might locate themself is if they have a shared marginalized target identity that the client may not know about and sharing the therapist's location might help to keep the client safer. For example, a therapist who is involved in the kink community who lives in a lower populated area might be explicit with a new client who is also involved in the kink community so they can navigate how to avoid crossing over in a way that might make either of them uncomfortable.

Last, we feel that it is critical to name what you think is happening for clients both in the room as well as in their lives in an open, honest, and uncomplicated way. The archaic idea of a therapist being a blank slate and not sharing affect, thoughts or feelings with clients misses an opportunity for connection and growth. We have found that transparency operationalized with good boundaries creates a therapeutic environment that feels safer for our erotically marginalized clients. Billy's case offers an example of naming systematic and individual oppression that has occurred outside the bounds of the therapeutic context. The following is an example of naming an injustice or microaggression when the therapist is the person at fault.

Vignette

Harvey is a white 24-year-old transmasculine person who primarily uses they/them pronouns, but also is increasingly comfortable with he/him pronouns since going on testosterone and getting read as male more often. They came to therapy initially because they began identifying as nonbinary and was considering getting top surgery and didn't have many supportive people other than their boyfriend and a few close friends to discuss this with. We had been working together for seven months when we decided to start talking about bringing their family into session, as they wanted to try to bring their family along in their process due to their physical changes and before surgery. They were raised in a fairly conservative family. Their mother is a devout Catholic, and their father is a non-practicing Episcopalian. Their father is more socially liberal than their mother, but they both say that they "just can't understand the gender stuff." We arranged for a family session that also included their sister, who is a few years younger and very supportive. During the session, which proved to be challenging for everyone involved, Harvey's parents insisted on using their birth name and pronouns, although their father made some attempts to use the name "Harvey." At one particularly heated moment, when Harvey's parents and sister were all speaking over each other in increasingly loud voices, I tried to interrupt the momentum and frenzy of mixed up pronouns and names being used for my stunned seeming client and I said, fairly forcefully, "can we just take a moment here to allow some space for her to respond?" I immediately caught my mistake and said quickly, "Excuse me, for them to respond, I am very sorry, Harvey." My shame welled up inside of me, but I knew that the most supportive thing I could possibly do in that moment was to apologize and move on, to continue my job as working to create and maintain the container for all of the people in my office.

The session slowed and we were able to make some inroads with Harvey's parents, they seemed to soften some as the session went on, led by the guidance of their sister who was able to explain things to the parents in a way that Harvey and I were both unable. At the end of the session, I asked Harvey if they would stay back for a moment to check in. I apologized again for my mistake and asked them if we could set up a time to have a session over the phone, free of charge for them during which we could discuss what that session felt like for them, especially my mis-pronouning them in front of their parents. They said "it's really not a big deal, I totally get it," but with a little more prompting they took me up on my offer. I explained when we spoke that I had made a possibly understandable due to the extensive mis-pronouning that had been happening, but inexcusable, mistake. I told them that we could use that time to explore any feelings that had come up for them during or after the session, that it would be understandable if their trust in me had been shaken in any way. They were able to discuss their anger with me in a way that is uncommon for them and move through their feelings about what had happened.

Clinical Tools

Providing education, helping clients externalize negative feelings, and practicing solidarity with clients are tools that can be used to operationalize Principle One in the sex therapy office.

Education

One of the most fundamental and important ways to maintain transparency in a therapeutic context is to provide education for our clients about the ways in which power and oppression work in the world, in our clients' lives, and in the sex therapy office. This is not meant to be a top-down didactic form of education, but more of a gentle and nuanced approach to helping our clients along when the need arises. For example, the couple in the first vignette had relatively new identities and weren't aware of the ways in which society and people around them can oppress them, that what had happened in their group had been a microaggression.

Education can take the form of teaching a client about a concept, such as the idea of microaggressions, or more of a psychoeducational approach, such as how trauma affects the brain or of fight/flight/freeze/fawn reactions people have in scary or overwhelming situations. As with everything, we recommend using this tool only with thoughtful intention as it could be easy to reinscribe the power dynamic already inherent in the therapeutic context.

Externalizing

The concept of externalizing comes from Michael White and Narrative Therapy, which we discuss extensively in Principle Five. Externalizing is one of the most useful clinical tools, as it ideally helps clients become freer from the issues in their lives that are causing so much stress. Through externalizing, we help clients to see that struggles they are facing, like oppression or discrimination, are not issues that live in them, but rather are systemic problems that face many people with similar target identities. By giving these struggles some space, we can see how the toxic effects of discrimination function in our lives, and offer us the ability to combat it more fully.

Vignette

Alicia was a white upper-class cisgender heterosexual polyamorous woman in her mid-20s. We had been working together for some time when she came in feeling sad about her relationships and unable to explain why. As we traced back the last several days, she described watching an episode of a police procedural television show that was upsetting. In the show, one of the suspects was polyamorous and this plot point focused on demonizing her relationship models and therefore the suspect's personal integrity. My client felt that it was silly that she was so affected by a television show. However, as we began to unpack it, we were able to see the microaggression hidden in the plot. This television script had depicted polyamorous people as morally lacking with an expectation that the viewer would agree. If this plot point had been about sexual orientation, we would be able to clearly label that the television show was homophobic. However, we don't have easily accessible language to describe the experience of oppression in regards to relationship structure (open relationship or polyamory for example). Together Alicia and I created language that allowed her to see the microaggression and externalize her feeling or self-hatred that stemmed from what had seemed to her like an inconsequential experience. The fact that it seemed inconsequential also speaks volumes, Alicia had an expectation that any media depiction of polyamory would be a negative one.

Solidarity with clients

The last tool that we offer in an effort to increase transparency in the clinical context is to build solidarity with clients, to actively fight alongside of clients for justice and liberation. We can do this by being active allies, which we discuss in Principle Eight, both inside and outside of the therapeutic context. As therapists, we already have our clients' best interest at heart, we are their champions and advocates. In order to increase transparency and more fully meet our clients' needs, we must extend this further and actively fight for our clients' liberation.

Key Clinical Points

- A social justice framework is foundational to working ethically with erotically marginalized clients.
- By exploring their own privileged and marginalized identities, sex therapists can work to minimize reenactment of systemic oppression in their work with clients.
- Microaggressions can be difficult for erotically marginalized clients to name but can also create internalized shame.
- Maintaining transparency and naming systemic and individual oppressions helps to create a safe space for clients be open curious about their sexuality.

References

Beal, C. (2018). Preemtive Radical Inclusion. http://justiceandpeaceconsulting.com/preemptiveradical-inclusion/. Accessed July 11, 2018.

Bullough, V. L. (1995). *Science in the bedroom: A history of sex research.* New York: Basic Books.

Califia, P. (2003). *Sex changes: Transgender politics.* San Francisco, CA: Cleis Press.

Combahee River Collective. (1977). The Combahee River Collective statement in Taylor, K-Y. (Ed.) *How we get free: Black feminism and the Combahee River Collective.* Chicago, IL: Haymarket.

Crenshaw, K. (1989). Demarginalizing the Intersection of Race and Sex: A Black Feminist Critique of Antidiscrimination Theory and Antiracist Politics. *University of Chicago Legal Forum,* Vol. 1989: Iss. 1, Article 8.

Dee Watts-Jones, T. (2010). Location of self: Opening the door to dialogue on intersectionality in the therapy process. *Family Process, 49*(3), 405–420.

Hanna, F. J. (2011). Freedom: Toward an integration of the counseling profession. *Counselor Education and Supervision, 50,* 362–385.

The National Association of Social Workers. (2017). *Code of ethics.* Retrieved from http://socialworkers.org. Accessed November 9, 2017.

Singh, A. A. & Harper, A. (2012.) Intercultural issues in LGBTQQ couple & family therapy in J. J. Bigner & J. L. Wetchler *Handbook of LGBTQ-Affirmative Couple and Family Therapy.* New York, NY: Routledge.

Stryker, S. (2008). *Transgender history.* Berkeley, CA: Seal Press.

Sue, D. W. (2010). *Microaggressions in everyday life: Race, gender, and sexual orientation.* Hoboken, NJ: Wiley.

Sue, D. W., Capodilupo, C. M., Torino, G. C., Bucceri, J. M., Holder, A. M. B., Nadal, K. L., & Esquilin, M. (2007). Racial microaggressions in everyday life: Implications for clinical practice. *American Psychologist, 62*(4), 271–286.

THE CASE OF WANDA: INDIVIDUAL THERAPY WITH A QUEER CISGENDER FEMME OF SOUTH ASIAN DESCENT

Lourdes Dolores Follins

Introduction

This clinical case study describes aspects of clinical sex therapy with a queer-identified, cisgender woman of South Asian descent who was partnered with a Black person who identifies as trans and genderqueer[1]. In this case narrative, I begin by identifying my psychosociohistorical position as a therapist, then I describe the client's presenting concerns and case history followed by portrayals of segments of our therapeutic work together. The case study ends with possible implications of this type of clinical work with erotically marginalized ("EM") people of color and suggestions for future practice and research.

Psychotherapist's Location

I am a Black, queer, cisgender femme clinical social worker from a working-class family that has been in the United States since the 1800s. I live and work in a large, ethnoracially diverse urban city on the East Coast and am a psychotherapist, an independent researcher, and a Yoruba/Lukumi[2] priest. In my private psychotherapy practice, I focus on the needs of same-gender-loving, intersex, and other EM communities of color. More specifically, I work with EM people of color and EM indigenous people struggling with grief and loss, relationship challenges, anger management, unresolved trauma, identity issues (ethnic, gender, sexual, and religious identity), career changes, and life transitions. My research and academic writing have largely focused on resilience and resistance in EM people of African descent.

As a priest, power and Spirit are always in the forefront of my mind and naturally inform my work. In my clinical work, I help my clients access and reconnect with their innate power so that they can be *power-filled* and learn how to share or exchange that *power with* others as they see fit. I believe that people intuitively know what they need and that psychotherapy provides a space for us to get in touch with those needs, so I view my role as a facilitator of that process. My approach to psychotherapy is a trauma-informed, strengths-based, sex-positive, kink-affirming, eclectic approach that blends intersectional theory, womanism, transfeminism, harm reduction, Eye Movement Desensitization and Reprocessing (EMDR), and psychodynamic psychotherapy.

Presenting Concern

This composite client, who I refer to as Wanda (a pseudonym; pronouns, her/hers/she), is a queer, Asian American, cisgender femme who is not living with a disability. She contacted me because she wanted to manage her depression more effectively and heal unresolved childhood traumas.

Case History

Wanda is 29 years old and was raised Muslim. Her parents migrated to the United States from a South Asian country when they were in their twenties, and Wanda and her siblings (one sister, two brothers) were born in the United States. She is the youngest of the four children and was raised by a stay-at-home mother and a father who was a physician. Wanda described her mother as "passive-aggressive" and her father as "an alcoholic" who was emotionally and physically abusive towards her mother and her siblings when they were children. Wanda noted that of the four children, she is the only child who was not physically abused. Although she no longer wears a hijab and occasionally drinks alcohol, Wanda identifies as a practicing Muslim.

Wanda has been in a relationship with her 35-year-old, Black, trans/genderqueer partner, Bec (a pseudonym; pronouns, they/theirs) for three years, and they moved to the East Coast a year before Wanda and I began working together. Wanda and Bec met in a large, progressive city on the West Coast where they both had an extensive community of friends, allies, and healers. Both partners were politically active progressives who view the world and their relationships with an intersectional, Marxist lens. Before moving to the East Coast, Wanda worked with a psychotherapist and a somatics coach. The couple moved to the East Coast because Bec got a high-paying job in their field. Since the move, Wanda felt isolated and alone, and struggled to both find progressive queer and trans people of color communities in her new city and remain connected with her old friends. She had a white-collar, remote job that barely paid her bills.

When Wanda and I began working together, she shared that she had been diagnosed with Major Depressive Disorder and prescribed Prozac ten years prior and that she struggled with depression off and on ever since. Her symptoms at the time of our initial meeting were lethargy, tearfulness, and feelings of hopelessness and helplessness. As a harm reductionist, I asked how she was managing her symptoms and she shared that she smoked marijuana two to three times daily. We discussed the physiological interaction between marijuana and the human brain for many people with depression and Wanda admitted that the frequency and amount of her smoking had become a point of contention between her and Bec. She also shared that her sister has been on antidepressants for many years and that they "saved her life." As a result, Wanda was "open to exploring medication."

Application of Principles of Clinical Support

Wanda contacted me after reading my profile on a national website for queer and trans therapists of color because she specifically wanted to work with a queer woman of color. In my online professional profiles, I deliberately self-disclose my gender identity (femme) and EM status from the onset (Zur, Williams, Lehavot, & Knapp, 2009). My intent is to ensure that potential clients can make more informed decisions about whether to work with me, especially those who believe that they will be better understood by an EM person who is also a cisgender femme woman of color. As a womanist and transfeminist, I have found that the shared experiences of erotic marginalization and/or being a person of color often facilitates the creation of basic trust, enhances the therapeutic alliance, and fosters a more egalitarian relationship (Zur et al., 2009). So, my self-disclosure laid the foundation of my work with Wanda.

During our work together, Wanda and I discussed how various sociopolitical events (the 2016 election, the "#MeToo" movement, the Charlottesville killing), along with daily oppressive experiences as a South Asian queer femme who is "read" as heterosexual (Sandil, Robinson, Brewster, Wong, & Geiger, 2015) psychologically, physically, and spiritually impacted her and her self-care practices. One of the challenges that Wanda faced in interpersonal relationships was difficulty expressing her disappointment and anger towards others. The origins of this issue are rooted in both the Asian cultural value of emotional self-control (Inman, Ladany, Constantine, & Morano, 2001) and witnessing how her parents dealt with their own disappointment and anger. Her father was only able to express his anger and violence when he drank alcohol and her mother was passive-aggressive towards her loved ones when she was angry or disappointed. I occasionally repeated the metaphor that Wanda used to describe how she tended to express her anger – volcanic – and voiced my concern that she would "explode" if she did not communicate her feelings when they arise.

Another challenge Wanda faced was when she began to feel uncertain about whether her relationship with Bec would continue. Wanda reached a point where she noticed that although Bec had complained about her depressive symptoms and asked Wanda to enter therapy, Bec was not addressing their own depression, gender minority stress (Giammattei, 2015), or gender identity concerns. I encouraged Wanda to explore her discomfort to even articulate this concern aloud in my office and then allowed her to discuss her fears about the dissolution of their relationship and the basis of those fears. At some point during our conversation about Wanda's concern about Bec needing support around their gender identity and body image concerns, I self-disclosed that I had partnered with transmasculine partners in the past (see detailed description in the next section). As described later, this self-disclosure appeared to solidify Wanda's perception of me as an ally.

Therapeutic Work

We initially focused on Wanda's depression and her unresolved feelings about her relationships with her parents. Within two months of beginning our work, Wanda began taking antidepressants because her previous attempts to somatically address her depression – boxing, Reiki, and acupuncture – no longer worked. Within three weeks of beginning Zoloft, Wanda had more energy and motivation and said that she wanted to focus on her dissatisfaction with her relationship with Bec. Wanda shared that Bec experienced gender minority stress in the form of racialized transphobia and cisgenderism in every aspect of their life (Giammattei, 2015). She described Bec as exhausted every day after work because they are "constantly misgendered" at work. According to Wanda, Bec's ways of coping with these stressors were to withdraw and self-isolate: eat quickly and quietly, binge on Netflix, and remain at home on the weekends because they were "too tired."

At one point, Wanda tearfully said that she was afraid that she would have to leave Bec because they were not dealing with their depression or their "gender dysphoria." When I asked her to elaborate on the latter, Wanda said that Bec does not discuss their body image or experiences of their gender with *anyone*. She added that Bec's gender-related body dysphoria[3] led to changes in the nature and frequency of their sexual activity (Brown, 2010; Pfeffer, 2017). When I asked about the couple's sexual history, Wanda lit up and shared that in the beginning of their relationship, she and Bec connected through dancing together and used to spend hours in bed having sex. She understood that typically the amount of sex that couples have gradually decreases after a few months into relationships, but the shift that Wanda experienced with Bec was dramatic. Bec rarely wanted to have sex with her, no longer wanted to have sex with the lights on, no longer wanted to be touched in a sexual manner, was only interested in having sex in sexual positions that did not allow them to fully see one another during sex, and no longer wanted to be naked during sex.

When I then asked when was the last time they had sex and Wanda replied, "I don't even *know*!" She paused as she thought a bit. "Nope. I can't even remember the last time we had sex and I need to be touched!" Wanda was sprawled out on my couch at this point, looking both despondent and exasperated. We discussed how complicated it was for her to navigate sex and desire while having compassion for her partner's experience as a person with multiple marginalized identities and trying to be supportive of them. We spoke more about her concerns about the fact that she had briefly considered asking Bec if they could "open" their relationship just so that Wanda could be sexual with someone. She quickly added that she decided against making that request and planned on asking Bec to seek help and "to find people they can talk with" about their depression and gender identity. Something stirred in me and almost without thinking I asked, "Who do you speak with about your experience of being with a trans, genderqueer partner?" Wanda briefly looked puzzled and then chuckled. "No one!" "How come?" I continued. Brief pause. "I don't know . . . " Wanda said thoughtfully.

I off-handedly added that when I had transmasculine partners, it was helpful, grounding, and validating to speak with other cisgender partners of transmasculine people. I asserted the importance of cisgender partners having the opportunity to discuss and explore how a trans partner's transition impacts their life as well (Bockting, Knudson, & Goldberg, 2006; Theron & Collier, 2013). Wanda's eyes widened as I briefly shared my experiences and although she usually listened intently when I offered suggestions, this time Wanda was rapt with attention. I told her that at that time – in the late 1990s to early 2000s – we were referred to by the rather unflattering term, SOFFAs: significant others, friends, family, and allies. I encouraged her to go online and type in the term so that she could see what she could find for herself. My intention was to open up a dialogue about what Brown (2010) and Pfeffer (2017) refer to as "a process of negotiating bodies and sexual connection" (Brown, 2010, p. 566) and Wanda's thoughts and feelings about that process. At that point, Wanda perked up and looked more hopeful.

Implications and Further Questions

This case study has clinical, training, and research implications for therapists working with EM cisgender femme partners of transmasculine and genderqueer people. To begin with, Wanda contacted me specifically because she wanted to work with "a queer woman of color". This was because not only had she had negative experiences with White cisgender female therapists (e.g., not taking her concerns seriously, insisting that she take psychotropic medication without exploring her feelings about it, not having an intersectional lens), but also because she believed working with an EM woman of color would be restorative for her. The majority of my EM clients of color have expressly stated that they wanted to work with an EM woman of color because they thought I would "be able to relate" to them or would "get them." More research is needed about EM people of color's experiences with and perceptions of both therapists of color and White therapists. In addition, it would be useful to learn more about the level of training that social workers, sex therapists, and other allied health professionals receive about using an intersectional perspective to clinical work with multiply marginalized people.

Another implication of this case study is that it provides a unique opportunity to give voice to the experiences of Asian-descended, EM cisgender femmes. Historically, the social science and public health research literature has failed to explore the experiences of EM people of Asian descent when it comes to their sexual health. Exceptions to this are when members of these communities are sexually objectified by non-Asian individuals (Dang & Vianney, 2007), rendered invisible by non-Asians (Alimahomed, 2010), or when researchers note ethnoracial differences in the HIV/STI infection rates of cisgender EM men (Chen et al., 2012; Wei et al. 2010). In centering the experiences of an Asian-descended femme, I am highlighting the fact that not only is "femme" is a marginalized identity unto itself (Brown, 2009; Levitt, Gerrish, & Hiestand, 2003), but also that heteropatriarchy, xenophobia, and racialized sexism negatively affect Asian-descended cisgender femme EMs. Clinicians working with Asian cisgender femme EMs will need to ask how about various aspects of these clients' identity (ethnoracial, religious/spiritual, gender identity, sexual identity, class identity, ability), the level of importance they have, and how they impact their lives.

Additionally, Wanda's dissatisfaction with her relationship with Bec *was* and was *not* about sex: it was about wanting to be emotionally, sexually, and spiritually reconnected with her partner. Having the opportunity to openly discuss how various types of systemic and individual oppression (the binary gender system, xenophobia, racialized sexism, homonegativity, cisgenderism, etc.) negatively impacted her life and her relationship provided Wanda with the validation that she needed and prepared her to speak with Bec about her concerns. Unfortunately, clinicians seeking guidance about how to support cisgender EM femmes of color will find little in the social science literature. A cursory review of the relevant literature reveals that, with one exception (Theron & Collier, 2013), the unique experiences of cisgender EM femmes of color continue to be left out of the theoretical and research literature about the experiences of those who partner with trans and genderqueer people (Brown, 2009; 2010; Lenning & Buist, 2013; Pfeffer, 2010).

Theron and Collier's (2013) study of South African cisgender female partners of transmasculine partners utilized the term "co-transitioning" (p. S66) and found that many of the women in their study needed both informational and emotional support. More information is needed about how cisgender EM female partners of color – who have their own experiences with multiple types of oppression – are affected by and adapt to their role as a partner of a transmasculine or genderqueer person (Theron & Collier, 2013). Depending on the presenting concerns, clinicians working with cisgender partners of transmasculine or genderqueer persons should ask about the support network for both the individual and the couple (Brown, 2009; 2010; Pfeffer, 2017). The latter is especially important if the trans or genderqueer partner has additional aspects of their identity that are stigmatized. Culturally competent and culturally humble clinicians also need to make as few assumptions as possible in order to create a space where clients can discuss their experiences around the negotiation of both partners' bodies, sexuality, and intimacy (Brown, 2009; Pfeffer, 2017).

Conclusion

This case study provided information about how one can utilize a framework of privilege and power in clinical work with erotically marginalized cisgender femmes of color who have a transmasculine, genderqueer partner. Historically, the literature about the impact of transition on cisgender and trans couples has neglected to include an analysis of the needs of the cisgender femme partners of color. In this case study, the client depicted fully comprehended how oppression impacted her life – both individually and her relationship with Bec. As suggested by Pfeffer (2017), "sexual interactions that validate each partner's gender identity are critical for the health and well-being of most relationships" (p. 101). A culturally competent and culturally humble clinician needs to be able to broach these topics and discuss them with cisgender EM femmes of color in their clinical work together.

Notes

1 Genderqueer: "An umbrella term for those whose gender identity and/or expression does not normatively align with the sex into which they were categorized at birth and/or whose gender expression may not be static" (Pfeffer, 2017, p. xxxv).
2 A West-African based religion.
3 A negative view of one's own body when it fails to reflect one one's gender self-image or identity, or is societally misrecognized by others (Pfeffer, 2017).

References

Alimahomed, S. (2010). Thinking outside the rainbow: Women of color redefining queer politics and identity. *Social Identities*, *16*(2), 151–168. doi: 10.1080/13504631003688849

Bockting, W. O., Knudson, G., & Goldberg, J. M. (2006). Counseling and mental health care for transgender adults and loved ones. *International Journal of Transgenderism*, *9*(3/4), 35–82. doi: 10.1300/J485v09n03_03

Brown, N. B. (2009). "I'm in transition too": Sexual identity renegotiation in sexual-minority women's relationships with transsexual men. *International Journal of Sexual Health*, *21*, 61–77. doi: 10.1080/19317610902720766

Brown, N. R. (2010). The sexual relationships of sexual-minority women partnered with trans men: A qualitative study. *Archives of Sexual Behavior*, *39*, 561–572. doi: 10.1007/s10508009-9511-9

Chen, Y.-H., Raymond, H. F., Grasso, M., Nguyen, B., Robertson, T., & McFarland, W. (2012). Prevalence and predictors of conscious risk behavior among San Franciscan men who have sex with men. *AIDS Behavior*, 1338–1343. doi: 10.1007/s10461-012-0169-2

Collins, P. H. (2000). *Black feminist thought: Knowledge, consciousness, and the politics of empowerment* (2nd ed.). New York: Routledge.

Dang, A. & Vianney, C. (2007). Living in the margins: A national survey of lesbian, gay, bisexual and transgender Asian and Pacific Islander Americans. National Gay and Lesbian Task Force Policy Institute. Accessed from www.theTaskForce.org. Accessed August 31, 2009.

Giammattei, S. V. (2015). Beyond the binary: Trans-negotiations in couple and family therapy. *Family Process*, *54*, 418–434. doi: 10.1111/famp.12167

Inman, A. G., Ladany, N., Constantine, M. G., & Morano, C. K. (2001). Development and preliminary validation of the cultural values conflict scale for South Asian women. *Journal of Counseling Psychology*, *48*, 17–27. doi:10.1037/0022-0167.48.1.17

Lenning, E. & Buist, C. L. (2013). Social, psychological and economic challenges faced by transgender individuals and their significant others: Gaining insight through personal narratives. *Culture, Health & Sexuality*, *15*(1), 44–57. doi: 10.1080/13691058.2012.738431

Levitt, H. M., Gerrish, E. A., & Hiestand, K. R. (2003). The misunderstood gender: A model of modern femme identity. *Sex Roles*, *48*(3 /4), 99–113. doi: 0360-0025/03/0200-0099/0

Pfeffer, C. A. (2010). "Women's work?" Women partners of transgender men doing housework and emotion work. *Journal of Marriage and Family*, *72*, 165–183. doi: 10.1111/j.1741 3737.2009.00690.x

Pfeffer, C. A. (2017). *Queering families: The postmodern partnerships of cisgender women and transgender men*. New York: Oxford University Press.

Sandil, R., Robinson, M., Brewster, M. E., Wong, S., & Geiger, E. (2015). Negotiating multiple marginalizations: Experiences of South Asian LGBQ individuals. *Cultural Diversity and Ethnic Minority Psychology*, *21*(1), 76–88. doi: 10.1037/a0037070

Theron, L. & Collier, K. L. (2013). Experiences of female partners of masculine-identifying trans persons. *Culture, Health & Sexuality*, *15*(S61), S62–S75. doi: 10.1080/13691058.2013.788214

Wei, C., Raymond, H. F., Wong, F. Y., Silvestre, A. J., Friedman, M. S., Documet, P., McFarland, W., & Stall, R. (2010). Lower HIV prevalence among Asian/Pacific Islander men who have sex with men: A critical review for possible reasons. *AIDS Behavior*, *15*(3), 535–549. doi: 10.1007/s10461-010-9855-0

Zur, O., Williams, M. H., Lehavot, K., & Knapp, S. (2009). Psychotherapist self-disclosure and transparency in the internet age. *Professional Psychology: Research and Practice*, *40*(1), 22–30.

THE CASE OF LAYLA AND MICHELLE: MOST WELCOME, BONDAGE, FOR THOU ART A WAY, I THINK, TO LIBERTY

Laura Jacobs

"Most welcome, bondage, for thou art a way, I think, to liberty."
William Shakespeare,* Cymbeline, *Act 5, Scene 4

We erotically marginalized individuals have complex relationships with our bodies. Often tormented by stigma, trauma, dysphoria, disempowerment, and otherness, it can be challenging to resolve one's identity and sexuality. But as providers, erotically marginalized or not, an openness to alternative interventions allows us to "meet clients where they are at" – i.e. outside the traditional – and to use innovative techniques to heal.

The following case documents one situation in which a recommendation that a couple open themselves to BDSM, along with a therapeutic environment in which we could safely process the experiences that followed, offered clients the opportunity to explore safety, boundaries, communication, and embodiment, the very things so often lacking in the experience of erotically marginalized people. It simultaneously afforded them a means to political liberation and pleasure[1], and illustrates many of the principles set forth in this book.

As a trans and genderqueer provider actively engaged in BDSM (an abbreviation linking Bondage and Discipline, Dominance and Submission, and Sado/Masochism) for decades, I have counseled many erotically marginalized individuals and couples, making use of my own experiences alongside those of others and my training in clinical social work. The preponderance of my personal activism concentrates on educating other mental health and medical professionals (most especially on transgender issues and those of BDSM) as well as on improving healthcare access for marginalized communities in New York City and worldwide. My practice is located in Manhattan and the nearby suburbs, a region welcoming of queerness and nontraditional identities.

This chapter proceeds from an avowedly trans/sex/kink/poly-affirmative position.

Layla and Michelle[2] approached me in late 2015, stating "we are experiencing a little 'lesbian bed death', but we both love each other and need help determining if staying together is a good thing or if we should just be good friends." Like so many they had avoided addressing their crisis until a deadline loomed as Layla was due to leave for Thailand a few weeks later with Michelle to follow a few after that. I replied that my magic wand was temporarily under repair but we agreed to sessions as often as feasible and to continue afterwards via teletherapy.

Layla was a 34-year-old pansexual cisgender woman of African American, Caucasian, and East Asian ancestry. An accident left her with prominent scar tissue along her left hip and upper leg, and while she recovered full mobility she remained insecure about exposing her body. She reported having been very sexually active earlier in life with partners of various genders, but that she was now more reserved.

Michelle was 35, Caucasian, lesbian, male-recorded-at-birth but identifying as female, and several years of hormone treatment had feminized her body dramatically but she reported ongoing dysphoria. She expressed ambivalence about vaginoplasty[3] and was somewhat comfortable using her penis during sex. Partners had been few and far between; she felt a victim of the transphobia still present among some women who date other women, and when partnered often felt unable to advocate for her needs or compelled to engage in sex against her wishes to not be alone.

They had met a year earlier and progressed within weeks to "Uhaul" stage[4] due to Layla's unexpected displacement, initially living with Michelle's family, later couchsurfing and house sitting. Both were established authors who did not feel geographically bound, and past travel had liberated them from the American capitalist society they viewed as oppressive, a feeling they hoped to recapture.

During their honeymoon period sex was consistent though not fireworks-worthy. Sharing a bed afforded them easy access but also presented difficulties; their lack of a courtship stage left them without scripts for seduction and they had little clue how to "turn each other on." The prospect of traveling together worried them that the pattern would continue. Early sex also involved alcohol and marijuana, but after deciding to decrease they were unable to be as uninhibited and they regularly dissociated or performed out of rote. They craved nothing more than breathtaking, heart-trembling, electrifying sex.

The therapeutic bond formed easily. Their affection was clear as they intertwined on my couch or exited with hands in the other's back pockets, and I experienced a fondness for them immediately; as someone creative and queer myself, I imagined them as potential "pizza and beer" friends had we met in another setting. My own queer- and trans-ness are stated openly on my website and facilitated trust. We all recognized a commonality[5], though I worried about my possible countertransference.

We started traditional sex therapy techniques the second session with a homework assignment of hand caressing exercises in which each partner was to deliberately stop and restart the other to improve communication and body autonomy. We also brainstormed methods of fostering the excitement of longing, such as one partner working at a nearby coffee shop, distinct friend groups, and mischievously flirtatious texts throughout the day. Our goal had been to make initial progress that might continue in Thailand, but both interventions proved impossible as the couple was too preoccupied with the upcoming move.

Teletherapy lasted only briefly; the 12-hour difference meant my brain was still muddled from sleep as they were preparing for bed themselves, something not ideal for any of us. We lost contact and I was left frustrated, unsure whether I had impacted their relationship in any way.

A full year later I was startled by an email: they were returning to New York briefly, still a deeply committed couple, and while the sexual difficulties persisted so did their love and wish to improve. I was eager to continue (both to rectify what I viewed as my initial failure and to fill an open appointment with people I liked), so we resumed.

The novelty of Sapphic sex on the coasts of Thailand at dusk had dissipated quickly. Their stories again described dull, depressingly mediocre and largely conventional acts including oral, the use of hands and vibrators, even Michelle's occasional penetration of Layla with the aid of Viagra, none of which were any more thrilling than they had been in New York. The two had sex simply because they believed couples should have sex, but were impatient to find a smoldering passion they saw in others. Once again we only had weeks.

The metacommunication was clear: sensate focus and simmering were useless if they only led to monotonous sex. Tension permeated the room so I confronted them directly: "Sex can be so much more than traditional fucking. Have you ever considered multiple partners, toys, kink, bondage, paddles, crops, wooden spoons, roleplay, maybe even a sexworker? Or anything else? You pride yourselves on your 'outside the box' lifestyles . . . why are you limiting yourself when it comes to sex?" Layla's eyes widened and Michelle's head tilted with curiosity.

Each admitted to BDSM fantasies they had felt too incorrect to share. The topic evoked stereotypes of a stiletto-clad, authoritarian dominatrix indignantly subjugating others through punishment, restraint, and the command of her presence, imagery that was distressing to them as compassionate individuals actively opposing a culture of inequality. They were utterly unable to reconcile their fantasies with their politics, yet their bodies responded. And knowing of my interest in BDSM (though no detail about my engagement in it), transference left them with another dissonance: what they perceived as my desire to inflict torture was incongruous with my career as a therapist.

Yet BDSM can be loving and passionate even when done in torn pajamas. I loaned copies of *The Topping Book*[6] and *The Bottoming Book*[7], texts featuring a wide diversity of bodies and identities written by queer women who regard kink as mutual pleasure. Layla and Michelle read voraciously. Over the next six weeks I gently tutored them through communication and basic BDSM technique, and once open they longed to try more; in doing so they became closer with each other and themselves. There was a flicker of newfound passion before they again moved away, and I can only hope they gradually cultivated a bonfire.

BDSM allowed them to sexualize their bodies outside the areas that caused difficulty. Layla became aroused at any offhand mention of crops, paddles, a hand, a spatula, or anything suggestive of a spanking, while Michelle, now enamored with bondage, was distracted each time they passed Home Depot, daydreaming of ropes and twine and delicious tortures everywhere but her penis. They recognized that sex need not focus on Michelle's genitals nor Layla's areas of scarring, and thus could safely and consciously reinhabit their bodies.

Negotiation provided a structure within which they could articulate desires and establish boundaries. Explicitly defining what acts were permissible – where, when, and to what degree they each could be touched – improved sexual communication. Outlining what was prohibited was crucial as well; both suddenly recognized that they had the authority to say "no." Unthinkable before, they each began to appreciate their body autonomy. Now cautiously safe they could be increasingly vulnerable, their limits allowing trust and their newfound ability to communicate offering freedom.

But the intersection of power and race remained disturbing. As racially conscious individuals they could not set aside the notion that Michelle's domination of Layla was a replication of slavery until they discovered a particular story of interracial BDSM in which a 'submissive' of color unmistakably took possession of her own sexuality, insistent and unwilling to settle until her own needs were met. This clashed with their conviction that submission equaled powerlessness; Layla and Michelle concluded that all power can be problematized and that what occurred within their bedroom (or elsewhere) was for them alone.

Ultimately BDSM became a form of sexual resistance; they reinterpreted BDSM as a "fuck you" to heteronormativity and to an oppressive culture that would restrict their identities and limit their expressions, a method of disrupting the fetishization and marginalization of multiracial and transgender people so prevalent in our culture. Every act of bondage, every spank, every orgasm was defiance. Submission was now subversion; they became empowered through their nonconformity.

They found a way to radicalize sex, and through this, a craving for each other.

Undeniably sex is not a silo unto itself; both partners also had outside concerns which interfered with their intimate lives. Nor was treatment as straightforward as depicted.

But many principles outlined in this book aided the work. My transparent use of self through disclosure of my gender, race, orientation, and interest in BDSM, as well as my avowedly nonjudgmental stance, humanized both my presence and the process. Michelle and Layla, like all my clients, were told up front that all I sought was their happiness and that I would support any decision thoughtfully made[8], culturally conforming or not. And I modeled ease with the nontraditional, all of which established a safe therapeutic frame.

That the couple existed outside heteronormative binaries troubled none of us nor did their queer and lesbian identities, but at their request our conversations did examine any possible distinction between queer and non-queer sex, the relationship between acts and identities, even whether Michelle's penis invalidated their identity as a lesbian couple. Intersectionality and transparency were frequent topics, especially around race, yet we again navigated the issues (including my own whiteness) through unfiltered communication, approaching the subjects from multiple perspectives and with no preconceptions.

My trepidation at encouraging them to explore BDSM (something possibly retraumatizing) mirrored their apprehension of engaging in it, and we recognized that in probing the identity issues we threatened to destabilize their narratives. We confronted our fears and together experienced the anxiety of uncertainty. The metacommunication provided information the couple was unable to articulate, directing treatment away from interventions that were unproductive. And all our discussions began from an acknowledgement of their narratives and their wisdoms of the self. Never (I hope) did I place my interpretation of their identities before theirs.

Nontraditional lifestyles sometimes require nontraditional techniques, and modern clinical work with erotic marginalized clients has spawned methods and perspectives especially relevant to these communities. Gender, orientation, ethnicity, trauma, socioeconomic status, ability/disability, kink, dysphoria, all intersect to complicate our daily existence; the philosophies outlined here, as well as those of others engaged in similar work, can only benefit us as providers and thereby those of us with erotically marginalized identities with our healing and exploration of the human experience.

Notes

1 A more comprehensive discussion of BDSM and Alternate Lifestyles as environments for healing and self-exploration can be found in my chapter "Hormones and Handcuffs: The Intersection of Transgender Identity and Alternate Lifestyles" in the upcoming book *Trans+Sexuality*, due to be published by Jessica Kingsley Publishers in mid-2018.
2 Names and other details have been altered to protect privacy.
3 The surgical reconstruction of the penis and scrotum into a vulva, vaginal canal, and clitoris.
4 Referring to the stereotype that women in relationships with women often move in together quickly.
5 As a provider of services to communities I myself inhabit, this happens often. I am mindful of boundaries, transference, and countertransference, and only share occasional snippets of my own story when they seem especially relevant, often 'third person-izing' the details. I also make clear that their identities need not match my own, and that I have no bias toward any particular outcome besides happiness.
6 Easton, D. & Liszt, C. A. (1997). *The Topping Book: Or, Getting Good at Being Bad.* Greenery Press.
7 Easton, D. & Liszt, C. A. (1997). *The Bottoming Book: How to Get Terrible Things Done to You by Wonderful People.* Greenery Press.
8 I will support any thoughtful decision even should it be at odds with my own clinical judgment.

Principle Two

CHALLENGE BINARY THINKING AND ITS CONSTRICTIONS

Binary Thinking

This principle, which challenges clinicians to move away from the common experience of thinking in binary models, emerged late in our writing process because it is so foundational to our work with erotically marginalized clients that we hadn't yet put a name to it. Binary thinking describes a way of understanding that reduces complex ideas down to only two opposing choices (Budge, Rossman, & Howard, 2014). This system of thinking creates a framework of seeing the world that limits possibilities. As sex therapists we are as at risk of being immersed in this frame as anyone else; "therapists are 'very ordinary' people 'situated within culture' and are open to the same prejudices and ignorance as lay people" (Moon, 2008, 2). In this case the prejudices and ignorance that we are susceptible to are the binary assumptions that permeate and influence our culture.

Binary thinking creates a world where there is an either/or. You are either with us or against us; people are good or bad, right or wrong. However, this perspective creates distance and separateness, "from their inception, binary categories have been the centerpiece of modernity, separating men from women, male from female, black from white, homosexual from heterosexual, able bodies from disabled bodies" (Moon, 2008, 2). This way of thinking influences the field of psychotherapy itself (Moon, 2008) including the models and modalities that we use as sex therapists. We believe that this distance, this act of separating and sorting, is painful and hurtful to people and works against the task of creating a safe and supportive environment.

Queering Sex Therapy

A queer theory lens is one way to conceptualize an alternative to a binary model. It is not explicitly about describing a person's sexual orientation or

Common Binaries in the Field of Sex Therapy:

Male/Female

Man/Woman

Gay/Straight

Gay/Lesbian

Transgender/Cisgender

Female-to-Male/Male-to-Female

Vanilla/Kinky

Monogamous/Polyamorous

Top/Bottom

Normal/Pathological

Figure 2.1 Common Binaries in the Field of Sex Therapy

identity (Barker & Scheele, 2016). Queer theory can be applied to any type of client or presenting problem, it creates an opportunity to frame our work in a way that provides the most freedom for clients to have live their own truth without being boxed in by binary assumptions. Queer theory originated from the field of gay and lesbian studies as a reaction to the assimilation of gay and lesbian identities (Jagose, 1996).

Instead of assuming that lesbian and gay people want to and should be just like straight people, queer theory makes visible the power dynamics that are at work in these assumptions and challenges them. The ambiguity of queerness provides an alternative for a binary perspective. Applying queer theory to psychotherapy in general and sex therapy specifically, challenges therapists to resist the temptation to apply a binary frame to the experiences of their erotically marginalized clients (Moon, 2008). Queer theory provides an alternative to a binary frame, "the overall purpose is to challenge our binary thinking to prevent the either/or rhetoric that has been a purposeful tool of modernity, pervading most theoretical and applied social systems" (Moon, 2008, 3).

Psychology and Pathologization

Pathologization is in essence a binary act of categorizing people's behaviors into "normal" or "pathological" and is foundational to the field of psychology. Although the American Psychiatric Association's Diagnostic and Statistical Manual of Mental Disorders, Fifth Edition (DSM-5) now states the behavior must be seen as a problem for the client in order for a diagnosis to be made, historically it was the medical professional who made that decision. This is especially relevant for mental health providers because it is a part of our history, and important for us to hold in mind. The mental health and sex therapy fields have participated in, and continue to participate in, the oppression and discrimination of sexual minorities and gender minorities (Lev & Sennott, 2011; Singh & Dickey, 2016). Each member of an erotically marginalized community carries with them a communal experience of trauma perpetuated at the hands of the medical or mental health care system. We have worked with many erotically marginalized clients who have fears and anxiety about seeking help not because they have had a negative experience themselves, but because so many of their peers and community members have. As clinicians it is our job to be aware of this dynamic and to be sensitive to the ways that it might impact our clinical work. For example, the process of joining for an erotically marginalized client may take more time than anticipated or require a different level of disclosure in order for them to feel safe simply by virtue of being in a mental health care office. Additionally, the beginning process of therapy may need to include processing and healing from past traumatic experiences with other mental health care providers.

Erotic Marginalization

Using the term erotic marginalization provides us with a way to talk about the shared experience of oppression related to sexuality without having to neatly categorize people into identity labels. It is also, in and of itself, a way to challenge binary thinking. Categorical thinking shows up in the world and in our offices affecting how we think about clients, how we work with clients, the language that we use, what we see as possible, and what our clients see as possible. Shifting away from a categorical or a binary frame, makes space for intersections, complexity, and change; it opens up possibilities.

These principles invite us to shift our therapeutic frames to include queer and strength-based approaches. This framework is most interested in what is possible and strives to move away from limiting ideas of preconceived notions. Perhaps the most common and fundamental use of binary thinking in our culture is the assumption that there are only two gender choices. Centralizing this foundational binary, helps us to understand the power of binary thinking and the liberation that comes from dismantling it. Challenging binary thinking and its constrictions creates a practice that is inclusive of all clients, including and especially those with nonbinary gender identities.

Gender Identity

The gender binary is perhaps the most entrenched and prevalent of binaries that exist in our culture, and we are all socialized to believe that designated sex is a biological imperative. From the moment that a baby is born, and for many people, from the moment that a baby's chromosomes or genitalia are determined in utero, humans are divided into male and female, boy and girl. In fact, these two identities get collapsed and a baby that is designated male is called a boy, a baby that is designated female, a girl. The reality is that male and female refer to the components of a human's genitalia or chromosomes, but are not a biological truth and gender identity can only be determined by a person's self-determined sense of themself.

Nonbinary Gender Identities

There are multiple ways that a person can identify outside of the binary gender system and many different types of language that they might use[1]. From a sex therapy perspective, the most important thing to understand is how your clients identify and what language they use to describe themselves, their identity or sexual practices. This is an example of the clinical benefit of shifting away from a binary frame, learning about a client's gender from an intersectional perspective provides an opportunity to know more about them and how they move through the world. For example, it is affirming for most transgender clients to be asked what pronouns they use. In our culture people who identify as men typically use he, him, and his and people who identity as women use she, her, and hers. People who have nonbinary gender identities may use alternative pronouns, for example, they, them, and theirs or ze, hir, and hirs. The way that a person presents their gender does not dictate what their gender is or what pronouns they use. The act of asking about name and pronoun usage establishes the provider as someone who respects the client and begins to create a safe working relationship. Including a space that allows for multiple names as well as pronoun usage on intake forms creates this foundation from the beginning. In the case example that follows, the client discussed uses the pronouns ze, hir, and hirs. This vignette exemplifies the importance of shifting away from a binary frame when working with erotically marginalized clients who are exploring their gender identity.

Vignette

Andy came to me for therapy because ze wanted to "figure out this gender thing." Andy was 19 years old, African-American, and in hir second year of college. Andy was assigned female at birth, and when we first met, identified as male and used

(continued)

(continued)

male pronouns. Shortly after we began working together, Andy asked me to begin using ze and hir pronouns instead of he and him. Ze was feeling more and more that ze was trans and nonbinary. Andy had begun identifying as transgender during hir last year in high school, but didn't tell anyone until hir first semester in college. Ze was concerned about experiencing physical danger if hir had told hir parents or teachers in high school. Instead ze waited until college and purposefully chose a university far from hir hometown. Ze originally came out to friends and professors on campus as a transman. Andy was an active member in several queer and trans student organizations and felt supported at school. During the summer between hir first and second year of college ze came out as a transman to hir parents and siblings, one older sister with children of her own and one younger brother still in high school. Andy was surprised by the positive reaction of hir family. However, as ze continued to explore hir gender identity, ze found that more and more hir felt like ze wasn't a man or a woman. Identifying as a man became as alienating as identifying as a woman. Andy felt pressure from hir friends and family, and from society at large, to either be a man or a woman. Andy sought a therapist to get help deciding when and to whom to tell about hir gender identity. I was the first person that Andy used ze/hir pronouns with. Within the safe boundaries of my office and our relationship Andy began to learn more about hir gender, what felt right, and what words ze wanted to use to describe hirself.

Non-Binary Gender Identity Sexual Intimacy Model

Gender identity and sexuality are intimately connected in our culture and our individual experiences. This is also true for people who have nonbinary gender identities. Constantinides's Non-Binary Gender Identity Sexual Intimacy Model (NBGI Sexual Intimacy Model) is a visual model that illustrates one way that gender identity, sexual behavior, and intimacy interact for people with nonbinary gender identities. In this model these three parts of a person's experience interconnect with each other while always being influenced by the experience of otherness. It demonstrates the way in which otherness can dominate the landscape of sexuality and sexual behavior when operating outside of a binary gender system. This model is a useful tool for therapists working with nonbinary clients, because it helps to demonstrate the ways in which applying a binary rooted assessment or understanding can actually further alienate or isolate a client. Ignoring the way in which otherness can be at the center of identity, sexual behavior and intimacy help to frame the unique constellation of concerns a person is grappling with. Additionally, separating intimacy from sexual behavior elucidates the fact that these are distinct experiences, sexual behavior is not always experienced intimately and intimacy does not always include sexual behavior.

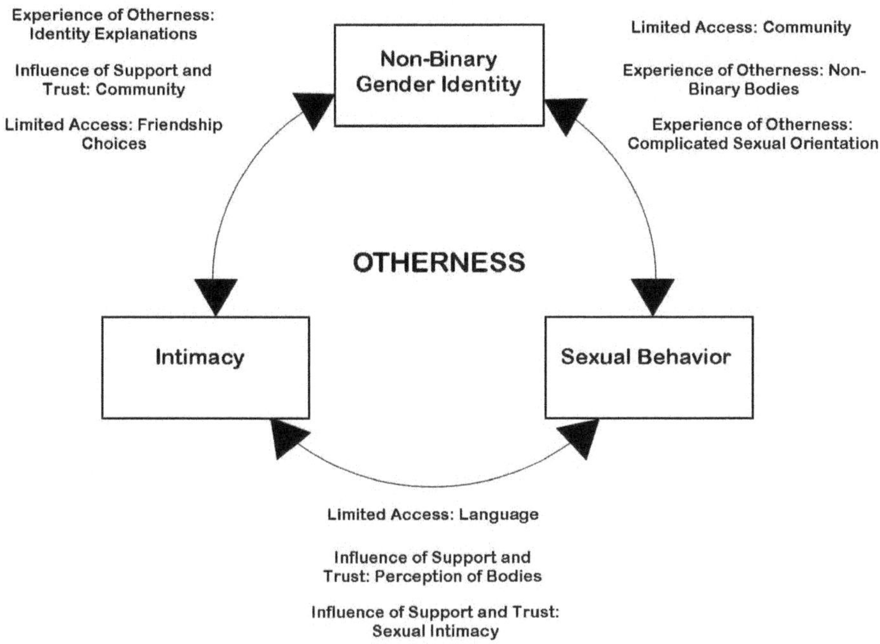

Figure 2.2 Non-Binary Gender Identity Sexual Intimacy Model

The NBGI Sexual Intimacy Model, based on qualitative interviews and using a grounded theory approach, exemplifies the ways in which oppression and discrimination can adversely affect people who are erotically marginalized. One study participant explained,

> *I don't fit the scripts, and people are both excited, because I don't fit the script, and both don't know how to function. So we don't necessarily get anywhere . . . I mean, it's lovely being a unicorn. And at the same time, you're a unicorn. . .when I show up, I am the unicorn. And . . . I get fag hags in this, like, totally strange, bizarre way. It's just like, "Oh, my God. You look amazing. What are you wearing? Your eyelashes are so great . . . Let's hang out." And I'm like, "You're hot. Okay." And – and I – I'm desexualized.*
>
> *(Constantinides, 2011, 144)*

In this example the participant describes how as a nonbinary person, they are simultaneously desexualized and fetishized. On one hand they experience others as being attracted and drawn to them because of their physical appearance and gender identity, while at the same time, our culture offers few sexual scripts for those who have nonbinary gender identities. This lack

Table 2.1 NBGI Sexual Intimacy Model Themes

Emergent Themes	Sub-Themes
Experience of Otherness	Identity Explanations Complicated Sexual Orientation Non Binary Bodies
Influence of Support and Trust	Sexual Intimacy Community Perception of Bodies
Limited Access	Community Friendship Choices Language

of sexual scripts can lead to desexualization as the validity of their experience is rendered invisible. As sex therapists, utilizing the NBGI Sexual Intimacy Model offers us a way to legitimize clients' experiences as well as understand in a deeper way the nuances of sexuality and gender identity. A client presenting for therapy with a sexual concern may carry with them similar experiences that call on sex therapists to have an awareness of the possible impact of oppression and discrimination not just on gender identity, but also on sexual desire, sexual behavior, and sexual intimacy.

The NBGI Sexual Intimacy Model identifies areas in which clients with NBGIs might experience challenges including having limited access to communities, friends, and language that adequately describes their gender and their bodies. Two other common experiences were the experience of otherness, particularly when one needed to describe or explain their gender identity, sexual orientation or body to others, and, how important support and trust was in their experience of community, their experience of their bodies, and in building sexual intimacy.

Even in transgender communities, participants with a NBGI felt on the outside, "I feel like when I'm around other trans people I fit in, but don't necessarily belong" (Constantinides, 2011, p. 159). Another participant discussed not participating in the transgender community at all because, "I obviously don't fit in there and all the resources that are out there are very binary-orientated . . . even trans people don't get it because . . . they just want to live their life." (p. 160). For clinicians working with clients who have NBGIs, it is important to be aware of possible isolation and challenges of finding community.

Vignette

Aaron was a white 45-year-old who sought out therapy in order to better understand their gender identity. They were assigned male at birth, and had been raised male, but never fully identified as male. From their first sexual relationship Aaron can remember describing to their female partners that they felt like they had no gender, or that gender was not important to them. Recently they have experienced an increased discomfort with their male body and increased comfort with a feminine identity. Aaron has always been sexually attracted to and dated women. They have had previous relationships with partners who were accepting and loving in regards to their gender identity. However, as their current relationship deepened, Aaron's partner began making clear indications of her discomfort with Aaron's gender identity including stating that she only experienced sexual attraction when Aaron was dressed and acting masculine. I presented the NBGI Sexual Intimacy Model to Aaron during session as a way to increase both our vocabulary and as a possible mirror to Aaron's experience. Aaron was not connected to transgender community and felt like they were not feminine enough to be a part of trans-feminine spaces. After discussing the model, I asked Aaron what they thought of it and if there were any parts of it that resonated with them. Aaron talked at length about how the type of sex that they participated in either increased the comfort with their gender identity (anal penetration) or decreased their comfort with their gender identity (penetrating). Before this moment Aaron had not connected the way in which sexual behavior impacted their feelings about their gender. They also revealed a recent pattern of erectile dysfunction and we began unpacking possible connections between this and their partner's feelings about their gender identity.

Sex, Sexual, and Relationship Identities

The gender binary is perhaps the most central and obvious way that binary thinking appears and is deeply problematic in popular culture. In this principle, we are asking clinicians to liberate their thinking from rigid categories of male/female, man/woman, masculine/feminine. These notions are socially constructed and intensely regulated within popular western culture. We are then asking them to take this expansion of thought and apply it to a larger clinical realm involving sex, relationships and sexuality. In this next section, we unpack binaries or dichotomies that exist in notions of sex therapy and how to think outside them, to problematize the very foundation in which they are rooted.

Sexual Orientation

Sexual orientation is also often a site of unchallenged binary assumptions. "Sexual orientation" describes a person's erotic attraction towards another person (Shively & DeCecco, 1977) and is most often categorized into "gay or straight" or "heterosexual or homosexual." "Heterosexuality and homosexuality, as relationship models, both rely on a bi-polar construct of sex and gender, a distinction between women and men that is seen as fundamental to human existence" (Green, 2004, p. 279), however this binary approach to sexual orientation erases a great many people, including those who identify as bisexual, pansexual, and queer. In order for someone to be "gay" or "straight," they and their partner need to identify with the binary gender system. These identities rely on the two categories of man and woman to describe the experience of same gender desire.

As we know from our work with clients, identity and relationships are much more complicated. Some people experience sexual desire for transgender people, or people with nonbinary gender identities. Others may experience sexual desire for more than one gender, or their experience of sexual desire may not be based on gender at all. For example, someone who identifies as demisexual only experiences sexual attraction if they also feel a strong emotional attraction, there may or may not be a gender component to this type of sexual orientation (www.asexuality.org/wiki/index.php?title=Demisexual). Bisexual can be interpreted as either supporting the binary gender system, or challenging it. For many people it indicates a sexual preference to "men" and "women" and therefore implies that there are only two gender choices available. Another interpretation of bisexuality is that it simply means sexual attraction towards two genders; which two genders is up to the individual person. For example, a person might be attracted to transgender people and women, but not cisgender men and use bisexual to describe their sexual orientation.

Queer and Pansexual

The term "queer" has multiple definitions both because it can be used in different ways, and because that is the intended nature of the term itself. In *Queer Theory: An Introduction* Jagose states, "In recent years 'queer' has come to be used differently, sometimes as an umbrella term for a coalition of culturally marginal sexual self-identifications and at other times to describe a nascent theoretical model which has developed out of more traditional lesbian and gay studies" (Jagose, 1996, 1). Queer studies as a field has only continued to evolve and grow since this was written, as does the use of queer as a personal identifier. Queer theory itself influences this principle by asking us to question and expand our understanding of the world around us by shifting away from binary models or understanding. For the purposes of this principle however, we are more interested in queer as a personal identifier. The elasticity of the word queer continues into its use as a sexual identity, it is often used to describe someone being "not straight" or "not participating in typical sexual relationships." It can describe a wide range of sexual attractions and behaviors and it is inclusive of all gender identities including transgender and nonbinary gender identities; as an identity category, it inherently defies the binary.

While queer tends to serve as an umbrella term that includes a political positionality, preferences related to sexual behavior and overarching identity, pansexuality is an identity more focused specifically on sexual orientation and practices with a focus on liberation from binary thinking or orientation. Callis (2014) describes that "for those people inhabiting this borderland, it is a place of sexual and gender fluidity, a space where identities can change, multiply, and/or dissolve." Just as people choose the identity label of "bisexual" or "queer" for a myriad of personal reasons, people similarly adopt "pansexual" for a variety of reasons. Inherent in the use of the term is a defiance of binary thinking, as the prefix "pan" is defined as "all-inclusive."

Kink and BDSM

Sexual orientation can also expand outside the constraints of gender. For example, "a primary identification as a sado-masochist can cut across and invalidate traditional descriptions of sexual orientation which regard the sex of one's object choice as definitive" (Jagose, 67). In other words, the practice of BDSM (bondage/discipline, dominance/submission, sadism/masochism) is often based on the behavior, not the gender of the practitioners. A client who identifies as part of the BDSM community may fall outside of a binary view of sexual orientation that assumes a person is either gay or straight.

Kink and BDSM sexual identity and sexual practices also challenges a binary idea of sexuality in which as a culture we prioritize heterosexual penetrative intercourse (Barker, Iantaffi, & Gupta, 2008). Sex that falls outside of that model is seen as incomplete or false. This can clearly be seen by the culture phenomenon of lesbian sex being seen as "confusing" or not real. Clients who participate in kink and BDSM may also find this kind of disregard of their sexual behavior and identity based on its incongruence with "real sex." Maintaining our nonbinary frame allows for the possibility of all different kinds of "real sex" that are equally and/or individually meaningful.

Relationship Models

Clients seeking sex therapy may participate in a variety of relationship models, and may be looking for support in the maintenance of those models. The historical focus on monogamy in the field of sex therapy (Berry & Barker, 2014) is an example of the way that a binary model is reflected in our culture's acceptance of relationship models. Monogamy is often centralized and seen as the only healthy choice and any divergence is viewed an infidelity or even psychopathology (Chatara-Middleton, 2012; Finn, Tunariu, and Lee, 2012). A nonbinary perspective allows for the possibility that there are many different types of relationship models, and our job as therapists is to help our clients find the model that works best for them; free from morality, judgment, or pathology.

Non-monogamy and polyamory are not new ideas, and polygamy has been a part of many cultures both historically and today. Working with non-monog amous and polyamorous clients in a field that is historically binary/monogamy focused may require an element of translation. For example, both Gottman and Emotionally Focused Therapy are relationship therapy models that are based on monogamous relationships that can be adapted to other relationship models. Our culture, and field, is monogamous-centric. Our erotically marginalized clients may need support in managing and navigating this form of sexual oppression.

Goal Oriented versus Pleasure Orientated

Sex is primarily viewed as a linear and goal-oriented behavior. Our vernacular language is filled with sports analogies that equate having sex (presumably cisgender heterosexual intercourse) with winning or scoring. What does someone really mean when they say, "I struck out last night!"? This euphemism is widely used in our culture, on the surface to say that someone didn't have sex last night. Let's look at some of the underlying assumptions that are hidden in this statement. Firstly, there is an assumption that "sex" means to the same thing to every person. Vernacularly "sex" describes penetrative penis-in-vagina intercourse. Using "sex" generally is at best confusing and at worst explicitly excluding anyone who does not participate in intercourse involving a penis and vagina. As sex therapists, we know that there are many different ways that people participate in sex and sexual pleasure. Secondly this statement assumes sexual intercourse as the goal of the interaction. Sometimes this is true and is a consensual decision made by all parties. However, this overarching idea that the goal is intercourse limits erotic and sexual relationships. In our culture we get even more specific, when we say "I had sex" what we mean (but usually don't clarify) is "I had intercourse and I had an orgasm." Striking out is a baseball reference, a goal-oriented sport. However, goal-oriented sex creates anxiety and is the root cause of many sexual dysfunctions (Timmers, 1976). Maintaining a pleasure-oriented model of sex provides clients with more options for a successfully and fulfilling sexual experience.

Application

Tools for Clients

Identifying Client Need

Clients feel the impact of a clinician's commitment to challenging a binary frame through our language and actions. Challenging binary thinking is not the same as rejecting binary thinking. Our clients come to us with their own beliefs and value systems. For some clients, a binary frame is an essential way that they understand themselves. For example, Malpas suggests that transgender people can be grouped into those with binary gender identities and those with nonbinary or more fluid gender identities (2008). A transgender client with a binary gender identity, for example someone designated male at birth who identifies as a transwoman, and articulates clearly their binary identity, has a very clear understanding of their gender identity and how it works. It unnecessarily and possibly harmful to apply a nonbinary frame to this individual person's experience. Alternatively, it is the clinician's responsibility to meet the client where they are without assigning a pre-conceived narrative of gender. Even the idea that there are "binary" and "nonbinary" gender identities is essentialist and uses a binary frame. A nonbinary frame doesn't adopt the nonbinary stance as a rigid alternative, but instead remains curious about possibilities and intersections.

Circle of Sexual Pleasure

One tool that we have found useful for use with erotically marginalized clients seeking sex therapy is the Circle of Sexual Pleasure, adapted from Timmers,

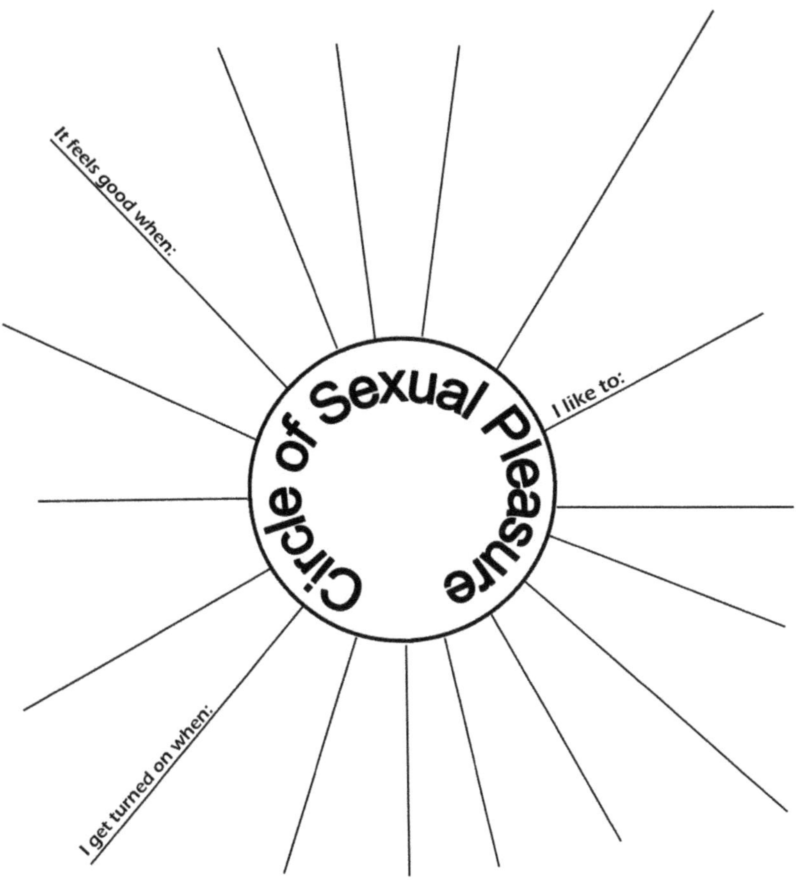

Figure 2.3 Circle of Sexual Pleasure

Sinclair, and James' (1976) Non-Goal Directed Sexual Experience. The traditional goal-oriented model of sex that is normalized in Western Culture can be described as steps. Each step is closer to the goal, which is heterosexual penetrative intercourse. In the United States we often encounter this step model superimposed on the analogy of baseball. Sexual participants try to get to First Base, Second Base, Third Base, and then Fourth Base, also known as a homerun or "scoring." Not getting to that fourth step means that you Struck Out – no runs. The entire sexual exchange is written off as a failure and you lose (Vernacchio & Foster, 2014). As discussed earlier, a nonbinary approach is an opportunity to step away from goal-based sex and move to a pleasure-based model. This is especially significant for erotically marginalized clients because their sexual experiences are rarely included in mainstream models of sex, media, or sexuality education.

The Circle of Sexual Pleasure model can be used in session during individual or relationship counseling to help clients expand their own sexual possibilities and desires. It looks like a sun, a circle with lines coming off of it. In the center of the circle is the client. Each spoke is one behavior that the client finds sexually arousing or pleasurable. This can include a wide range of sexual or erotic behaviors including holding hands, taking a shower together, giving a massage, oral sex, intercourse, watching a move, going for a walk, consensual hitting or slapping, consensual voyeurism, service, specific fetishes, or any other behavior that is pertinent to your client. With this model, any combination of any of the spokes constitutes a "good date" or a "positive experience." The pressure to perform both physically and socially is lifted and clients can create their own sexual menu.

Vignette

Phil was a Latino cisgender bisexual man in his early 30s who identified as kinky. He sought therapy to resolve recent erectile dysfunction that he experienced. At the time of treatment, Phil was currently in a long-term relationship with a woman. Six months prior, Phil began to have difficulty maintaining and keeping an erection during intercourse. Phil was terrified that something was wrong with him and ashamed of his inability to keep or maintain an erection. He talked about himself as "broken" and wanted to be "fixed." After connecting Phil to a urologist, he learned that nothing was physically wrong with him, although this knowledge further fueled his anxiety. From the beginning of our work together I refrained from using pathologizing or binary language. For example, I did not refer to his erectile difficulties as a "problem." Although I prefer to follow the client's lead in terms of the language they use, in this case I also refrained from using "broken" or "fixed" as ways to refer to his body or how it was functioning. I was transparent regarding my use of language with the client, explaining that sometimes our bodies don't do what we expect, but that shaming and blaming ourselves can often make us feel bad and take away from understanding our bodies better. I worked with Phil to make space for his feelings of disappointment and sadness, and to help him deepen his emotional vocabulary (figuratively and literally). As Phil was more able to identify his feelings both in the relationship, and during sex, he found that he was able to create situations where he was less likely to experience "erectile dysfunction." When Phil was able to move away from seeing himself as "broken" there was more opportunity to learn about the intersection between intimacy, desire, and his body. Phil found moving from a goal-oriented model of sex to a pleasure-oriented model of sex especially freeing.

Key Clinical Points

- Binary thinking describes a way of understanding that reduces complex ideas down to only two opposing choices (Budge, Rossman, & Howard, 2014). This system of thinking creates a framework of seeing the world that limits possibilities. As sex therapists we are as at risk for being immersed in this frame as anyone else.
- Maintaining a pleasure-oriented model of sex provides clients with more options for a successfully and fulfilling sexual experience.
- A nonbinary frame doesn't adopt the nonbinary stance as a rigid alternative, but instead remains curious about possibilities and intersections.
- The Circle of Sexual Pleasure model can be used in session during individual or relationship counseling to help clients expand their own sexual possibilities and desires.

References

Barker, M., Iantaffi, A., & Gupta, C. (2008). Kinky clients, kinky counseling? The challenges and potentials of BDSM. In Moon. L (Ed.), *Feeling queer or queer feelings? Radical approaches to counseling sex, sexualities, and gender* (pp. 7–22). London: Routledge.

Barker, M. & Scheele, J. (2016). *Queer: A graphic history*. London: Icon.

Berry, M. & Barker, M. (2014). Extraordinary interventions for extraordinary clients: existential sex therapy and open non-monogamy. *Sexual and Relationship Therapy, 29*(1), 21–30.

Budge, S. L., Rossman, H. K., & Howard, K. A. (2014). Coping and psychological distress among genderqueer individuals: The moderating effect of social support. *Journal of LGBT Issues in Counseling, 8*, 95–117. doi: 10.1080/15538605.2014.853641

Callis, A. S. (2014). Bisexual, pansexual, queer: Non-binary identities and the sexual borderlands. *Sexualities, 17*(1–2), 63–80.

Chatara-Middleton, A. (2012). Working with non-monogamy: Dance/movement Therapists' Experience of Working with Individuals in Non-monogamous relationships. *American Journal of Dance Therapy*, *34*(2), 114–128. doi:10.1007/s10465-012-9138-6

Constantinides, D. M. (2011). *Intersections of gender and intimacy in the lives of transgender people with non-binary gender identities* (Order No. 3456031). Available from Dissertations & Theses @ Widener University; ProQuest Dissertations & Theses A&I (871211349). Retrieved from http://0-search.proquestion.com.libcat.widener.edu/docview/871211349?accountid=29103.

Finn, M. D., Tunariu, A. D., & Lee, K. C. (2012). A critical analysis of affirmative therapeutic engagements with consensual non-monogamy. *Sexual and Relationship Therapy*, *27*(3), 205–216. doi:10.1080/14681994.2012.702893

Green, J. (2004). Centering: An alternative perspective. In J. Alexander and K. Yescavage (Eds.), *Bisexuality and transgenderism: InterSEXions of the others*. (pp. 277–285). New York: Harrington Park Press.

Jagose, A. (1996). *Queer theory: An introduction*. New York: New York University Press.

Lev, A. I. & Sennott, S. L. (2011). Understanding gender nonconformity and transgender identity: A sex positive approach. In P. J. Klienplatz (Ed.), *New Directions in sex therapy: Innovations and alternatives* (2nd ed.). New York: Taylor & Francis.

Malpas, J., MA, LMHC (2008) From otherness to alliance. *Journal of GLBT Family Studies*, *2*(3–4), 183–206, doi: 10.1300/J461v02n03_10

Moon, L. M. (2008). Introduction: Queer(y)ing a psychosocial approach to sex, sexuality and gender in therapeutic settings. In L. Moon (ed.), *Feeling queer or queer feelings? Radical approaches to counselling sex, sexualities, and genders* (pp. 1–6). New York: Routledge.

Shively, M. G. & DeCecco, J. P. (1977). Components of sexual identity. *Journal of Homosexuality*, *3*(1), 41–48. Retrieved from Humanities International Complete database.

Singh, A. A. & Dickey, L. M. (Eds.). (2016). *Affirmative Counseling and psychological practice with transgender and gender nonconforming clients*. Washington, DC: American Psychological Association.

Timmers, R. L, Sinclair, L. G., & James, J. R. (1976). Treating goal-directed intimacy. *Social Work*, *21*(5), 401–402.

Vernacchio, A. (2014). *For goodness sex: Changing the way we talk to teens about sexuality, values, and health*. New York, NY: HarperCollins.

THE CASE OF WILLIAM: HETERONORMATIVELY QUEER AND KINKY, AN INTEGRATION STORY

Amy Basford-Pequet

I am the Clinical Director of Northampton Sex Therapy Associates, LLC (NSTA), a group practice comprised of eleven sex therapists. I am also the Program Director of The Center for All Men and Sexual Health, a clinic for men's sexual health focused on working with men who engage in Out of Control Sexual Behavior. Encountering sex therapy, I felt lucky to have found a specialty with potential to combine many of my interests, beliefs, and values as a long-time social justice activist, therapist, group therapist, and queer person in the world. The founder, Jassy Casella Timberlake, created NSTA with the expectation that all sex therapists working there would be actively using a social justice framework, including a health at every size framework, as a part of the sex therapy provided. I was so fortunate to find a place to work, a kind of work, and a brilliant mentor who understands and operationalizes the importance of unpacking the impact of white cissexist heteropatriarchy on the body, sexuality, desires, intimate connections, and eroticism.

I am white, queer, cisgender, fat, femme, and of working class descent. I am mostly able-bodied, a survivor, and consider myself to be erotically marginalized. I am fluid sexually, meaning I like to switch, can easily move toward kinky play, and am attracted to many kinds of bodies and genders. I am married to a brown, queer, Filipinx, nonbinary, more masculine presenting immigrant. We have two children. We were each a gestational parent. One of our children is Filipinx and brown and one is mixed race, Filipinx and white, and is white presenting. I am well-educated and am solidly middle class and am without a legacy of financial or resource support to rely on.

Many of my identities are visible: my whiteness, my femmeness. And. I am fat. I identify as a person of size. When I started working with William I was not as fat. At least he did not know that I was usually fat. I happened to be in a "normative size" moment in my life. I remember receiving his intake and feeling nervous and unsure. He had requested to work with me and there was something about this request that made my skin crawl and my sixth sense perk up. He was the first person who had requested specifically to work with me and his request was vague saying he had read through our website and liked my bio the most. I immediately felt uncomfortable and unsafe in my body, but did not know why. I spoke with my director about it and she set me up with a hand-held alarm to have beside me during our first session.

William is a 54-year-old white cis man who is heterosexually identified and wealthy. During the last decade, with increasing exploration and intensity throughout the last five years, William started to explore his sexuality and found: he is attracted to trans women, likes to be penetrated with penises whether the person identifies as trans or cis, he likes being in the role of sissy, and amateur boudoir photography. William has a growing interest and desire to be dominated and penetrated as well as spanked while wearing a chastity device and for many years has enjoyed cross-dressing and intense nipple play.

Early in our work he described his ideal romantic partner: a brown-skinned Latina with dark hair, dark eyes, and a "big round butt, big thighs, and small breasts," and he explained that he thought he would find true love with a cis woman from a Latin American country and had pursued relationships with women who fit this ideal. I am not Latina and my skin is white and I identify as white, however, my hair is dark brown and curly and at that time I was the only member of our team with dark brown hair, brown eyes and curly hair. Even at my most normative sizes I have a lovely, larger-sized butt, large thighs, and am small-breasted. It became clear that, out of the clinicians in our practice, I was in closest proximity to this fantasy of his ideal romantic type. It became clear that I was holding a space, with my body, for his fantasies and desires to be present in the room. That, in turn, brought clarity to why, in those early moments when I was handed his intake, I was having such a visceral and intuitive response.

Hearing that I, in many ways, fit some sort of ideal body fantasy for William was also very confusing. Early on he very clearly let me know that he is "shallow" and "narcissistic" and "probably cares too much" about how he looks and how his partners look. He recounted stories of going to a hot tub with an ex, whom he was dating again when he first entered treatment, and feeling "kinda grossed out" and "turned off" by how her stomach looked as compared to how it had looked twenty years prior when they were first together. He told me another story of feeling sick at the sight of cellulite on a woman's legs that he had been dating. These stories left me feeling confused, rageful, and flooded in shame. On paper, William is the picture of who I have been expected to want to be desired by – of who has been handed the power to determine if I am desirable. He was in his early 50s when we began our work together, he is tall, white, skinny, has wavy hair, handsome, and wealthy. He is heteroromantically identified and a cisgender man. Why would *I* be flooded in shame? Why would *I* want to hide under the cushion of my turquoise faux-leather therapist's chair while he spoke of his valuation of women's bodies in his life? Shouldn't *he* be the one ashamed of his misogyny, objectification, and sexism while talking about women as well as added layers of racism, colorism, and fetishization when talking about cis Latinas and trans women from Thailand?

Session after session I tolerated the shame as it skidded along my fascia. I breathed deeply to stay present with William and not swept away with rage. I planted in my body and talked myself into re-owning my belly as it bulged and the perfect pockets of cellulite on the backs of my thighs. I slid my therapist hat back up to the top of my head as I slowly started to peer out from behind my turquoise cushion. I realized William needed me to be activated and responding. He was using his reactions and experience of my physical form to support deepening his own understanding of attraction, eroticism, and desire. My body, in those moments, was a symbolic and actual container to hold the complexity of his emotional and erotic landscape. As I started parsing out what was mine and what was his and the importance of being such a container, I was able to step back, self-soothe and settle into the work in a different way. I started looking for openings, moments of incongruence, and curiosity, and used them to sometimes gently, sometimes not so gently, but almost always directly; challenge William's language and frameworks. As I settled in, he started settling in in a different way.

As William felt more grounded in the work my sense of my being as a "container" for his emotional and erotic landscape was confirmed. Erotic transference started to arise; it felt as though William was attracted to me, like there were moments he wished I would dominate him, want him. He would flirt with me and started pushing boundaries of the therapeutic relationship. Boundaries like not paying his co-pay after each session along with asking me very personal questions and holding long moments of charged and intense eye contact. I could also tell that the erotic charge was increasing in the room, as I would periodically feel turned on during the sessions. I have learned that this is an important cue to pay attention to and not to be afraid of or push away (it is also a cue to get *really* good supervision to talk out the attraction in the room and how to work in the erotic transference!). In my experience, feeling turned on in the work could mean many things, but most often means that the person has brought a part of their sexuality into the work, that they have arrived. They are trying to communicate something to me about their lived experience. The mounting transference coincided with William opening up about the kinky solo play he was engaging in, his desires to be penetrated by a penis, as well as his fears of having penis-in-vagina (PIV) penetrative sex with cis women.

We sat in the erotic transference for weeks. I decided to bring it up and explore what it would mean for our work if William found himself attracted to me. I normalized that this happens quite readily in sex therapy, as I am a caring kind person who is holding his vulnerabilities in a compassionate and non-judgmental way. William became very rejecting of the idea that he could be attracted to me. He denied the possibility of it. It may have been too early in the work to bring this up *and*, during the experience, it felt as though there was great value in William rejecting me and almost shaming me in the sessions where I gently brought up the possibility of attraction in the room.

My wild ride of feeling desired and rejected repeatedly in the therapeutic work paralleled the emergence of two distinct and compartmentalized parts of William, his "feminine" and "masculine" parts, about which he used binary and gendered language to discuss. He would swing from solidly inhabiting one part to rejecting it in order to inhabit the other part, sometimes on a weekly basis. He referred to the part of him that wanted to be penetrated, dominated, spanked, etc. as the "feminine" part of him. This "feminine" part is the part that desired to be penetrated by a trans woman, but could not imagine being in a long-term committed relationship with a trans woman. While deeper into the "feminine" parts William would often feel less depressed at first. He would allow himself to have long solo sex play sessions, taking sexy photos, and playing with lots of toys. This is the part that *loved* to dress up in fancy panties with pink bows and beautiful matching tank tops with knee-highs and powerful and sexy high heels. He expressed feeling "cute" and "sexy" in this place. He would spend hours at a time on Tumblr re-posting pictures, mostly of trans women penetrating cis men and some depictions of himself or other cis men cross-dressing. He would often talk about his experience on Tumblr as an "addiction" as he would spend hours using Tumblr and felt he had no control over. William would stay in this "feminine" place for a few days to a week and then crash out into a very lonely hopeless place. This part would often feel liberated and full of immense pleasure while engaged in the sex and then flooded in shame and guilt afterward, often leading to days and sometimes weeks of depression.

In periods of depression William would swing the other way into the "masculine" part of him. This was the part that wanted to be in a normative long-term hetero-romantic relationship with a cis Latina woman and expressed feeling like it was unattainable. He would spend sessions tearful, angry, hopeless, and lonely and would dip in and out of talking about his fears of having PIV sex with a cis woman and historical difficulties in maintaining an erection in these scenarios. He would become very punitive toward the "feminine" part of himself and vow to stop looking at any sexual imagery that was not cis and hetero oriented as, when he was in this place, he was convinced that he was making himself not straight and not cis by watching the porn and looking at the still images that he was looking at while in the "feminine" part.

William's work has been largely focused on integration of self through the integration of these two parts in combination with a lot of differentiation and self-soothing work. Throughout William's first year, it became clear that this growing internal split between what he characterized as the "feminine" and "masculine" parts was causing discord, discomfort, turmoil, depression, and anxiety. William took the brave step into exploring the "feminine" side of him in our work. He used sessions to figure out ways he might be able to safely explore this part. He contemplated going to play parties or kink/BDSM conferences. He had been cross-dressing for about 30 years, but until about 5 years prior, had never shared this part of his erotic self with anyone else. During this time, he met a Latina cis woman online and they became play partners. He had the opportunity to dress up in front of another person and experiment with sex that started to move toward some kinky play, which was new territory for him and was eye opening and affirming. It also increased his internal discomfort around his sexuality and highlighted his internal erotic conflicts, as he wanted more, to be penetrated, dominated, to be a sissy, to dress up in panties and lingerie, wear a chastity device, to be spanked and to get off with someone sucking, pinching, and clamping his nipples. Delving into this territory, he began to wonder if he was a sex addict or a sinner.

In our work, he was able to delve into his "feminine" with me as a witness. I became a cheerleader for this part of him, affirming, validating, and normalizing. We discussed local resources and ways he could access kink and BDSM communities and occasionally he would allow himself to fantasize about a partner that held all the qualities he desired. At one point, William went to a day-long tantric workshop led by a woman who was also a professional dominatrix. He hired her for a package deal of individual sessions which was quite profound and ushered in a new wave of integration, comfort, and acceptance of his kinky/BDSM parts.

There was point in our work around his "feminine" parts where William started to wonder aloud if I knew enough about how to work with the masculine. He wondered if he should work with a cis male therapist who would be "better equipped" to explore this part of him. I felt another round of William trying to reject me and our work together and also wanted to stay open to his concerns. We decided to bring in a colleague of mine who focuses on masculinities, for a joint session. This colleague is a white cis gay man but William was unaware he identified as gay.

Prior to this session I had dreams that what William wanted was to see this colleague and I demonstrating sex acts in front of him in the session. These dreams did not feel erotic. It felt like the purpose of the dreams was to model something, almost to demonstrate possibility, or re-parent. In these dreams I positioned my colleague and was penetrating him wearing a strap on with a dildo and then the colleague was, very academically, positioning me and penetrating me vaginally and then anally with his penis.

During the collaborative session, my colleague gave a history of the development of the modern day construction of the normative/binary version of masculinity and its roots in homophobia and transphobia, and shared that the work we were doing was similar to the way he approaches masculinity work. After this collaborative session, William expressed not feeling like the other therapist was "masculine" enough and felt "bothered" by the session, but was not able to say much more than that about his experience of my colleague. Ultimately, that session brought to the surface a lot of fear that William was sitting with about whether or not his "masculine" parts would go away or be wiped out by such intensive work with his "feminine" parts. My willingness to bring the gay cis male therapist (the "expert" on masculinities) into the room pushed William's integration process along. What he really wanted to know was whether I could hold all of his parts. It became clear that I had successfully demonstrated that I was holding space for the versions of masculinity within him. I believe the collaborative session was somehow a reminder that those parts would not just disappear--that I would not forget or dismiss the entirety of him.

During this deep exploration of the "feminine" and "masculine" parts, William would still vacillate from week to week between the different parts of him and in and out of more and less depression and anxiety, but in general, stayed with over two years of work exploring many aspects of these parts. He shared the depths of shame, disgust, fear, and curiosity about the "feminine" part of him. At times he was able to confront his feelings of self-hatred, worthlessness, and ignorance and connect them to how he was using his money as a way to wield power and influence women, and mostly the cis Latinas not from the U.S., to be with him. He started to confront his racism and question why it has felt so compelling and important for his idealized long-term partnership to be with brown curvy cis Latinas. He started questioning why he is most often in relationships with women who are of a very different class background from him.

While doing this very pointed work around his sex, gender, and sexuality, William was also doing *a lot* of therapeutic work around other life factors. Factors such as: his relationship to his spirituality, coping with mental illness in the family, differentiation with family of origin, exes, and friends. There were many parts of William that needed to be attended to for him to even be able to believe that he can make space for his full sexual self. There were parts of him that needed to be shored up for him to feel stable enough to take more risks in expressing both his kinky self and his desire for deeper emotional intimacy with a cis woman he started to date. He needed to do work to be able to feel like he could stand on his own, rely on his full self, in order to be able to do the integration work around his gender and sexuality.

William is now moving fluidly through his parts and rarely refers to them as the "feminine" and "masculine" parts and when he does it is with love and affection and respect. He engages in nights of solo sex play while cross-dressing and penetrating himself with dildos and does not spend days or even hours flooded in shame or guilt afterward. He spends limited time on Tumblr and when he does it feels in his control and choice. He has started anti-depressants and is dating a light-skinned cis Latina whom he believes, will quite likely, engage in some kinky play with him. He is not putting his needs and wants away. He allows himself to express the more exhibitionist parts by being around his family of origin with shaved legs or wear tiny swim trunks to gatherings with wealthy, more conservative friends and relatives.

I chose to write about William because the many ways our identities intersected in a relationship of oppressor/oppressed was uncanny. For example: he grew up wealthy, I grew up working class. He fetishized brown trans people; my partner is brown and nonbinary. He expressed a lot of fat-phobia and sizeism with ease and I am fat. The places where we were able to join were around being erotically marginalized, his perception of me being kinky and on the dominant end of the dom/sub spectrum, and being white and not from the area. I also chose to write about him because I have felt more activated and more complex feelings in my work with him than I have with possibly any other client to date. There was a real turning point in our work together when William started talking about the complexity of his relationship to past lovers –especially in reference to past cis Latina lovers and the trans Thai woman he had been in a relationship with. It was simultaneously settling to hear how affectionately and respectfully he spoke of these past lovers and partners and still unsettling to hear some of the ways he talked about these same past lovers and partners in respect to their bodies and sex. He was clearly presenting me with the splits that lived inside of himself while trying to talk about all of the ways he was fetishizing, loving, rejecting, and desiring these women.

It was a relief to know that he deeply loved some of the cis Latina women he had dated. It was a relief to know that he had the capacity to connect and the yearning and desire for deeper, more intimate connections and that he was not completely and entirely objectifying and fetishizing these women. It settled something in me and helped me sort out his gaze (both his gaze in the room and the gaze I felt he walked through the world with) after hearing these stories. I was able to see and feel the complexity of this person sitting in front of me; and not just swim/drown in the presence of the gaze of his white cissexist heteropatriarchy pouring into the room as he described these past relationships. I got to see his tears of loneliness and emptiness and desperation for a different kind of connection with others. I got to see the regret in his eyes at how he treated some of his past lovers and partners. I got to hear the grief and sadness about being in his 50s and not having someone to go out to dinner with and cuddle up with in bed at night. I was presented with the paradoxes of being human, the manifestations of self-hatred and powerlessness gone unseen and unchecked and the violence this same self-hatred was causing toward others.

As a sex therapist I have had the opportunity to uncover the layers and layers of ways my own sociopolitical positionalities and identities impact my experience of body and sex as well as how these same positionalities impact how I do, experience, and am able to show up for the work with whomever is sitting on the couch across from me as my client. We are not immune to each other. My identities are constantly interacting with theirs and vice versa. There are ways my identities support work in moving along and ways they create places that make it hard for me to see and maybe even help my clients--especially in the moments where I feel flooded with the jab of a microaggression or the punch of a strong projection that happens to intersect with how my body looks or how my spouse presents in the world or how I understand and see the impact of experiences such as othering and violence through fetishization on people I know and love.

What does it mean to not consider how our bodies are entering the room as an avenue/conduit/container for the work even if our bodies never touch our client's bodies? What does it mean to not notice when we are turned on, flooded in shame, confused? What does it mean to not hide that we, as therapists, have bodies and that when we, as sex therapists, are talking about sex, sexuality, and eroticism, our bodies with all of their particular shapes, sizes, colors, and histories are also in the room? It is a disservice to our clients to not take the risk to explore our own bodies, eroticism, internalized messages about desirability politics and shame. William pushed my edges in all of these regards and I am deeply grateful for my work with him.

I can even honestly say, that I love him.

Note

1 We encourage therapists to use the language "what pronouns a person uses" not "preferred pronoun." The introduction of the notion of preference implies that there is a "real" pronoun and a "preferred" one, which is a binary into itself. Additionally, this then implies that the "preferred" pronoun is not authentic or real, that there is something not being said or to be discovered.

Principle Three

SUPPORT WILLINGNESS TO EXPERIENCE THE ANXIETY OF UNCERTAINTY

Introduction

Clients seek out a therapist because they are looking for answers. Our job, as sex therapists, is not just to help clients find their own answers, but to also help them learn to survive in the murky gray areas without answers. Human sexuality is complicated and by honoring those complex intersections we can help clients learn to be whole and suffer less. To hold our whole selves (and our clients) we need to be able to sit with the awe of not knowing.

Vignette

Before I met Jacky (16 years-old, white) I talked to his dad on the phone. A single parent, his dad expressed concern about the phase Jacky was in. Six months ago Jacky told his dad that he was a boy, despite a history of dressing and presenting as a feminine woman. His dad wanted Jacky to meet with me to determine if he really was transgender, or if he was just influenced by his group of friends at school, two of whom had come out as transgender in the last year. As a transgender therapist, it is sometimes difficult to sit with the discomfort of the parents of the trans youth with whom I work. Implicit in dad's concern about whether or not his child is "really transgender" is the assumption that it would be a bad thing to be transgender. In the best case scenario being trans is seen as dangerous; parents often talk to me about their fears that their children will be suicidal, lonely, ostracized, experience violence, or be unable to find a job. Worst case scenario parents understand being transgender as disgusting, a sin, or unacceptable.

(continued)

(continued)

Because I have the privilege of being open about my own identity, I am more likely to get parents who are feeling the former. They have made a choice to contact a transgender therapist to "help" their gender questioning child. My use of self becomes complicated. Do I share my own "success" as an "example?" Do I join with Jacky's dad around the dangers of being transgender and the fears that he is feeling? What approach is going to be best for Jacky?

I was clear with Jacky's dad, as I am with any parent who approaches me looking for validation of their child's gender identity, that I am not going to tell you whether or not your child is transgender; that is only something that they can share with us. What I can offer is a safe space for them to explore their understanding of themself and their gender, my years of experience working with gender questioning and trans youth, my training and clinical skills, and my own experience as a transgender person. What I am asking from Jacky's dad is that he join me in experiencing the anxiety of uncertainty. He's looking for a quick answer that will provide some guidance for his behaviors and how he can best support his child. In reality, what Jacky needs is a space for it to be ok to not know. I believe that holding this space is a gift.

Influences

This principle is influenced by the Freedom Paradigm (Hanna, 2011; 2013), key elements of Dialogic Practice (Olson, Seikkula, & Ziedonis, 2014), and Mindfulness, which stems from Buddhist thought (Chodron, 2012; Germer, Siegel, & Fulton, 2005; Kabat-Zinn, 1994; Suzuki, 1995). Although influenced by each of these paradigms or schools of thought, the origin of this principle lies more closely in the lived reality of our erotically marginalized clients whose experiences of their sexuality, intimate relationships, family building, bodies, and gender identities are pushing and expanding the definitions we currently have available to us. Erotically marginalized clients are often trailblazers in their experience, and it can be scary when there is no clear path to follow. As sex therapists we have found our own ability to tolerate uncertainty to be helpful in our work with erotically marginalized clients because it models and therefore opens up space for clients themselves to tolerate uncertainty. When we establish tolerating uncertainty not only as a possibility, but an expectation, we create a safer container to hold the anxiety that may arise.

The Freedom Paradigm's focus is helping clients attain freedom from oppression. Hanna believes that just helping clients learn how to cope with and be ok with the results of living with oppression is not enough and only contributes to the experience of living with oppression (Hanna, 2013). He identifies seven precursors for change:

1. A sense of necessity for change
2. A willingness or readiness to experience anxiety
3. Awareness
4. Confronting the problem
5. Effort or will toward change
6. Hope for change
7. Social support for change. (2013, p. 352)

The second precursor, a willingness or readiness to experience anxiety, recognizes acknowledging and feeling feelings as an important part of healing. We call on sex therapists who work with erotically marginalized clients to not only help their clients through this process, but to also experience it themselves. This is intended to shift the power dynamic between client and therapist. The therapist truly cannot be an expert, but they can work with the client to help them. The client themself is the expert of their experience. Acknowledging that we don't have all the answers and are ready to help, communicates to the client that it is ok to not know. There is an opportunity for modeling the skill of tolerating uncertainty.

There is a subtle but significant difference here between holding a stance of "not knowing" and not having the knowledge and skills to work with a population or client. We believe that therapists working with erotically marginalized clients should access education for best serving these populations through workshops, conferences, and other resources that we mention in this book in order to have a general knowledge base. We then hope that therapists will hold their education with a light touch, to assume that every client who walks into their office is the sole expert on their own lives.

A dialogic perspective to tolerating uncertainty is focused on shifting the goal of therapy away from diagnosing a pathology and creating an intervention as the expert, to creating space for all voices to be heard and valued equally. The therapist's aim is then to help a client or a system create language and to give meaning to unspeakable dilemmas. These principles are explored in greater depth in Principle Four. Sex therapy, like most therapeutic orientations, is built on a model of pathology and diagnosis. Masters and Johnson's Model of Sexual Functioning provided an original blueprint to identity and define when sexual behavior is functional or dysfunctional. Sexual dysfunction is diagnosed and treated accordingly, either based on a physiological or psychological etiology. This version of sex therapy, which laid the foundation on which we have built the work that we do today, is based on a behavioral model consistent with the mainstream model of what sex is, a procreative physical behavior between two heterosexual cisgender adults. The sexual experiences of erotically marginalized clients often fall outside of this limited definition of sex and therefore challenge traditional sex therapy models.

The use of mindfulness practices has grown dramatically in the field of psychotherapy in recent years, has its roots in Buddhist thought and finds a helpful application in clinical work through the idea of mindfulness based stress reduction. Buddhist thinkers and writers have long worked with the idea of uncertainty, or not-knowing, sometimes referred to as "beginner's mind." Suzuki reminds us "in the beginner's mind there are many possibilities, but in the expert's there are few" (1995, p. 21), which is an important message for meditators, for therapists and for clients. Pema Chodron (2012) explores Buddhist thought and its practical, daily application. She discusses that this sense of not-knowing is one of the most fundamental anxieties of being human and encourages all of us to work with our own minds through meditation to create a culture of awareness and acceptance of the dilemmas of being human. Mindfulness based stress reduction reminds us about the importance to remain present and in the moment to moment with our clients and with ourselves. As a clinical tool the definition of mindfulness, "expands to include *nonjudgement*" (Germer, Siegel, & Fulton, 2005, p. 6). This stance of non-judgmental not knowing encourages our clients to both experience and define themselves outside of the relentless weight of marginalization, or in spite of it.

Uncharted and Uncertain Narratives

Clients who experience erotic marginalization are often blazing uncharted and uncertain narratives. This can include the first transgender student at her high school, the first poly triad navigating the foster care system, or the only person of color at a BDSM munch. As sex therapists, our job is not to have the answers, but to hold space to help our clients discover them for themselves and to be able to sit with our own uncertainty and discomfort.

Tools

Normalizing and Modeling

We can model tolerating uncertainty with clients by being transparent about their own process. The following case offers an example of using the therapist's own experience to normalize and model what might be an unsettling and frightening experience.

Vignette

Eli and I had been working together for two years. Eli was a white transgender person with a nonbinary gender identity who also struggled with severe depression and anxiety. They were blazing new paths as they came to understand their gender identity and sexuality. Questions that we discussed included: What does it mean to be trans? What is a man? What is a woman? Can my gender change? What does the kind of sex that I like mean about my gender identity? What does it mean to transition? Who will accept me? Who will love me? What do I want? One day when Eli turned to me for answers my response was, "I don't know what happens next, which feels uncomfortable to say but is true. What is it like for you to hear that I'm not sure what the next step is?" They expressed that they felt scared and we both talked about what it was like to not know what to do. Eli's anxiety decreased throughout this session as we together made space for feelings of fear and not knowing. We brainstormed together the things that helped Eli to feel safe during times like these. They talked about how helpful it felt to talk to their friends and partners about it and to be in their apartment with their dog – ways they could feel both emotionally and physically safe. Together we took a moment to both breathe, notice our bodies, and to feel the floor beneath our feet. These physical markers helped Eli to use their sense of touch to stay present and have this hard conversation with me.

Mindfulness

Mindfulness-based stress reduction is a research-based approach to teaching people to stay present developed by Jon Kabat-Zinn that has been found to be effective treating anxiety (Hoge et al, 2013), mood disorders (Hofmann et al, 2010), and stress disorders (Kearney et al, 2012). It uses a combination of meditation and mindfulness to help clients to experience their feelings and experiences in the present moment. Remaining present is also a strategy that we use to help clients reduce anxiety in general. Anxiety always focuses on the past or the future. If you are truly present (and not experiencing direct stress or trauma) then there is no space for anxiety to co-exist. There are many excellent resources for learning more about mindfulness-based stress reduction and how it can help sex therapists to be more present clinicians as well as ways to use with clients.

Using the Body

We believe that our connection with our body is a powerful tool to help clients both understand and tolerate their feelings. Using the body is not right or helpful for every client. Clients who have experienced trauma or abuse may find body work to be triggering, it is important to check in with clients before suggesting interventions that involve the body. Body work can include recommending that clients seek out alternative therapies such as massage. It can also be helping a client feel more aware and in touch with what is happening in their body. Body work is an extension of mindfulness, it is a way to manage anxiety through the body itself (vs using the mind to control the body).

Key Points

- Erotically marginalized clients may find themselves without a clear path to follow.
- Therapists who work with erotically marginalized clients need to be willing to not have all the answers and model for their clients the practice of tolerating uncertainty.

References

Chodron, P. (2012). *Living beautifully: With uncertainty and change.* Boston, MA: Shambala Publications.

Germer, C. K., Siegel, R. D., & Fulton, P. R. (Eds.) (2005). *Mindfulness and psychotherapy.* New York: Guilford Press.

Hofmann, S. G., Sawyer, A. T., Witt, A. A., & Oh, D. (2010). The effect of mindfulness-based therapy on anxiety and depression: A meta-analytic review. *Journal of Consulting and Clinical Psychology, 78*(2), 169–183. doi: 10.1037/a0018555

Hoge, E. A., Bui, E., Marques, L., Metcalf, C. A., Morris, L. K., Robinaugh, D. J. Worthington, J. J., Pollack, M. H., & Simon, N. M. (2013). Randomized controlled trial of mindfulness meditation for generalized anxiety disorder: Effects on anxiety and stress reactivity. *Journal of Clinical Psychiatry, 74*(8), 786–792. doi: 10.4088/JCP.12m08083

Kearney, D. J., McDermott, K., Malte, C., Martinez, M., & Simpson, T. L. (2012). Association of participation in a mindfulness program with measure of PTSD, depression and quality of life in a veteran sample. *Journal of Clinical Psychology, 68*(1), 101–116.

Kabat-Zinn, J. (1994). *Wherever you go there you are: Mindfulness meditation in everyday life.* New York: Hyperion.

Olson, M., Seikkula, J., & Ziedonis, D. (2014). The key elements of dialogic practice in open dialogue: Fidelity criteria. Version 1.1: September 2nd. http://umassmed.edu/psychiatry/globalinitiatives/opendialogue/

Suzuki, S. (1995). *Zen mind, beginner's mind.* New York: Weatherhill.

THE CASE OF DERICK: A FRAMEWORK FOR INTEGRATION

Thomas Wood

Jose Saramago wrote "inside us there is something that has no name, that something is what we are" (1999). The time, effort, and energy it takes to locate that "something" can seem monumental. Additionally, to construct language to describe the depth of one's identities can be even more difficult. As a queer person, I am intimately familiar with the struggle to integrate different parts into some semblance of an identity. I am also familiar with succumbing to pressures to disintegrate, or to section off certain parts of myself, to seem more presentable and, therefore, acceptable. I know the personal and social impacts of these pressures that can leave us nameless, without communities to belong to, and without validation that our experiences are real. This experience has informed my work as a social worker and psychotherapist in that I use the clinical space to explore the forces and motivations to integrate and disintegrate parts of the self. I also use this approach to structure sessions around processing the trauma and loss of this experience.

In going over Derick's intake form, I recorded that he was a 36-year-old, Vietnamese-American, partnered, gay-identified, cisgender male with no religious affiliation. As soon as he sat down, I could sense a mix of anxiety and uncertainty. After chatting for a few minutes, Derick confessed that he was "not interested in being in therapy forever." I responded with "you know a trained psychoanalyst might call that a fear of commitment." We bonded over a good laugh and got started. Derek asked for help to manage some sexual activities he described as "addictive" and "out of control." He was in a relationship at the time and was hiding his frequent use of crystal meth and much of his sexual behavior from his partner. Feelings of guilt, shame and fear overwhelmed his daily existence and made running an architectural firm difficult. He feared he would soon lose his relationship, his business, and possibly his life if he kept up this behavior. There was also a great deal of unwanted violence associated with his meth use. Over the prior two years, Derick had been beaten, robbed, cut with broken glass, sexually assaulted, and burned with cigarettes. While high, some sexual or using partners would become angry and assault Derick in various ways. Violence also occurred during drug procurement. It seemed like Derick was hurting, being hurt, and sometimes hurting himself at every turn. When talking about these events, Derick referenced them in ways that ranged from joking to self-deprecating, which I noted but did not comment on. With little emotion, Derick also revealed he became HIV positive and contracted Hepatitis C after he started using meth.

After these details were provided, I moved into an initial assessment. This assessment involved an invitation for Derick to tell me as much as he would like to share during our first session together. I emphasized that I was relying on Derick to determine what information he thought was important, not just what he thought I needed to know. With clients whose lives are clouded by guilt, fear, and shame, I find it valuable to establish early on that their voice and their story (as told from their perspective) is central to the therapeutic relationship; to let their voice be the grounding element in our work. Initially, Derick focused entirely on wanting control and shared a rather long list of how his behavior needed to change. He presented some "all or nothing" thoughts around his goals by stating that he "never wanted to use any substance again and wanted to stop having sex with other men." When asked if he would like to talk about a plan to accomplish these goals, Derick brought up deleting drug contacts from his phone, avoiding spending time with people who use crystal meth, and changing his route to work to no longer pass bathhouses. We examined the pros and cons of this plan together. Towards the end of session, I gently brought up the idea of our self being made up of different parts by stating that, "while creating plans effectively refocuses anxiety on tasks and can reassure fears, in the future we may be talking about other ways to cope with uncertainty and how to cope with those parts of life and ourselves that are outside of our control." We agreed to the plan and made another appointment. Derick left our first session reporting feelings of hope and renewal.

Derick missed his next two appointments. When he returned a few months later, he acknowledged he had relapsed out of fear. He disclosed he was overwhelmed with the possible loss of his sexual outlet. This insight allowed us to revisit the notion of all or nothing thinking which oversimplifies parts of the world into two opposing categories that hold incredible emotional weight. For Derick, he thought his choice was between a sober, sexless life of responsibility or a sexually hedonistic life of abandon and ultimate demise. I reassured him that it is normal during periods of frequent substance use to feel out of control and desperately want to gain control by going to the opposite extreme. However, Derick seemed to, in that moment, understand he could lose something very important to him if he chose total control – his sexuality. This conversation provided a foundational understanding to later broach Derick's association between vibrant sexuality and total abandonment of his responsible self.

A few weeks after Derick returned from his relapse, I chose to check in on any possible role my identities played in his absence from therapy. I wondered what it was like for Derick to be seen as "unable to control himself" by me, a white, cis, gay male. We discussed what it was like for him to fully show up in this dynamic, even when he was not at his best. This check in led to a bigger conversation about what it was like for Derick to grow up in the rural south. He was one of very few people of color and felt as though that gave him the ability to fit into or "blend" with white, Western culture. He softly reflected that he could act like he belonged but never actually "felt belonging." This discussion revealed that, in times of embarrassment and shame, he would hide from white scrutiny (or as he later called it "white eyes") so that even if he didn't belong, his differences could be mitigated. Derick could stay somewhat in touch with friends of color but he noted it was different with white men. We discussed his reasons for choosing a white male therapist and what he would like to do going forward: possibly work with a therapist of color or try to work through the feelings of shame and embarrassment with me, a white therapist. Derick took a week to think about it and came back to our next session with a desire to feel through our potential differences. He recognized a repetition of the same dynamic of only showing his cultivated self and hiding anything deemed shameful in other areas of his life. He asked that we go forward together. Through presenting parts of myself as possibly being important to our connection, I gave an example of how discussing the interrelational experience of our identities can positively or negatively impact connection. Exploring gaps in our connection genuinely mattered to Derick because he described his suffering as coming from a place of disconnection. His attendance became more regular and I believe our therapeutic relationship grew stronger from this discussion along with Derick's interest in knowing himself in deeper ways.

Further assessment revealed that Derick's sexuality and desire for sexual and affectionate touch was deeply tied to his drug use. Derick felt unsure how to be excited about sober sex. It was as though Derick needed to go to the crystal meth and request permission to be his whole sexual self. I challenged him to consider the vast middle ground between sober and substance-influenced sex. Those two options only seemed to embody a loss of aspects Derick did not want to part with. On one side, he didn't wish to lose his sexual abandon, on the other, he didn't wish to lose everything he had worked for and invested in. Our further exploration blended Cognitive Behavioral, Internal Family Systems, and Acceptance and Commitment therapies to broaden Derick's thinking so that he could see potential for his integrated self rather than simply loss. These clinical modalities were employed to create language for what an integrated self might be like for Derick, identify the authentic values that would guide him through his toughest times moving towards integration, and unpack the unhelpful thoughts that blocked his way forward. By refocusing from fear to possibility, he felt more hopeful that recovery wasn't only about loss.

Having grown up as a gay male in a conservative/fundamentalist Christian community, I am aware of the ways in which I have been asked to separate my sexuality into a "closet" to preserve some of my self-esteem and to survive emotionally and, sometimes, physically. This process causes a banishment of the sexual self to a distant place with a gulf of fear, shame, and denial in the space between. Having an understanding of the ways in which heteronormative pressures can split our selves, I wanted to assess whether Derick had a similar or different experience with his sexual identity. To start this conversation, I asked questions about shame and any pressure felt to be different then who he knew himself to be. When we looked into possible sources of his sexual shame and need for substances to liberate him from inhibiting emotions, Derick revealed significant physical, emotional, and verbal abuse from his father. This abuse was even more pronounced when his father drank, which was a lot and often. As a "flamboyant, fat Asian kid", Derick felt unworthy around his father and rejected by his peers. However, he found validation and recognition in his academic achievements. Derick avoided sexual intimacy of any kind until he graduated high school and moved to a major American city, choosing instead to focus on his studies. In his first sexual and romantic relationship, Derick found himself pulling away from his partner sexually and engaging with other men without his partner's knowledge or consent. When his secret sexual behavior was discovered, his partner decided to end the relationship. Derick continued to thrive in his architecture program but his next few relationships also ended due to undisclosed/discovered sexual behavior and/or drug use.

As we saw this pattern of outward projection of togetherness and achievement with periods of partner discovery and shame, Derick realized his "failures" only made him more determined to present perfection. I also noticed that the words Derick was using like "flamboyant, fat, Asian, gay" were words that typically are used to identify those who do not fit into western ideals for masculinity. I wondered if not fitting into masculine ideals also fueled his drive to hide his sexuality and present a cultivated persona. I asked "Can you think of any place or relationship in which you feel free to be Asian, gay, flamboyant, intellectual, and sexual all at the same time?" Derick first reported a belief that being high allowed him to be himself completely. We explored this idea a bit more and it became clear that, when high, he could be everything but his intellectual self and acknowledged that this part of himself was and is equally important. This realization was a turning point in our therapy as it was in this moment Derick recognized how his lack of identity integration had him using substances, environments, and relationships to try and access different parts of himself that had been compartmentalized through abuse, trauma and survival. The more significant the trauma, the more he needed extreme methods of numbing, avoiding or escaping his inhibitions to access his disowned self. With a belief that he had the power to bring and hold his parts together, Derick's goal became valuing integrity and setting boundaries in his life to claim some space for his whole self to exist. When I asked how Derick would like help from me in this effort, he stated that he needed support and encouragement to talk more openly about his sexuality, his HIV status, his racial identity, his recovery, and his past trauma.

To focus on open communication, we explored the meaning of courage as being the experience of fear along with the commitment to go forward anyways. Derick expressed a desire to disclose his secret sexual behavior and drug history to his current partner to face his fear that if he revealed himself, he would be abandoned. Although he was not physically abandoned, his partner reacted with disgust and demanded that Derick find ways of "making it up to him." As we talked about his partner's reaction, Derick realized he was, again, being asked to split himself into parts and compartmentalize to only show his partner what he wanted to see. Soon after this realization, Derick ended his relationship. This was the first time Derick had ended a relationship and brought about his most empowering insight, that his embodied self was not a vessel for meeting the needs of others. This insight meant that he could allow himself the right to be uncomfortable, the right to set terms, the right to have boundaries and limits, and, ultimately, the right to exist.

Once the groundwork for integration was established, we moved on to Derick's goal of finding connection in his life. Our work shifted to focus on locating supports and creating communities that would not ask for, or expect, a perfect persona. While this state of social presentation allowed Derick to survive scrutiny and abuse, it blocked him from connection in all directions. This new direction in treatment included locating an LGBTQ recovery group (Crystal Meth Anonymous). This group gave Derick the room to incorporate both his sexual identity and his experience with substance use into his whole life story. From there, Derick connected with a few folks in recovery and together they started an exercise group. At first, it was difficult for Derick to connect with a group of gay men and not sexualize the dynamic. What became clear through this dynamic of compulsively sexualizing connection with other gay men was that sexuality was used by Derick to relieve his social anxiety around gay men. However, the shadow side of this coping mechanism was that it also repeatedly confirmed a belief that his only worth to gay men was as a body to be sexually used. In time, he determined he wanted to find other sources of self-worth and esteem around gay men that didn't deny or ignore erotic dynamics but centered mainly around regard for mutual personhood. This insight led our work to a disclosure that allowed us to begin processing Derick's seroconversion.

Through our discussion around compulsive sexualization of gay men, Derek made important connections which led to him asking the question, "this dynamic explained why I wanted to get HIV?" I asked him to elaborate and he responded with "I think because I felt worthless all the time, I believed I deserved to get HIV. Maybe deep down I just wanted to get it over with." Derick acknowledged that there was also an erotic component to being infected with HIV and Hepatitis C. Initially, Derick could not reconcile his desires with his rational mind that did not want to live with these conditions. Because we had spent a great deal of time recovering lost or disowned parts, Derick soon identified that he felt terrorized by HIV and STIs growing up because it was the way in which his father would abuse his gender nonconforming behaviors. An early recollection for Derick was when his father observed him talking to a friend on the phone and thought he sounded feminine. His father asked him if he was "some kind of fag?" and then asking if he wanted to "die of AIDS" because that is what happens to "those people." This interaction sent a clear message to Derick, that something about him, his gender expression, and his sexuality was dangerous and worthy of disgust. To mitigate his fears, Derick compartmentalized his sexuality to focus on school. Later, when he started having sex with men, Derick believed that seeking out and eroticizing HIV transmission, as well as the behaviors that he believed would bring about transmission (bareback intercourse, multiple partners, injection drug use, etc.), allowed him to access his sexuality in ways that were otherwise inhibited by fear and self-judgement. Eroticizing transmission seemed to allow Derick to take back his sexuality from the fears which inhibited it – to paradoxically make desirable the very thing that terrorized his early life. Through our processing of the impact of childhood abuse on his sexuality, Derick began to identify the difficult feelings surrounding his behaviors and set out to claim his right to have a sexuality that didn't leave him feeling the way his father's abuse and the childhood bullying did – ashamed and afraid. It was in the following weeks that Derick took full grasp that he had many options in between and outside of the shame-based binary of sexual abstinence or total, unsafe abandon. Derick's continued momentum built on the notion that he could go to himself, his values, and his intuition to guide his sexual choices and connections rather than going to a substance that promised freedom but only ever left him deeply ashamed and afraid of himself.

Our efforts to unpack shame, guilt, and fear to create space for integration and connection were made possible by our combined willingness to try and name that "something" that makes us who we are, that something that either connects or disconnects us from ourselves and others. This process asked for vulnerability and courage from both of us that ultimately created an open space for Derick to give a voice to his experience, his identities, and ultimately, his truth.

Reference

Saramago, J. (1999). *Blindness*. Boston, MA: Harvest Books.

THE CASE OF NIAM: RACE, CLASS, SEXUALITY, AND GENDER WHILE BEING AND BECOMING

Jaycelle Basford-Pequet

Agency Context

Niam is engaged in individual psychotherapy at The Institute for Emerging Adulthood, Inc., an independent psychotherapy practice with offices in Northampton and Amherst, Massachusetts. I am the Director of The Institute for Emerging Adulthood, Inc (IEA). IEA compassionately engages adults in the Five College Area – Smith College, Amherst College, UMass-Amherst, Hampshire College and Mount Holyoke College – in therapy for being and becoming in changing terrain. IEA clinicians treat individuals navigating trauma, depression, anxiety, couple and poly relationships, race-based trauma, POC (people of color), and LGBTQ individuals in an anti-oppression framework and a creative and embodied process. Treatment at IEA consists of weekly individual and/or couple/poly group long-term psychotherapy.

Specificity of identity is meaningful for me as a 36-year-old queer, brown, immigrant, AFAB/nonbinary individual, parenting and loving in an interracial relationship with a white cis woman. *I come from somewhere.* I was born in the Manila and am part of the Filipinx diaspora. *I come from nowhere.* I am AFAB and nonbinary and do and do not remember what has been erased. *I come from everywhere.* I am brown and accompanied by the global majority. I am an uneasy transplant. As a parent *I come and will go.*

Client Information and History

Client system and identifying information

Niam is a 22-year-old undergraduate at a historically women's college. They are a black-identified Afro Latinx masculine of center nonbinary individual. They are temporarily able-bodied and a U.S. citizen. They were, per client, "raised white" in an upper middle-class socioeconomic status, both of their parents are software developers in major tech firms, they attended private schools for the entirety of their primary and secondary education. Their family's experience of SES has at times been mutable but was largely of upper middle class status.

Presenting concerns

Niam presented with issues related to self-worth, anxiety, and existential dread. They named their gender transition as "a process, I am figuring it out." Niam identified as monogamous in a poly-oriented relationship and described that there was a level of codependency in their primary relationship that felt isolating and confusing. Consuelo, Niam's primary partner, is a femme, nonbinary, Latinx individual of Chicanx and Salvadorean lineage. They live in a nearby metropolitan area and recently graduated from college as a first generation undergraduate. Consuelo identifies as both queer and poly. Over the course of being together Niam has felt pressure to perform sexually with Consuleo. The pressure to be sexual was exacerbated by Consuelo's responses to Niam if they didn't want to be sexual. Consuelo would cry for hours, act in punishing ways, or completely stop speaking to Niam. Niam also presented with social anxiety related to experiences of being in the out group following a break up with a charismatic upper classman. They made choices to step away from student groups, and had ruptures in a theatre group. Niam grew up in a somewhat high conflict household where fights often resulted in yelling and then stonewalling.

Histories and Theories

Sex and bodies

In middle school Niam developed an eating disorder, describing their restrictive eating as "control oriented" as they navigated "being black in a predominantly white setting." They described eating less and "if no one listened to me I starved myself." During this time in middle school they presented as femme and they linked an increased experience of internal pressure in the face of having to perform femininity, specifically, performing gender adjacent to white upper class, straight, and cis femininity in a black body. Niam shared that through primary and secondary education they were often "the only" black person in their classes, extracurricular activities and sports teams. In high school Niam was hospitalized briefly and then engaged in outpatient eating disorder treatment. This experience of treatment ended abruptly, Niam reasoning that "I just wasn't doing it right, and they basically kicked me out."

Coming to college Niam began transitioning socially and "moved away from the eating disorder." One important resource that supported this move away from the eating disorder was a love of creating playlists. At several points in our work they developed playlists that centered around compassion, grief related to social and physical transition, and a playlist that was informed by an emerging self-part that "is grown enough to take care of me/themself."

Niam described their process towards a masculine of center gender presentation as coinciding with a changing relationship with their body, in particular decreased restrictive eating and purging cycles, remission of binge exercising, and decreased body dysmorphia.

Niam's relates experiences as a gendered individual being multiply defined as a black transmasculine individual. Niam "feels seen as transmasculine in a way that I don't consent to." Niam named that at their historically women's college their experience was that transmasculinity was associated with promiscuity and aggression. In one session they animatedly described what they were *not* trying to be "a trope of angry, possessive, insecure masc trying to lord over a happy fleek femme, you know, that's just so 1990s." I laughed out loud with them enjoying their flawless delivery, exuding a with-it-ness with which I could just barely keep up.

Niam continues to navigate sex, gender, race and sexuality in the wake of formative phenomenological technologies – both personal and historical – namely, a recent sexual assault and U.S. chattel slavery. Christina Sharpe in her 2016 book *In the Wake: On Blackness and Being* offers as a siren meditation on the leitmotif of the wake, in summary, an "instantiation of the wake as the conceptual frame of and for living blackness in the diaspora in the still unfolding aftermaths of Atlantic chattel slavery". In this work Sharpe locates being woke, the wake, and the wake work evoking DeLoughrey's (2010) image of "the American ship of state . . . the ark of the covenant that authorized both liberty and slavery." In considering the wake work we are called to consider Sharpe's words, "a region of disturbed flow . . . Wake; the state of wakefulness; consciousness . . .Wake; in the line of recoil of (a gun) . . .Wake: a watch or vigil held beside the body of someone who has died . . . Wake: grief celebration, memory" (Sharpe, 2016).

Wake Work

Niam considers woke. Niam considers woke in the wake of their sexual assault. One day Niam entered session in a powder pink windbreaker and announced with a frozen smile that their partner had sexually assaulted them. It seems that some of work since then has been about choosing between narratives. In *Sister Outsider*, Audre Lorde says, "If I didn't define myself for myself I would be crunched into other people's fantasies for me and be eaten alive." (Lorde, 2007). Niam considers the possibility of "not prosecution and persecution but a restorative justice model", making choices about "calling in" and "calling on" chosen family and family of origin, giving themself permission to access material resources to change student housing and restructure academic workloads. They tell a chosen few some details of their sexual assault. A moment of great importance for Niam was choosing to share some details about their sexual assault with their Latinx mother and Black father. Their parents are upper middle-class professionals, whose relationship was shaped by desire and anxiety related to hyper-performance, specifically academic and vocational excellence in institutions of higher education. Niam felt seen and received in this moment of conversation with their parents, this moment of vulnerability when their mother heard and responded with, "Niam, do you need to take a semester off?"

Niam chose *not* to name Consuelo as the perpetrator of acts of assault to mutual friends. They perceived in the sequela of social distancing from peers, narratives that they felt as disciplining and regulatory. Narratives related to notions about the promiscuity and aggressiveness of transmasculine individuals, i.e. Niam as a "fuckboi," as well as social perception of them as a shifty player in racialized erotic borderlands with the potential "to hurt" a "white femme baby queer" and "the POC status quo". Largely, they chose to take the fall for other people's fantasies for the ending of their relationship with Consuelo dealing with race, sexuality, gender, and class narratives beyond their choosing.

In the wake of their sexual assault Niam considers their familiar sense of *being in trouble.*

In *Aberrations in Black: Toward a Queer of Color Critique* Ferguson follows in his author's eye the "black drag-queen prostitute [who] sashays along a waterfront" in Marlon Rigg's 1989 film *Tongues Untied* a film whose closing line is "Black men loving black men is the revolutionary act." Between these opening and closing images naming fiercely race, sexuality, class and gender, Ferguson (2004) invites us to accompany closely the black drag-queen prostitute naming, "that engagement has borne a range of alienations, each estrangement securing another: her racial difference is inseparable from her sexual incongruity, her gender eccentricity, and her class marginality . . . She is multiply determined, regulated, and excluded by differences of race, class, sexuality and gender" (Ferguson, 2004).

An alienation that both Niam and Ferguson point to is the notion of home. Niam named student groups, a black student group, a POC group, a queer POC group, and fellowship programming, as one of many spaces that produced racialized space that were both home and not home. Niam's dystopic experience was one of feeling relegated to the margins of their campus's queer-trans (QT) groups and people of color (POC) groups. Metaphorical and figurative houses, student groups and housing, in the margins for not being "black enough" in their particular constellation of race, sexuality, gender and class. The discipline inflicted in the face of this double bind is their experience of expulsion by the black and QTPOC community. Their transgression was leaving their aggressor, Consuelo, who was read by the majority of the proverbial houses as the victim. In the wake of their sexual assault Niam was left to consider literally and metaphorically, just where do they live.

Bodies and Social Being

Niam was also aware of the ways their black body engenders in others a preoccupation with their physicality, a watchfulness about "what they might do." As a high school athlete, in the distinctly queer space of their lacrosse team, and in their sexual engagements with other queers, there was a way their being was watched as a sort of doing, a sort of trouble. Like the black drag-queen in Ferguson's meditation, we might consider the ways Niam's navigation through the wake was, "multiply determined, regulated, and excluded by differences of race, class, sexuality and gender." As a high school athlete when their gender presentation was "distinctly femme" their blackness engendered a sense in young white track and field competitors a somatically visible anxiety about athletic domination. Niam's being, ever in the transition of becoming, becomes a doing.

Niam described their experience of black transmasculinity on the lacrosse team as "complicated". Their lacrosse team was a social microcosm where the visibility and shared experience of physical and sexual aggression were a fluid currency. This exchange was accompanied by words, by substances, acts and intrigue. Niam named being watched with curiosity and wonderings about who they would "hook up with", with anxieties about being seen as a calculating "fuckboi" (deeply incongruent with their caregiver-identified sense of self), and acts of discipline related to miscegenation fears from both white-identified and POC peers alike.

Niam is certainly *in*, and perhaps positioned to *stay in, trouble.*

The Trouble with Freedom

Trouble. Freedom. Being in. Becoming.

Considering Niam's presentation (we might insert for the word "presentation" the words "assault," "playing field," or "work") the clinical position I posit might be to ground in the being and becoming of changing terrains. *Redefining. Devising. Altering. Constructing. In trouble.*

Sara Ahmed, the independent scholar who works at the intersection of feminist, queer and race studies, excerpts Judith Butler (1990) in *Gender Trouble*,

> *To make trouble was, within the reigning discourse of my childhood, something one should never do, precisely because that would get one in trouble. The rebellion and its reprimand seemed to be caught up in the same terms, a phenomenon that gave rise into my first critical insight into the subtle ruse of power: the prevailing law threatened one with trouble, even put one in trouble, all to keep one out of trouble.*
>
> *(Butler, 1990, p. vii)*

As a QTPOC sensorimotor psychotherapist, considering Niam's experience of their blackness, gender, and sexuality, Ahmed's treatment of the body in considering Butler's trouble resonates in my chest as crucial, "Trouble becomes even more of a threat for those who live at the edges of social life: you are more likely to get in trouble, to fear the consequences of this "in" or to fear this "in" as a consequence, the more you stray from the paths that are supposed to lead to happiness. Your body, your desires, might be registered as error: to err is to stray; to err is to go the wrong way. When you slip out of what or who you are supposed to be, you slip into trouble."

Ahmed's treatment is important in considering Niam's experience as an individual "multiply determined" and *determined* to – in the face of it all to, in their own words, declared most emphatically to describe, post-assault, the expansiveness of new loves, heightened eroticism and hot hook-ups – their goal to "stay engaged in the petty dramas of life." Ahmed asks, "Can we think of trouble making as a collective struggle?" ultimately offering, "We learn from being in trouble. We stay in trouble. We aim to stay in" (Ahmed, 2015).

Being in Trouble with Niam

And where was I in all this trouble? I think I was guilty in moments, as a member of a so-called and not historically aptly named 'helping profession' of moving from the fantasy that sidestepping trouble is in fact virtuous, or in the very least possible. As a final reflection vis-à-vis the case of Niam I offer the scene of the orgy, "We learn from being in trouble. We stay in trouble. We aim to stay in" (Ahmed, 2015).

In *Funk the Erotic: Transaesthetics and Black Sexual Cultures*, race, sexuality, class and gender scholar L.H. Stalling troubles the polarity of sacred and profane sites of memory in her treatment of black women's memory, specifically, the ocularity of the orgy and participatory ecstasy contrasting with the ocularity of spectatorship, that is, "the visual economy sustained by a singular male authoritarian gaze." Stallings writes,

> *I demonstrate what happens when black women enact memory of black orgy's communal erotic gaze over a visual economy sustained by a singular male authoritarian gaze. The communal erotic gaze exemplified in voodoo initiations, carnival, chitlinality, the soul-train line, or orgies enact an interior ocularity that reorganizes the senses to detect sacred energies of others in relation to the self so as to produce a new metaphysics of political struggle, rather than a movement that will simply mediate sex through a public sphere created and maintained by the authors of sex as knowledge, terror or violence.*
>
> *(Stallings, 2015)*

Stallings reminds us, "that the eyes feel as well as see." As a QTPOC in trouble with and enamored by the petty drama of life and the new metaphysics of struggle I find myself troubled as much as moved by the yearning evoked in hearing Niam's sense of integrity – operationalized in their frame of restorative justice in a moment of violence, in hearing about their "of course, so hot" queer threesomes and trysts, and in their fluent and intellectualized sense of compersion as they wondered and wandered in their sense of self as poly, monogamous, in an open relationship. If only I knew and felt then what I learn now from my clients. From my considered distance of my therapist's chair and author's laptop I am left to sift through, at the end of a semester and the beginnings of a hot summer, the communal erotic gaze of one other QTPOC like and unlike myself, their memories which are also my bread and butter, and what my eyes feel as well as see.

References

Ahmed, S. (2015). Being in trouble: In the company of Judith Butler. *Lambda Nordica, 20*(2/3), 179–189.

Butler, J. (1990). *Gender trouble: Feminism and the subversion of identity.* New York: Routledge.

Deloughrey, E. (2010). *Routes and roots: Navigating Caribbean and Pacific Island literature.* Honolulu, HI: University of Hawaii Press.

Ferguson, R. A. (2004). *Aberrations in black: Toward a queer of color critique.* Minneapolis, MN: University of Minnesota Press.

Lorde, A. (1984, 2007). *Sister outsider: Essays and speeches.* Berkeley, CA: Crossing Press.

Sharpe, C. (2016). *In the wake: On blackness and being.* Durham, NC: Duke University Press.

Stallings, L. (2015). From the freaks of freaknik to the freaks of Magic City: Black women, androgyny, dance, and profane sites of memory. In L. Stallings (Ed.), *Funk the erotic: Transaethetics and black sexual cultures* (pp. 176–204). Urbana, IL: University of Illinois Press.

PART II
Practice

Principle Four

PRACTICE A RELATIONAL AND DIALOGIC APPROACH TO SEX THERAPY

The fourth principle builds on the frameworks of relational and dialogic therapeutic approaches. The foundation of this principle is a clinical acknowledgment of the multiple intersecting identities of privilege and oppression that can impact both a client and a clinician. Within the relationship between the client and clinician there exists the work of tending to unspeakable dilemmas, that which there is not yet language for, and meta-communication. This includes naming and creating language for the power differential within the therapeutic relationship. What is the clinician bringing into the room and how aware of their own identities are they? Is the therapist attuned to their own visible and invisible identities that are alive in the therapeutic relationship? We will move further into location of self and meta-communication in the fifth principle, but first we want to provide some scaffolding for dialogic and relational therapeutic contexts of sex therapy.

When we talk about the use of dialogic principles we are considering the use of attention, movement, images, memories, and personal resonances in the context of the therapeutic relationship (Olson, 2015). We utilize our awareness of power dynamics between the therapist and the client and our ability to create language around these differences in individual privileges and target identities (Watts-Jones, 2010). For example, a way that one of us begins their work with a new client is to offer the client(s) a locating statement about themselves, saying,

> *As a therapist who is committed to social justice and a relational therapeutic orientation, I share with all new clients, in the first couple of sessions, that I work very hard to create open space to discuss all identities, included target identities – such as, but not limited to – race, ethnicity, gender identity and expression, sexual orientation, sexual practices, disability, size, citizenship, religion, and age.*

In this example there is a self-identification of the clinician's stance on identities that might not have been spoken about for a client before, and the client knows that the therapist is able to navigate these areas of curiosity and concern with an affirming lens. It is also important, if a clinician is working with a wide range of clients, perhaps in a community mental health setting or a generalist private practice setting, to consider saying this at the end of every first session with every new client, not just the clients that are known to the therapist as erotically marginalized. The reasoning behind telling every new client, no matter who they are, is that a clinician cannot know by looking at a person if they experience erotic marginalization, therefore, it would be considered profiling of clients based on appearance and expression to not share this statement with all clients, no matter how they present in the therapeutic context. This also exemplifies the stance of Preemptive Radical Inclusion outlined in Principle One.

Vignette

My first job out of social work school was in a secondary city in western Massachusetts, near the New York state line. The organization that I worked for was the local community mental health clinic that served all the surrounding hill towns in the area, with over 50,000 people in the greater area. Historically, this city was a thriving mill and manufacturing hub but in the late 80s most of the larger employers in the area were forced to close due to production competition overseas. Many people were left under or unemployed and the social and economic climate of the city shifted drastically, with empty store fronts on the main street of town and smaller business also closing due to a mass exodus out of town. Every single one of my 65 clients was white, with the population of the area at 93% Caucasian, 2.5% Asian, and 4% "Other." Over 80% of my clients were on some sort of fixed income that usually afforded little opportunity to save financially.

At this time in my practice, I was a new clinician and had been greatly influenced by dialogic and narrative approaches. I was seeing individuals, couples and families using as many different practices from these theoretical frameworks as possible. In both of these therapeutic orientations there is a commitment to naming that which is the unspeakable dilemma in a person's relationship, family, or worldview. Also important in these approaches is a privileging of voices and storylines that are not the dominant but rather the subordinate, and this often meant helping clients create language to make meaning of the most difficult and unspoken aspects of themselves. I had always felt deeply committed to locating myself with clients, even if I was not sharing personal identities of oppression, I felt it was critical for me to let clients know from the very start of our work together that I greatly valued making space for invisible and visible identities that a person might embody. I would share with all new clients, no matter what their presentation, that I try my hardest to be open to people's intersecting identities, including (but not limited to) race, gender, gender expression, sexual orientation, class, ability, size, age, religion, and citizenship.

When I first met Bruce he was a mechanic at a shop in a hill town about 40 minutes north of the city. At his intake session he came directly from work in order to make the appointment on time, in coveralls caked in grease and grime. He declined to sit because he was worried that he would get my chair dirty, so he stood next to the chair with his stained hand resting on the back. Bruce was in his mid-40s, white, and had lived in the hill town that he worked in for his entire life. He met his wife in elementary school, though he was invested in assuring me that they never dated until he was in his late 20s. He had finished 10th grade and then dropped out of school to work for his uncle at his garage, fixing motor cross bikes and ATVs. He had worked for that same garage, for his uncle and then his cousin, for almost 30 years. When I asked Bruce what was bringing him into therapy at this point in his life (he had never sought therapy before), he said that he and his wife could not agree about how they wanted to live their lives and raise their child together and that it was causing him enormous distress. This seemed understandable enough to me, and so we agreed that we would meet weekly for a few months to see if I could be helpful in clarifying things for Bruce so he could have better communication with his wife about his hopes for their life and their future.

In the last five minutes of the session I let him know that we were getting close to time and asked him if he had any questions for me. He said what many clients say, "not that I can think of." I remember like it was yesterday, thinking to myself, "I don't need to give this guy my spiel, just skip it . . . no . . . you promised yourself you would not profile clients, and that you would say this to every new person no matter how they presented." And that was true. I still believe that when I tell clients my position on identities of oppression they can take what they want and leave the rest, if they need to hear it they will and if they don't, it will just wash over them and we will move on. I told Bruce, as he stood next the chair that he would eventually come to sit in week after week, for, all totaled almost three years of therapy. Bruce looked at me blankly, as if I was speaking a different language, and then said, "Okay, good to know."

Over the course of his first year of therapy Bruce came to weekly sessions, rarely missing an appointment. We worked together in supporting him to learn about his authentic self, which he felt had been hidden away from even his own awareness due to extremely rigid and toxic messages growing up, from both family and community, about masculinity and what it meant to be a man. We named notions of his "true voices" and "true selves" and how these parts of him could be access as guides and beacons to help lead him through his experiences as a partner and a parent. Lastly, I supported him in learning the strategies for making changes in how he communicated with his wife, and how he could assert his perspectives and needs, while also making space for her desires to be voiced.

(continued)

(continued)

I remember clearly the day that everything shifted and how, consequently, it shaped my work as a clinician and educator. Bruce and I were beginning to discuss his therapeutic accomplishments and my thought was that we were winding down our work together, as he had felt stabilized in his roles at home with his kids and his wife, and all other parts of his life seems to be "running smoothly." As I reflected back to him all that I had witnessed him accomplish and move through, he looked pensively at the enormous jade plant by the window. I asked him if some feelings or thoughts were coming up for him, and he said, "Well, yeah, I guess that now that things are goin' better with home and work stuff, I might want to start talkin' about other stuff." I was a bit surprised but asked him what kind of "other stuff," and he said, "Well, you know how you said that thing the first day I met you, about it being okay to talk about wearin' women's under clothes? Well I do that, I've done it for years, I don't even have any men's underwear anymore, so I thought we could talk about that some."

Obviously, I knew that I did not say anything in our first meeting about Bruce possibly wearing women's underwear but what I learned is that when I gave him my speech about making space for erotically marginalized identities to be discussed, he heard exactly what he needed to hear and it made it possible for him to share this with me, after a year of working together. Bruce and I did talk more about it that day, and for almost two more years after that day, up until I left the agency and referred him to another clinician. When I left the agency, nothing about Bruce's life had changed, he was still very happily wearing women's undergarments under his coveralls every day and his wife knew everything and was his biggest support in his life. We talked about all the possibilities for him in the future and I left knowing that he would have support in his new therapist who I had met with and trained over the course of three months before leaving. About six months after I left the agency I received an email from Bruce's clinician saying that Bruce was now using the name Bridget and female pronouns in therapy sessions and that Bridget would like to start gender affirming hormones in the near future. I was so grateful that the therapist I referred Bridget to had taken me up on my request to be in contact at any time in the future if she needed support in supporting Bridget. I was able to email the therapist a sample letter of referral for an endocrinologist in Bridget's area, and we met by phone a few times to consult on how to best support Bridget in accessing affirming healthcare and hormone treatment.

This type of locating statement, at the end of the first session, is not everyone's style, and many clinicians have said to us that they feel that this is not psychoanalytic. They feel that it gives the client too much information about the therapist and the therapist's beliefs, to the point where the client cannot see the therapist as a "blank slate" to make of the therapist what they need them to be to work through internal and relational impasses in their lives. Those that argue this stance have often said that they prefer to take a more nuanced approach to getting this information across, usually through having visible postings in one's office about their perspective and positionality, with affirming stickers in visible places and affirming books on their bookshelf. We would argue that this is not enough, that giving passive signs of one's position is still a holding on to one's sense of clinical power, and not allowing for a relational and dialogic component to fully emerge between the therapist and the client. In Bridget's situation, it seems clear that she may never have broached topics related to her gender if she had not explicitly heard the locating statement that was made in the first session.

For a clinician to be transparent and open about their stance on working with erotically marginalized identities and other identities of oppression is to prioritize the relationship between the client and therapist as a tool of meaning making, which creates a space for growth and change for the client, instead of a problem saturated model of treatment, which is often mired in a pathologizing discourse of sexuality and desire (Sennott, 2011). In this chapter we introduce a sexual history form that is a consent based information gathering tool that we use to aid in the process of creating a dialogic environment in the therapeutic setting.

The sexual history form was developed by Jassy Timberlake, the director of Northampton Sex Therapy Associates (NSTA), and Shannon Sennott. This sexual history form continues to evolve and grow to support therapists in aiding clients in finding new meanings. As we move through the sexual history form we will bring to life the dialogic environment, through a thoughtful examination of the individual procedures of this tool and the use of vignettes.

Sexual History Questionnaire

The sexual history questionnaire (SHQ) is meant to be a guiding tool for clinicians to consensually begin the process of naming that which is often unspoken or unnamed for clients who are erotically marginalized. The notion of consensual conversation about such private and personal landscapes for a client must be explicit. It is most helpful to think of the SHQ as a container that allows clients to feel that they have the right and ability to pass on questions if they are not interested in answering them. In the first session with someone who may identify as erotically marginalized one must make clear what enthusiastic consent looks and feels like, in order for clients to be able to chose what they are ready to share freely about. This is also the place in the work where a clinician could introduce the concept of Preemptive Radical Inclusion, which is described in detail in Principle One. If a client understands that their therapist is coming into the therapeutic relationship with a stance that radically includes any aspect of their identity that might be unspoken, produce shame, or not yet have language to describe, this knowledge acts as a relational container that is accountable and as safe as possible for the client to explore and try language on, getting closer to an integrated understanding of themself.

Sexual History Questionnaire (SHQ)

In a first session it can be helpful to lay out the trajectory of the next few sessions, to help with anxiety that the client might be having, and to create some expectation management for them. In the dialogic tradition this practice is understood as "talking about talking about it". This means that often, when there is an unspoken dilemma or concern, there has not yet been a safer and more accountable way for the client to discuss their experience. The practice of talking about *how* things will be discussed is a way of acknowledging that language has not yet been linked to this experience. It allows for a meaning to begin forming that is not secretive (as many unspoken experiences are) but rather, very slowly and cautiously transparent and relational.

CURRENT CONCERN:

> *What prompted you to come at this point for therapy?*
>
> *Who initiated seeking therapy?*
>
> *Have you seen therapists previously? What were your experiences with these professionals?*

The first area of inquiry in the sexual history questionnaire is the current concern section. In this section the clinician is asking specifically dialogic and relational questions. It is important to know what prompted the client to come at this point in their life for therapy. Often it becomes apparent that it was not initially the client's idea, but rather a family member, a loved one, or a partner. From a dialogic stance, this is important information to gather because it clarifies who in the client's world see their experience as a predicament or concern. If it is the case that the client was not the initiating party it is important to ask if they feel that therapy would be helpful at this time. If they say that they don't know or don't think so that is an understanding that the clinician will want to honor and hold for the client, and, be even more thoughtful about the idea of enthusiastic consent when moving through questions about their sexuality, desire and intimacy. The last question in this section addresses the dialogic practice of "learning the history of the idea" for coming to therapy. It is valuable to have conversations about previous therapists and what those experiences were like for the client. Also, all professionals, mental health and medical health professionals, can be damaging to erotically marginalized people without even knowing that they are doing it, this makes the third question important, to understand the pace and movement of the session.

Vignette – Example of a First Call

Jenya's initial intake message stated their name and their pronouns (they/them), and that they were looking for therapy to support them in beginning gender affirming hormones and help figure out issues related to sexual intimacy with their partners. They said that they feel their sexuality and the things they desire are shifting as they move more deeply into an understanding of their gender identity and their desire to be a testosterone bodied person. They are worried that they will alienate their partner through the process of transition and becoming their "true self."

With a message like this there are multiple areas of erotic marginalization and all must be attended to in the therapeutic context. First, there is Jenya's request for support around beginning gender affirming hormones, which means that part of what the therapist needs to find out is if Jenya is happy with their primary care provider and if they are not, it would be part of the clinical collateral work to help them locate a PCP who was competent in working with trans and nonbinary people, and ideally, comfortable prescribing hormones to them when they were ready for that. If someone feels that their PCP cannot work with them around issues related to their erotically marginalized identities it is extremely helpful to the therapeutic process to support them in finding a PCP who can support them. It is critical to have previously developed relationships with providers of all kinds, in the area, so that referrals and support can be offered (more on this in Principle Nine, when we discuss building a community of colleagues). Secondarily, the clinician could rely on the SHQ to aid them in gathering information around experiences related to Jenya's sexual relationships with multiple partners, which is a another aspect of their erotically marginalized identity landscape, both connected to and separate from gender affirming therapy and medical treatment.

DESIRED OUTCOME:

What is your primary goal for our work together?

If therapy is successful, what will you be able to do that you are unable to do now?

How will this change anything in your current life, relationship, personality, or partner's/partners' personality?

What significance does the concern have with respect to your own sexual functioning?

How does the problem affect your partner's/partners' sexual functioning?

The second area of questions focuses on the hopes and desire that the client holds about the process of therapy. These questions are important for the development of self-determination for the client. The client speaks to what types of freedoms and abilities they envision having through the process of sex therapy. They are asked to consider this question in the context of their own sexual and intimate life, their partner(s) life (if they are partnered), and their fantasy of their future self, both individually and inside of relationships.

Vignette

When I first met Ethan he identified as a white, cross dresser, with some kinky interests. He first discovered his "gender fluidity" as a young child, dressing up in his sister's outfits and using her make-up, when no one was home. Ethan was raised on a farm in a rural area of the mid-west and knew instinctively that if anyone were to ever find out about his desires to dress in female clothing that he could be badly punished by anyone in his family or religious community. He became an active user of drugs and alcohol as soon as he could get his hands on them and he married his first wife at age 19, "because she was a religious girl and would keep him out of trouble." Ethan spent 20 years with his first wife and though he was able to finally get sober around the age of 30, he could never tell his wife about his desire to dress in woman's clothing, until one evening she found his padlocked trunk in the basement and demanded that he open it for her. Ethan's wife left him the next day. For Ethan, this first relationship with his ex-wife has greatly influenced the belief system that Ethan adheres to for himself. He has since found a new partner and has remarried. Ethan swore he would tell the next person he started dating right away and he did that, on the first night, he told her that he likes to dress in women's clothing and she said, "is that all? Are you gonna kiss me or what?"

Ethan came out at the beginning of his next relationship and his new partner is genuinely open in a way that his first wife was not, but the blue print, the neuropathways, are all calibrated to his experience with his first wife, where she proved that his gender fluidity was something for him to be deeply ashamed of and that he could and would lose people that he loved the most over it. This beginning experience still haunts him.

When Ethan was asked the first question on this form, "What is your primary goal for our work together?" he had no idea how to answer. He had never seen his gender experience as having a goal, or having any positive things to offer in general. It was crucial for the clinician to understand and hold the complexity of his experience of both loving the way that he felt when he was dressed in his "femme" clothing, and, that all of this, his entire existence, was not a "desired outcome." This truth became particularly important to hold on to as he dove into the work of understanding his sexual relationship with his current wife, who was open to him wearing women's clothing while they were being intimate and has been open to wearing a strap-on and making love to him "as if he were a woman." Understandably, Ethan was reticent to believe that his current wife truly enjoyed these sexual practices with him based on his experience with his first wife. This, in turn, affected both of their sexual identities, because both Ethan and his wife ended up feeling, in some way, ashamed for either desiring or enjoying certain sexual practices. Understanding that they were moving from territory of heterosexual privilege to erotically marginalized identities was extremely valuable for them in making meaning of their shame and also their desires for different kinds of sexual practices.

HISTORY OF CONCERN:

> *When did the concern first occur? What was happening in your life at that time?*
>
> *(If there is more than one concern, or both/all partners have a concern): Which concern do you recall as having developed first?*
>
> *Is there any situation in which the concern improves?*
>
> *When does the concern occur? Is there anything that makes it worse?*
>
> *Alcohol/Substance use: How often and how much do you (and does your partner) drink/use?*
>
> *Have you ever had a blackout or memory loss while drinking/using?*

In this section, the history of the concern is elaborated on, in an effort to learn more about the way that the client came to be worried about this concern. It is also a way to find out what type of immediate attention this concern received when it surfaced. This can be critical to the entire work in that it will illuminate whether the client sees their concern as a deeply problematic and life altering situation. Having a shaming or dismissing experience of coming out to a loved one or partner about a sexual or gender related concern sets the neural pathway stage for all that is to follow for the client. If a client was mistreated after confiding in a trusted person about their concern it is important to continually hold this foundational experience with them in the therapeutic work, keeping an eye on other ways that this experience might affect their ability to feel pride, celebration, and excitement about their authentic identity.

Vignette

Toni, 53 years old, currently self-identifies as gender-fluid and pansexual. Toni also identifies as second-generation immigrant Chinese, assigned male at birth (AMAB), and uses they/them pronouns. When Toni first sought out sex therapy

(continued)

(continued)

they presented as cisgender male and used male pronouns. Toni described their experience of being "read" by their parents, who both only spoke Mandarin for the first ten years of their life in the United States, as "girlish" and "weak." Some of Toni's first concrete memories were of being called feminizing nicknames in Mandarin by their mother, older brother, and extended family, that were clearly not nicknames to be proud of, but Toni could not understand why because they were too young to comprehend. Toni waited until both their parents passed away to begin allowing themselves to acknowledge that they felt different than what was expected of them.

Toni sought out sex therapy in an effort to "fix" what they felt was wrong with them. Toni's entire experience of their identity and why they were coming to sex therapy was founded on the experience of culturally and socially condoned familial bullying and oppression for their entire life up until the present therapeutic work. This kind of context is critical to have in beginning work with erotically marginalized clients. Knowing a client's sexuality and gender blueprint is invaluable in working with those who have multiple intersecting identities of oppression.

SEXUAL HISTORY:

What was your major source for information about intimacy, sexuality, and sexual practices growing up?

In what ways has your religion and family background influenced your attitudes towards intimacy and sexuality? Were you allowed to ask questions?

What was the age of your first sexual feeling (in whatever way you define that)?

How old were you when you first masturbated? Where were you and what did you do?

With what frequency did you masturbate in your teens?

How did you learn about masturbation?

How did you feel about masturbation?

What techniques have you used for masturbation?

How often do you currently masturbate?

Are you able to talk with your partner about self-pleasuring/masturbation?

This section is an important place to revisit the notion of enthusiastic consent. These are very personal and private questions and it can often feel very difficult for clients to discuss these details with someone who they only recently met. This is something that the clinician will want to name and be explicit and transparent about. It is a mistake to assume that because a client has sought out therapy for sexual or gender related concerns that they are comfortable discussing and talking opening about it with a virtual stranger.

Vignette

Margaret is an upper middle class white cisgender social worker in her late 20s. She has recently begun group supervision with an AASECT certified supervisor, because Margaret is considering becoming a sex therapist. Margaret is considering this because she was raised in a very religious household and intimacy and sexuality were never discussed. When she became a teenager no one talked with her about sex and she found herself having sexual relationships with multiple older boys in her high school. When Margaret was a junior in high school she became pregnant and managed to have an abortion without telling anyone in her life about it. She does not want to see other people go through this experience so she wants to focus on working with people around issues related to sex. Margaret's supervisor has asked everyone in the group to consider filling out the sexual history questionnaire themselves. The one request that the supervisor had was that the clinicians in the group have someone else interview them so they have the experience of actually going through the process of doing their own sexual history and know the feelings of vulnerability. Margaret told her supervisor that she felt this assignment was unnecessary for her to do because she "wasn't a sexual trauma survivor or anything like that." Her supervisor asked her if she felt comfortable to talk about masturbation in detail with a client, and she responded that she believed that she could have a conversation about "it" if she needed to. Her supervisor asked her what "it" was and she mumbled, "masturbation" very quietly under her breath. It was clear to her supervisor that she was not at all comfortable using language that described sexual practices, sexual desire, or sexual fantasy and Margaret's supervisor shared this with her. At first Margaret was offended and taken aback. She left her supervisor's office in a huff and vowed to find someone with true expertise to supervise her moving forward. Then, over the next couple of days, she began to reflect on the observation that her supervisor had shared and she realize that there was not a single person in her life that knew about her sexual experiences in high school or the abortion that she had. She realized that even if she wanted to do the sexual history questionnaire there was no one in her life that she trusted to tell these private experiences to. Margaret called her supervisor and shared this new awareness with her, and her supervisor gently inquired if Margaret would consider seeing a sex therapist herself, to begin the process of learning how to talk about both her own experiences as well as ways she can help others down the line. Margaret agreed that perhaps that was the place to start.

Often, clinicians will say that they do not have anyone in their life who they would feel they could or would be completely open with about the answers to these questions. This section of questions target areas of sexual identity that are considered taboo to talk about, which means that usually clients have not been able to give true meaning and importance to these topics and sexual practices. It can be valuable to have had the experience of both being asked these questions and having answered them, in order to dialogically attune to the client. It can feel helpful for a clinician to meet with a sex therapist to explore this process for oneself, as a way to learn more about how to best offer this support to their own clients.

SEXUAL EXPERIENCES:

Any concerns with erection, early or delayed ejaculation?

Have you ever experienced physical pain during sexual practices? Please describe the nature of that pain. If yes, what have you done to address this issue?

Age of first sexual/sensual experience with another person, what was this experience like in detail?

Age of first erotic dream, and do you remember any of your erotic dreams?

Is there a theme to your erotic dreams?

Age of first sexual attraction. Who was it? How could you tell you were having sexual feelings?

Age, if at all, of first menstrual period:

What are any concerns you may have had about menstruation or pregnancy?

Have you, or a partner, had any pregnancy or birth difficulties or trauma?

Age of menopause:

Type of hormone supplement used, if any:

For how long?

Was it Rx or OTC?

What are any concerns you may have about being pre-/peri-/post-menopausal?

This section asks questions that are specific to assigned sex experiences, as well as early awareness of sexuality and attraction. This section calls for the dialogic tenant of "responding and reflecting" (Olson, Seikkula, & Ziedonis, 2014). Responding and reflecting in the context of with-ness thinking (Hoffman, 2007) allows for the clinician to be a support to the client who is feeling vulnerable and often ashamed. With-ness thinking is not solution or pathology focused, it aids the clinician in maintaining a stance of preemptive radical inclusion, by holding the larger socially and culturally condoned biases about erectile function and sexual pain accountable, instead of the individual, who is having the experiencing. Reflecting, in this context, "is the ability to engage in open, participatory, transparent and jargon free conversation" with clients as they share their experiences of feeling different from others (Olson, Seikkula, & Ziedonis, 2014). Specific questions about physical pain during sexual practices, pregnancy, birth and erectile function and ejaculation are important to normalize for clients, and always using resources and stats to back up this process when possible (McCarthy & Metz, 2004).

Vignette

Elaine (biracial, cisgender, woman, kinky) and Danny (white, cisgender, man, kinky) met while Elaine was in her last year of college in a small town in Western Mass. Elaine was diagnosed with MS in her teens and had struggled mightily to navigate her health throughout college. Elaine sought out sex therapy in her junior year of college because she had never been able to have intercourse due to her self diagnosis of vaginismus, which created extreme pain when she tried to have any kind of penetrative sex, including digital. Elaine was not able to use tampons because of her pain and found all of the symptoms of vaginismus to be "sexually disabling" in a way that brought up bigger feelings about having MS. Working together we came up with ways for Elaine to manage her symptoms of pain during sex, starting with not making penetrative sex the focus of the sexual or intimate encounter. She agreed to go to a pelvic floor therapist (which she did religiously for eight months), and she decided that the only way she would be able to overcome the fear of the pain was to only be intimate in "that way" with people that she truly trusted and could work on her symptoms with. When Elaine met Danny, she had already begun using tampons, which was a result of dilation therapy, and she was feeling very hopeful that he could be the person that she would be able to work up to having intercourse with for the first time.

Danny was a couple years older than Elaine and was very committed to being someone she could feel safe and comfortable with to work on her sexual pain. Danny was open to coming into therapy with Elaine to talk about how this might look and how to be the most supportive of Elaine. We met every other week to start laying the groundwork. We discussed openly what positions feel the most comfortable and safe for Elaine. We talked about the environment in the room, which room, what side of the bed, whether she wanted to be on her back or stomach or on top of him. We discussed how they would each work to stay differentiated and not take anything personally while they experiment with their

(continued)

(continued)

sexual practices to see what worked and what didn't. We talked about how with pelvic pain and vaginismus some days something will feel good and another day it will not, so it is even more important to ask for consent all along the way, even if in the past something has worked well. We discuss the idea of "exploratory experiences" versus "orgasmic experiences" and how it can feel good to start out with the intention to sexually explore with each other without being orgasm focused. Exploratory experiences can be slow and take time and include conversations with stops and starts. After there is an understanding that the exploratory experience is over they can then move into sexual practices that they know brings pleasures to both of them, things that are still very intimate and lead to orgasm but are not intercourse or penetration.

Elaine and Danny set off to explore each other's bodies and came back the next week feeling sad and defeated. I asked what happened and Elaine said, "My dysfunction is contagious, Danny was not able to keep an erection while we were doing our exploratory homework!" Danny was a young and sexually comfortable person and he had never had a problem maintaining an erection while being sexual. Danny was tender and kind with Elaine, he did not let Elaine get away with saying that. He acknowledged that it made him very nervous to try being sexual in a new way with Elaine that could cause her pain. I normalized this for him, that many partners of people that experience vaginismus will be sexually avoidant or unable to stay erect because of the concern of causing pain to their partner. I reminded them both that when two people are trying to have intercourse and one person is experiencing pain that can make the system of the other shut down because it does not want to do anything that might harm the person that they care about. Elaine had an "ah-ha" moment when I said this, because it made so much sense to her that if his body is reading her body as being in pain (that is not welcome) that his body would read this as a non-consensual sexual practice.

Elaine and Danny's experience of the intersection of sexual pain and concerns with erectile function are common and leave both partners feeling alone and isolated if they are not talking about the connections between the two. Often clients with either sexual pain or erectile function issues will be encouraged by their partners to seek therapy for their concerns. When these clients come into the office alone we will ask them if their partners who suggested they seek support for their worries be open to joining in the process of therapy. It is a dialogic tenant that concerns or problems do not live inside the person, but rather, live between people, within the relationships. Usually partners are very grateful to be included in the therapeutic work, as Danny was, because it supports them in supporting their partner.

ORGASM:

What have been your experiences with orgasm?

Alone?

With a partner?

Would time seem wasted without an orgasm with a partner?

A clinician must be thoughtful in this section not to alienate a client with these questions. Particularly if a person has never, to their knowledge, had the experience of having an orgasm. There are also many people who, due to a number of different life experiences, do not have orgasms with other people, only with themselves. Or they chose not to have orgasms for other reasons all together. This is something that is valuable to normalize for clients, giving them lots of possibilities of what "common" looks like and that there is a naturally occurring variation in sexual experiences and processes. We often begin by asking clients what their relationship is to orgasm, both for themselves and relative to their different relationships over time, asking if they feel comfortable to talk more about these relationships to orgasm and meanings in their life that they have made about orgasms.

Vignette

Arden is an ACE identified person who is panromantic and partnered with two people in what they term a polyship. Arden self-identifies as white, cis male, and a person of size. In my first session with Arden it was clear that he had no expectation that all his multiple intersecting identities could be held and honored by a therapist. He admitted to setting his expectations low so that he could work on concerns related to his romantic relationships. I asked him if I could at least offer to try to hold all the intersecting identities that he arrived with and he chuckled in a guarded and resigned way, and said, "good luck." It felt clear to me after he shared his presenting worry, that he was overwhelmed with himself, by the nuances and subtleties of his own personhood, and that if I could hold and normalize all the intersecting concerns with him he might understand his personhood to be a beautiful, complex and unique landscape, instead of something that was too much for any one person to handle.

Arden's specific concern that brought him to sex therapy, was that he struggled with his asexual orientation in the face of also feeling comfortable to be

(continued)

(continued)

sexual with himself. Both of his partners were sexual with other partners, and he worried that because his partners did not identify as ACE and they knew that he was sexual with himself, that they would eventually leave him because he was not going to be sexual with them. We spent a great deal of time unpacking all the meaning that Arden had made around his desire for self sexual practices and his relationship to the practice of having an orgasm. Arden's intersecting identities of being a cis white man (and all the traumatic gendering experiences that he went through as he was raised), and a man of size, both played a prominent role in his internal sexual and erotic world. Over time Arden was able to trust me to share that he had an internal sexual world that included other dimensions of time, other life forms, and universes, and his size and his maleness were both cherished and eroticized parts of his sexual self play and fantasies. He was in a D/S relationship with himself, or a fantasy of himself, that was very fulfilling and he had no desire to change this experience by being sexual with other people.

The work that Arden did over the next few months was to identify what he would feel comfortable to share with his partners about his fantasy world and the ways that his sexual needs were met there. This allowed him to share parts of his complexity with them and become closer to them. When he could see that his therapist, and his partners, could celebrate his sexual connection to himself and all the ways that it nourished him sexually, he was able to share more and more over time. In his last session Arden's therapist asked him if he felt known in a more supportive way by his partners and he said, "yes, I feel known by them in a deeper way, but I also feel known to myself in a more loving and encompassing way."

BODY IMAGE:

> *How did you feel about your body from ages 0–10, 10–20, 20–30? Please include distinct feelings about being pregnant and pre-/post-pregnancy if applicable.*
>
> *Have you experienced abortion(s)? If so, please describe these experiences in as much detail as you are able at this point.*
>
> *How would you like to feel about your body?*
>
> *Does the way you feel about your body impact your enjoyment of sexual experiences and practices?*

This section is one of the most important in the questionnaire because it focuses on the client's perceptions of self and body throughout their lifetime. As we know, the definition of a person who is erotically marginalized is a person who can be oppressed, fetishized, or discriminated against based on their sexual orientation, practices, or identity. Body image, starting from a very young age, is something that erotically marginalized people tend to be very attuned to, both their own and other people's bodies. The body is a site of focus for negative self-talk and critique, and is also a place that the world outside of the client can see. This makes it deeply personal and difficult to talk about, especially if there are issues of dysphoria, dysmorphia, concerns about body image in relationship to other body sizes, or post-pregnancy body understandings.

Vignette

Jessie and Serene both identify as Asian American, cisgender female, monogamous and queer. They sought out sex therapy a year after Serene gave birth to their first child. They both felt that they wanted to make time and space to prioritize their sexual connection, and Serene, since having their child a little over a year earlier was, "really struggling to feel open to being touched sexually, in any way." Jessie was feeling scared to initiate with Serene, because she didn't want to "make Serene feel pressured or obligated," but was also feeling de-prioritized and generally rejected. When a client has recently had a child it is important to find out as much as possible about their experience in their body, both sexually and generally, while being pregnant, and, to learn as much as possible about the birth. Often birth is deeply traumatic for people and there are very few narratives and resources that encourage gestational parents and their partners to seek support around the trauma of giving birth.

With most kinds of trauma, anniversaries are highly activating for the physiological system because a person's body memory of the traumatic experience is stored in the sense; smell, feel and touch, visuals, and sounds. Often these things will be the same a year later, such as the season, the temperature outside, the way the breeze moves, the color of leaves on trees, and generally the things that one does during that time of year. It was not surprising that Jessie and Serene were looking for support around their sexual connection just over a year after the birth of their child. After sharing this trauma lens and awareness about parenting with Jessie and Serene I asked for their consent in exploring the experience of pre-pregnancy intimacy, during-pregnancy intimacy, their birth story in detail, and post-birth experiences and embodiment, for both of them.

Over the course of the next four sessions we explored these different experiences of both intimacy and trauma during that time and it became very clear to both Jessie and Serene that they both had some unpacking to do around their connections to their bodies and to each other. Serene was able to make a direct connection

(continued)

(continued)

between her avoidance of being touched in an intimate and sexual way, post-birth, with the ways that she could not avoid (or have any choice in) the process of being in labor for 72 hours and then needing to have an emergency cesarean in what felt like a life or death moment for both her and the baby. Similarly, Jessie was able to identify that she felt completely "useless, helpless and alone" in the process of Serene's birth and the dangers of the labor that lead to her having to have an emergency cesarean, and that those feelings were being tapped into when she went deeper into her feelings in the present moments of being "rejected" sexually by Serene.

Embodiment and body image do not just effect an individual, they also can have an impact on partners and relational concepts of intimacy between people. If someone has not been pregnant or had an abortion themselves, it is common that they have been in connection with someone who has and it is worth asking if their experience of those close to them going through difficultly in these areas has had any lasting impact on them and the way that they understand themselves in their own body. It is important to remind clients that talking about their relationship to their body, over the course of their lifetime, can be activating and that all kinds of emotional responses (avoidance, irritability, sadness, relief, anxiety, etc.) would be completely common. Asking clients to track how they feel emotionally after sessions is also important, and if they are experiencing emotion dysregulation after sessions, there can be a plan put into place to slow things down during sessions, as well as making sure to complete exploration of harder topics with about ten minutes left in the session, to have time to ground and regroup for the client(s).

HISTORY OF SEXUAL EXPERIENCES AND RELATIONSHIPS:

Describe the history of your intimate and sexual relationships. Talk about the number of partners, what sexual activities you have experienced, and the issues and conflicts that have emerged for you in intimate relationships. If you have had a "type" please describe that type. (Clinician: add details on separate page and attach to the questionnaire)

If currently partnered:

Describe any feelings you may have about your sexual connection or sexual contact with your present or possible sexual partner(s).

Describe your present sexual interactions, such as intercourse or masturbation, turn-ons, your present pattern for sexual pleasure, frequency of sexual interactions, your current number of partners, etc. (Ask if partners cuddle, hug, spoon, kiss hello/goodbye. Who initiates what kinds of touch?)

Do you feel you most often "give your best" when being sexual or intimate with your partner(s)?

Are you proud of the way you express your feelings toward your partner(s) at this time? If not, what's missing in your opinion?

Do you WANT your partner(s) during sex (or intimacy?) or just "want sex"?

Do you WANT to be aroused and involved sexually?

What would you like from an ideal sexual partner, or your current partner? What would you be willing to give to such a partner?

Do you tell your partner what pleases you most sexually? What displeases you?

What do you want most in the way of attitude, behaviors, etc from your partner that they do not provide you now?

What attitudes or behaviors do you receive from your partner that you value the most?

What attracts, excites, and stimulates you sexually? Describe the situation you find most desirable and stimulating for being sexual?

What trait, behavior, or habit does your partner have which tends to diminish your sexual feeling for them?

Are you interested in sexual practices that include power and pain play, i.e. dominance/ submission/bondage?

Do you look at pornography? If so, with what frequency? Do you use pornography to masturbate? What kinds of pornography do you enjoy?

Are you currently seeing a body worker, i.e. chiropractor, acupuncturist, muscular therapist?

If yes, please described the nature of your physical discomfort:

Do you have any preexisting medical conditions that may affect your sexuality (for example, diabetes, hypertension, heart disease, etc?) Are you currently taking any prescribed medications (such as for hypertension, diabetes, depression, anxiety, or cardiovascular disease)? If yes, list:

What medications or drugs – including over the counter drugs and herbal supplements – do you use?

Please give the name and phone number of prescriber:

Describe anything else related to your past or present experiences. Include anything that may be important for me to know, so that I may assist you in reaching your sexual goals.

This section is the last in the sexual history questionnaire and it is the most detailed and comprehensive. In this section we are trying to learn about a client's sexual and relational history in a way that is not oppressive to their identity. These questions can feel too direct and personal for some people, so it is important to remind clients that they can always chose to pass on a question if they are not ready to answer of not sure how to answer. One of the things that clients are the most protective of in working with a sex therapist is their current relationship, if they have one. It is not uncommon for a person to be full of description and emotion in the past relationship portion and then have a complete change of affect and body language when they are asked to give language to their current sexual relationships. We try to remind folks throughout the process of this work that there is no right or wrong way to talk about their experiences and that this is not a skill that we were taught early in life, so building awareness and language to support the exploration of an authentic sexual and intimate self does not come easily.

Key Clinical Points

- Normalization of all different types of fears and experiences is key to the process of gathering sexual history information.
- Often both the client and the therapist learn more than they could have ever imagine when they do this work using dialogic practices and having a stance of preemptive radical inclusion.
- Taking the time at the beginning of working with an erotically marginalized person to explicitly describe to them what ones preemptively radical stance of inclusion includes is critical to acknowledging the power structures inherent to a therapeutic relationship.

References

Hoffman, L. (2007). The art of "withness": A new bright edge. In H. Anderson & D. Gehart (Eds.), *Collaborative therapy: Relationships and conversations that make a difference* (pp. 63–79). New York: Taylor & Francis.

McCarthy, B. W. & Metz, M. E. (2004). *Coping with erectile dysfunction: How to regain confidence and enjoy great sex.* Oakland, CA: New Harbinger.

Olson, M. (2015). An auto-ethnographic study of "open dialogue": The illumination of snow. *Family Process, 54,* 716–729. doi: 10.1111/famp.12160

Olson, M., Seikkula, J., & Ziedonis, D. (2014). The key elements of dialogic practice in open dialogue: Fidelity criteria. Version 1.1: September 2nd. http://umassmed.edu/psychiatry/globalinitiatives/opendialogue/

Sennott, S. L. (2011). Gender disorder as gender oppression: A transfeminist approach to rethinking the pathologization of gender non-conformity. *Women & Therapy, 34,* 93–113.

Watts-Jones, T. D. (2010), Location of self: Opening the door to dialogue on intersectionality in the therapy process. *Family Process, 49,* 405–420. doi:10.1111/j.1545-5300.2010.01330.x

THE CASE OF P: INTERNALIZED HETEROSEXISM AND THE SUBMISSIVE HETEROSEXUAL CISGENDER MALE

Dulcinea Alex Pitagora

Introduction

The fictional client presented in this chapter is a composite case incorporating the experiences and characteristics of a number of clients I have worked with who have similar intersecting identifications and statuses (heterosexual, cisgender male, monogamous, middle to upper socioeconomic status, 40s to 50s age range) and focal presenting problem: distress around having to stifle their kink-related sexual desires in the context of their non-kinky relationship. In the pages to follow, I will present a case study of "P," a 45-year old, white[1], heterosexual cisgender male (HCM), who, at the time of beginning therapy with me, had been married for 20 years, had two children (12 and 15), and had a high-stress, senior management position in a large company. P's presenting problems were distress related to compulsive thoughts about BDSM-related fantasies, and sexual functioning difficulties when attempting to have penis-in-vagina sex with his spouse. Associated with these problems, P felt relational and emotional constraints related to having kinky sexual desires, and distress around disclosing and expressing his desires. P is a client whose erotic marginalization is nested within multiple privileges, which provides a unique set of challenges in his experience and in the treatment of his distress.

P noted in our initial session that he was experiencing moderate to severe anxiety on a daily basis; had difficulty falling asleep and sleeping through the night; was experiencing intrusive thoughts and negative self-talk; compulsively fantasized about engaging in BDSM as the submissive participant; and had difficulty either achieving or maintaining erections when attempting to penetrate his spouse during sex, which he described as infrequent (i.e., once or twice a month). As a result of these symptoms, P experienced distress in functioning in multiple contexts, including work and relationships with family members. P had a previous history of treatment for generalized anxiety and panic disorders, though he reported that he did not find therapy to be helpful in the past. Perhaps not coincidentally, he had never been comfortable discussing his sexuality fantasies or functioning with previous therapists.

Clinician Positionality

Before going into more detail about this case, I will present my own background information as it relates to this type of case and to the type of work that I do. I am a clinical social worker, a licensed psychotherapist and certified sex therapist, and a doctoral candidate in clinical sexology. In my practice, I work predominantly with erotically marginalized people, including those who are LGBTQ-identified, transgender, gender nonconforming, BDSM-oriented, ethically/consensually non-monogamous, and/or current or former sex workers. As a person with intersecting erotically marginalized identities – I identify as BDSM-oriented, queer, poly, gender fluid, and a former sex worker – I bring a complex and complicated intersection of biases with me to this work. I have been an outspoken member of these groups and communities for a number of years; created an online network of local sex positive professionals (*ManhattanAlternative.com*); co-organized and co-produced the AltSex NYC Conference and the Sexuality Speaker Series; and created and hosted the pilot episode of the web series *Kink Doctor*, a forum for BDSM-oriented people to tell their stories, and a vehicle to model disclosure and "outness" in an affirmative context. While many therapists attempt to remain a blank slate, I feel an obligation to the individuals I work with to disclose my atypical identifications, to model that there is no shame in having atypical identifications, and that there can be pride in embodying who you are. The way that I incorporate this type of disclosure into my practice is a means of maintaining transparency and naming systemic and individual oppressions. I use the disclosure of my identities not only as a means of modeling transparency and sex positivity, but to lend my own experience to discussions around the intersection of oppression and privilege.

It is important to acknowledge that being out about atypical identifications is a privilege that not everyone has. Many people work and/or live in environments in which it would be dangerous to disclose difference; it is an individual and biopsychosocially-influenced decision. Some feel constrained by their cultural context, and may feel the need to remain closeted about non-mainstream identifications or sexual practices because they fear that their geographic location, community, family, friend and peer group, and work or academic environments would be unsupportive and intolerant of them.

In order to provide the most beneficial therapeutic relationship and environment as I can, I must remain conscious of the potential for countertransference, both in the form of under- and over-identifying. When working with a client like P, I regularly engage in self-reflection in order to make note of my thought process, and attempt to filter out the influence of constructed meanings associated with my personal history and identifications. For example, while I have a clear understanding of negotiated and consensual power exchange and power role orientations, my understanding and experience may be different than that of my clients. In order to avoid overidentification, I tell my client during our initial session that while I have a frame of reference and understanding of their BDSM desires and/or lifestyle, I will be asking clarifying questions to ensure that I am not making assumptions about their understanding and experience of these types of interactions.

I also emphasize that I collaborate with those I do therapy with; this is important because a notable power differential between clinician and client can increase the client's anxiety and make the therapeutic environment stressful (Gallo-Silver, Anderson, & Romo, 2014; Long, Burnett, & Thomas, 2006). I find this to be particularly relevant when people know about my history in the kink community and the focus is on power dynamics in their relationship(s). I find a constant and consistent practice of self-reflection is valuable in every therapeutic relationship, regardless of shared or unshared identifications and history.

Assessment

When we began working together, P reported being uncomfortable but eager to disclose issues related to his sexuality that he had long been compartmentalizing and suppressing. While it took several sessions for P to become comfortable discussing his sexual functioning issues in more detail, he noted in our first session that he felt an immediate and visceral sense of relief upon disclosing his kinky sexual desires. While he sought me out specifically because of my background and expertise in kink-related matters and my emphasis on sex positive and kink-affirmative treatment, he noted that he was extremely anxious prior to our session, which he attributed to anticipating such disclosure. P noted that he had been watching my face and body language for signs of judgment or disgust, and with the absence of those reactions to his disclosure, his body visibly relaxed and tears came to his eyes in gratitude and relief. He explained that he had never been able to voice his desires in an environment where his was so completely accepted and treated as "normal" and healthy. P noted in subsequent sessions that although he found therapy difficult, it felt good to know that someone was hearing and seeing him in a way that he never experienced.

In the first few sessions, P and I collaborated on fleshing out familial and sexual genograms. In childhood, P was well provided for, experienced no trauma other than a brief period of bullying during pre-adolescence, and had close relationships with his parents and siblings. P described his early sexuality as primarily isolated to masturbation to fantasies of submitting to dominant women. He remembered having these types of fantasies prior to puberty, and recalled a dramatic increase in frequency and creativity of the fantasies during and after puberty, once he discovered masturbation. P noted that he was more focused on getting good grades and being a competitive athlete in high school and college than he was on dating, and his first sexual interaction was with a woman in his undergraduate program who was four years older than him. During graduate school, P began to feel pressure from peers and family to think about marriage, so he began dating women with a specific vision of the future in mind, which he ultimately created with his current spouse and children. P met his spouse in his last year of graduate school, and got married two years after graduating. Since being married, he has engaged in BDSM interactions with professional dominatrices and full-service sex workers[2] about once or twice a year.

P had only spoken about his BDSM desires to sex workers. After changing jobs in his early 30s, he began to experience physical symptoms of anxiety, at which point his doctor prescribed anti-anxiety medications as needed for periods of heightened anxiety and panic attacks. The medication alleviated and helped P to manage his symptoms for a few years, but eventually he began experiencing intrusive thoughts comprised primarily of negative self-talk, despite presenting the appearance of being successful, and having what his family and peers considered the ideal spouse, children, and job. P sought out therapy at the advice of his primary care physician, but P never brought up his sexual functioning challenges, fantasies, or BDSM experiences. Many clients who have sought me out because of my identity disclosures and kink-affirmative approach noted that in working with previous therapists, have previously avoided disclosure of being kinky or tried to suppress their kinky desires after being pathologized by previous therapists; these are all too common occurrences among kinky clients (Barker, Iantaffi, & Gupta, 2007; Bettinger, 2003; Kelsey, Stiles, Spiller, & Diekoff, 2013; Khan, 2015; Kolmes, Stock, & Moser, 2006; Pitagora, 2016). After attending five sessions with his former therapist that did not feel helpful, he decided that therapy was not for him, and he terminated.

Shortly after his 40th birthday and subsequent promotion into a senior management position at work, P began experiencing difficulty with achieving and sustaining erections. P reported a decrease in libido over the past few years, and when attempting to penetrate his spouse during sex, he frequently is not able to maintain an erection, and at times is unable to achieve an erection His spouse became increasingly frustrated with the state of their sexual relationship, and their relationship has suffered. He described his spouse as one of his closest friends, though in the past years they have become more distant and their relationship feels less close to him. P was conflicted about visiting sex workers, because he did not like lying to his spouse. He did not feel she would be open to the types of sexual interactions he has with sex workers, during which he was always able to achieve and maintain an erection and experience orgasm. P also consistently achieved and maintained erections and experienced orgasms while masturbating to BDSM-related fantasies.

Interpretations and Interventions

Assessments and interventions are often interwoven as a means of strengthening the therapeutic alliance, to gain the client's trust and facilitate assessments with more depth and accuracy moving forward. At times assessments can act as interventions. For example, a genogram and sexual genogram and history can provide the client with psychodynamic insights about early systemic influences in their worldview and behavior. In P's case, there was no history of trauma in his childhood, and he was raised by loving, affectionate parents who were both doctors, and able to provide for their children's needs and wants. However, our conversation relating to his sexual history revealed that his parents would shut down discussions between siblings and friends when the content related to sexuality and attraction, and were not responsive and at times shaming in response to questions he and his siblings had when witnessing sexual content on television or in films. His parents taught him early on that sexuality was not to be discussed. During the assessment stage, P recognized that this pattern was repeating with his spouse and children, and was affecting the way he has always thought (or suppressed thought) about his own sexuality.

Diagnostic Information

The assessment stage includes obtaining as much diagnostic information as possible in the client's individual, intergenerational, and interactional systems. P's sexual functioning problems were confined to specific contexts (i.e., non-kinky interactions with his spouse, but not during kinky interactions or while masturbating alone), therefore it seemed unlikely that he had an organic condition that would present a risk factor for erectile dysfunction or act as a roadblock for treatment (Hertlein, Weeks, & Gambescia, 2010). Because my therapeutic approach with P was person-centered, collaborative, and transparent, I explained this to P, and that it is more common for erectile unpredictability to result from psychological or emotional phenomena like depression, anger, low self-esteem, or poor body image than physiological factors, though alcohol can also exacerbate symptoms (Hertlein et al., 2009). I also let him know that he could decide to visit his primary care physician for a physical, to be followed as needed by referrals to a urologist and endocrinologist, in order to rule out physiological issues related to sexual functioning.

P's upbringing revealed other relevant diagnostic information, in the form of cognitive distortions constructed during a childhood and young adulthood spent actively suppressing dialogue and thoughts about sexuality (Bettinger, 2003; Hertlein et al., 2010). Early on in our work together, I let P know that if and when he became comfortable with the idea and thought it would be helpful, we could schedule one or two joint sessions with his spouse. This could serve to facilitate conversations about his kinky desires that he felt were impossible to have, but could also be a valuable assessment of his communication style in the relationship. I recommended a couple's therapist, explaining that he might benefit from support in facilitating further discussions as we made progress in our work together.

P received heteronormative intergenerational messages related to his performance of masculinity in athletics and expected sexual scripts in dating. It is possible that P experienced a feeling of emasculation from his experience of erectile unpredictability (which, as determined through our conversations, was contextually predictable). P was linking his masculinity with being sexually active in the specific ways that were expected of him, regardless of his level of desire and sexual preferences. It is important to highlight the difference between unwanted emasculation due to not performing to social standards of heteronormative sexuality, and feeling humiliated and sexually submissive in a consensual and pleasurable BDSM interaction. The former sets P up in a lifestyle that provokes the fear of being seen as a "pervert" if his atypical sexual desires were revealed to his family, employer, or peer group, whereas the latter allows him a sexually affirming release from the pressures of the lifestyle he was conditioned to pursue.

Treatment Strategy

In order to collaborate with P on treatment goals, I asked him a miracle question: "If you no longer experienced erectile unpredictability, and you could have any kind of sex you wanted, what would your sex life look like?" This question provided space to fantasize about an alternate reality in which the problem no longer existed, in order to instill hope, and facilitate the articulation of clear and specific goals (Hertlein et al., 2009). This question also helped to externalize P's sexual functioning problems to make them feel more solvable, and helped us to create a roadmap with subordinate goals. P responded that he wanted his spouse to accept and support his sexuality, and ideally to participate in BDSM interactions with him from time to time. P hoped that if he could engage in kink with his spouse some of the time, he would feel more sexually connected with her, and be more able to perform conventional sex acts that he believed she preferred. When I asked him about her preferences, he noted that he was making assumptions since he had never explicitly asked her.

In conflict with his desire to engage in kink more openly, P feared that having more sexual freedom would lead to his wanting to engage in kink all of the time, and he did not want to lose the life he had built for himself in exchange for being a full-time submissive. I explained to P that many people who engage in kinky sex also engage in non-kinky sex, sometimes during or after BDSM scenes, or sometimes independently of BDSM scenes (Kleinplatz & Moser, 2004). Some engage mostly in BDSM and incorporate vanilla sex into their BDSM interactions, and others engage primarily in conventional or vanilla sex, and incorporate BDSM into their sexual repertoire from time to time. Interests in different sexual expressions may wax and wane over time, or they may remain fixed, but they usually plateau at some point as people hone in on their desires (Nichols, 2006). This helped to alleviate P's fears somewhat, though when we started talking about what having a conversation with his spouse about his kinky sexual desires would be like, his anxiety intensified. It was apparent that P was dealing with a significant amount of internalized heterosexism, which resulted in his experiencing shame around his sexual preferences.

P described fantasies of being in a submissive power role with a dominant female, engaging in role-plays that included humiliation scenes and anal play, and after disclosing his sexual desires, he asked: *Is there something wrong with me? Am I gay? Can I make these fantasies stop? Can I make these desires go away?* Along with immediate affirmation and validation that any consensual sexual interaction between adults can be healthy and that there is nothing wrong with having any sort of fantasy, regardless of content, early interventions included psycho-education on healthy kink practices, consent, and emphasizing the difference between fantasy and reality (Barker, 2017; Joyal, Cossette, & Lapierre, 2015).

Is there something wrong with me?

I reiterated that there is nothing wrong with having the kind of sexual desires and fantasies that P has, but that I could understand why he might ask that, given that it is a common fallacy to assume that BDSM is an expression of pathology (Kahn, 2015; Pitagora, 2013; Williams, Thomas, Prior, & Christensen, 2014). P had internalized this fallacy, handed down from a tradition of research that has pathologized BDSM practitioners by focusing on nonconsensual interactions that incorporate elements of sexual sadism or masochism as defined in the *Diagnostic and Statistical Manual Fifth Edition* (*DSM-5*; American Psychiatric Association, 2013; Khan, 2013). Over the past two decades, researchers have increasingly considered BDSM desire and expression as an atypical but naturally occurring variation of human sexuality that appeals to over 10% of the general population (Pitagora, 2013). Data also show that BDSM practitioners represent a cross-section of society, and though there is a lack of available research, there are studies emphasizing the wide range of demographics represented by BDSM practitioners, including various age groups, ethnicities, occupations, genders, and sexual identities (Connolly, 2006; Weinberg, Williams, & Moser, 1984). Normalizing and universalizing P's sexuality in this way helped him to feel less isolated and pathologized (Nichols, 2006).

Am I Gay?

Further exploration of what P meant by this question revealed that he thought his desire to be submissive, which at times included anal penetration by a dominant woman, might be a sign that he is repressing being gay. I explained that his body parts do not have a sexual orientation; the nerve endings in the anus and prostate react to stimulation, they do not experience attraction related to gender (Pitagora, in press). After P gained a fuller understanding of what sexual orientation means to him and how he self-identifies, we ascertained that when he stated he was attracted to dominant women and sometimes enjoyed being penetrated by them, it meant just that, and it did not mean that he was gay.

Can I make these fantasies stop? Can I make these desires go away?

This was another important place to check countertransference. For a clinician with different biases than mine, these questions could be understood as a request for help with changing the content of their fantasies or their desires.

This is a common question, and many clients newly aware of having kink-related desires have sought out therapy with me because of shame and fear due to socialization or internalized stigmatization, and have explicitly asked if I could help to "cure" them. My therapeutic approach requires an unambiguous answer: there is nothing wrong with their sexuality and it does not need to be cured, and attempting to do so would not work. Attempting to "cure" people of their kink-related desires is analogous to conversion or reparative therapy for lesbian-, gay-, bisexual-, and transgender-identified individuals, which is no longer considered an appropriate or ethical form of therapeutic treatment, does not work, and has been found to be harmful in many cases (American Psychiatric Association, 2009). Instead, I offer a sex positive, affirmative approach that works toward self-acceptance (Williams, Prior, & Wegner, 2013).

Before following my impulses to have this conversation immediately, I reminded myself to emphasize P's own words and narratives, and not to assume he is asking something he might not be when he may simply be information seeking. Therefore, I asked clarifying questions: *Are you asking me if it is possible to make the fantasies stop and the desires go away, or are you telling me you want that to happen? If you could enjoy the fantasies and desires without the negative feelings you associate with them now, would you still want them to stop and go away?*

The conversations we had in response to my clarifying questions revealed that P did not necessarily want to change his sexuality or sexual preferences, but he genuinely did want to know if that was an option. He noted that while it was hard for him to imagine giving up the pleasure he gets from his fantasies and desires, he often wished he could be "normal" because he thought it would make his life so much easier.

Termination

The majority of our work focused on affirmation, validation, psycho-education, and learning a new language for expressing and understanding his sexuality. Once P became more comfortable with his sexual desires, he was able to gain clarity around the deeper sources of his stress and anxiety, which were fears of being outed as a sexual submissive, and subsequently emasculated by his colleagues, peers, and spouse. This clarity led to awareness around the coinciding of stress and anxiety with compulsive fantasizing and sexual performance issues, and motivated P to actively work toward his goal of coming out to his spouse. This awareness and decision to some extent alleviated his compulsivity and performance issues, which provided further motivation, as he felt he was moving in the right direction.

Before having the conversation with his spouse, we roleplayed conversations with her in which he disclosed his kinky desires, and talked through the potential consequences of the conversation. What exactly did he want to disclose to her, and to what level of detail? What sort of reaction did he hope from her?

What sort of reaction did he expect from her? How would he react if she reacted badly? What would a bad reaction look like? What would a good reaction look like? If she did not want to explore BDSM in the context of their relationship, would he continue to see sex workers outside of his agreed upon monogamous relationship structure? Would he talk to his spouse about opening their relationship to consensual non-monogamy so that he could satisfy his kink-related desires without lying to her about it?

During our psychoeducational conversations, we had focused on the aspects of communication that are the scaffolding of BDSM interactions: negotiation, consent, safewords, and aftercare (Pitagora, 2013). We agreed he would employ and model this type of communication and care during his conversation with his spouse, in asking her consent to talk about his sexuality, checking in repeatedly about her comfort level, negotiating how they would move forward, and asking her if he could provide her with whatever aftercare she might need it after the conversation. This means of communicating was much different than what he was used to, both at work and at home, where his tendency was to think more about what he wanted to communicate and have happen, rather than engage in active listening and an exchange of feelings and ideas. Our work together ended at this point, though P contacted me some months later about couples therapy, and I referred him to a couples counselor who was well-versed in both BDSM and consensual non-monogamy at his request.

Reflections and Conclusion

Affirming P's atypical sexuality was an ongoing, central intervention throughout our treatment, from the first session through termination. Through repeated validation, affirmation, and reflection, P was introduced to his authentic self in therapy, and learned a new language with which to think and speak about his sexuality. P was an insightful and resilient client, bolstered by an intersection of privileges. P's privileges proved to be protective factors (Sheff & Hammers, 2011), but also acted as a wall of defense for his internalized heterosexist beliefs around masculinity and sexual expression, which ultimately manifested in the presenting problems he brought to therapy. Though I experienced spikes of countertransference when confronted with his tendency toward heterosexist microaggressions, they were easily overcome as I exercised compassion and empathy, and reminded myself of his internal struggle and the effort he was exerting toward overcoming it. My own experience with erotic marginalized identities provided a helpful frame of reference from which to remember that my role as a clinician is to validate my client's distress (Kleinplatz & Moser, 2004). Distress and dysfunction occur and must be understood in a context of the very real experiences of discrimination and stigma toward BDSM that P had internalized and was anticipating confronting (Bezreh, Weinberg, & Edgar, 2012).

Notes

1 While I have worked with many people of color in my practice, all of the clients with the noted demographic characteristics and presenting problem have been white, therefore the composite client described is also indicated to be white. It is important to note that the issues and treatment described herein do not apply only to white HCMs, and that there is a conspicuous gap in research on the experience of kinky people of every skin color (Sheff & Hammers, 2011), and it is a personal goal and a suggested goal to all researchers to work toward a more comprehensive representation of individual and group differences in the literature.
2 In many geographic locations, such as those where full-service sex work (e.g., typical sexual interactions like penis-in-vagina or oral sex with client, manual masturbation of client) is prohibited, professional dominatrices do not offer full-service.

References

American Psychiatric Association. (2009). *Report of the American Psychological Association Task Force on Appropriate Therapeutic Responses to Sexual Orientation.* Retrieved from http://www.apa.org/pi/lgbt/resources/therapeutic-response.pdf.

American Psychiatric Association. (2013). *Diagnostic and statistical manual of mental disorders* (5th ed., pp. 685–705). Washington, DC: Author.

Barker, M. J. (2017). *Good practice across the counselling professions 001: Gender, sexual, and relationship diversity (GSRD).* London: British Association for Counselling and Psychotherapy. Available from http://www.bacp.co.uk/docs/pdf/16237_gender-sexual-relationship-diversity-001.pdf.

Barker, M., Iantaffi, A., & Gupta, C. (2007). Kinky clients, kinky counselling? The challenges and potentials of BDSM. In L. Moon (Ed.), *Feeling queer or queer feelings: Radical approaches to counselling sex, sexualities and genders* (pp. 106–124). London: Routledge. Retrieved from http://oro.open.ac.uk/17272/2/4AD665D2.pdf.

Bettinger, M. (2003). Sexuality, boundaries, professional ethics, and clinical practice: The kink community. *Journal of Gay & Lesbian Social Services, 14*(4), 93–104, doi: 10.1300/J041v14n04_06

Bezreh, T., Weinberg, T. S., & Edgar, T. (2012). BDSM disclosure and stigma management: Identifying opportunities for sex education. *American Journal of Sexuality Education, 7*(1), 37–61.

Connolly, P. H. (2006). Psychological functioning of bondage/domination/. sadomasochism (BDSM) practitioners. *Journal of Psychology & Human Sexuality, 18*(1), 79–120. doi: 10.1300/J056v18n01_05

Gallo-Silver, L., Anderson, C. M., & Romo, J. (2014). Best clinical practices for male adult survivors of childhood sexual abuse: "Do no harm." *The Permanente Journal, 18*(3), 82–87. Retrieved from http://www.ncbi.nlm.nih.gov/pmc/articles/PMC4116270/pdf/permj18_3p0082.pdf.

Hertlein, K., Weeks, G. R., & Gambescia, N. (2009). *Systemic sex therapy.* New York: Taylor & Francis.

Joyal, C. C., Cossette, A., & Lapierre, V. (2015). What exactly is an unusual sexual fantasy? *Journal of Sexual Medicine, 12*(2), 328–340. doi:10.1111/jsm.12734

Kelsey, K., Stiles, B. L., Spiller, L., Diekoff, G. M. (2013). Assessment of therapists' attitudes towards BDSM. *Psychology & Sexuality, 4*(3), 255–267. doi: 10.1080/19419899.2012.655255

Khan, U. (2015). Sadomasochism in sickness and in health: Competing claims from science, social science, and culture. *Current Sexual Health Reports*, *7*(1), 49–58. doi:10.1007/s11930-014-0039-1

Kleinplatz, P., & Moser, C. (2004). Toward clinical guidelines for working with BDSM clients. *Contemporary Sexuality*, *38*(6), 1–4.

Kolmes, K., Stock, W., & Moser, C. (2006). Investigating bias in psychotherapy with BDSM clients. *Journal of Homosexuality*, *50*(2–3), 301–324. doi:10.1300/J082v50n02_15

Long, L. L., Burnett, J. A., & Thomas, R. V. (2006). *Sexuality counseling: An integrative approach*. Upper Saddle River, NJ: Pearson Education.

Nichols, M. (2006). Psychotherapeutic issues with "kinky" clients: Clinical problems, yours and theirs. *Journal of Homosexuality*, *50*(2–3), 281–300. doi:10.1300/J082v50n02_14

Pitagora, D. (2013). Consent vs. coercion: BDSM Interactions highlight a fine but immutable line. *The New School Psychology Bulletin*, *10*(1), 27–36. Retrieved from http://www.nspb.net/index.php/nspb/article/view/180/109.

Pitagora, D. (2016). The kink-poly confluence: Relationship intersectionality in marginalized communities. *Sexual and Relationship Therapy*, *31*(3), 391–405. doi:10.1080/14681994.2016.1156081

Pitagora, D. (2017). No pain, no gain? Therapeutic and relational benefits of subspace in BDSM contexts. *Journal of Positive Sexuality*, *3*(3), 44–54. Retrieved from http://journalofpositivesexuality.org/wp-content/uploads/2017/10/No-Pain-No-Gain-Therapeutic-and-Relational-Benefits-of-Subspace-in-BDSM-Pitagora.pdf.

Pitagora, D. (in press). The influence of BDSM-orientation on shame and heteronormativity in anoreceptive heterosexual males. *Journal of Humanistic Psychology*.

Sheff, E., & Hammers, C. (2011). The privilege of perversities: Race, class and education among polyamorists and kinksters. *Psychology & Sexuality*, *2*, 198–223. doi:10.1080/19419899.2010.537674

Weinberg, M., Williams, C., & Moser, C. (1984). The social constituents of sadomasochism. *Social Problems*, *31*, 379–389. Retrieved from http://www.jstor.org/stable/800385

Williams, D. J., Prior, E., & Wegner, J. (2013). Resolving Social Problems Associated with Sexuality: Can a "Sex-Positive" Approach Help?. *Social Work*, *58*(3), 273–276. doi:10.1093/sw/swt024

Williams, D. J., Thomas, J. N., Prior, E. E., & Christensen, M. C. (2014). From "SSC" and "RACK" to the "4Cs": Introducing a new framework for negotiating BDSM participation. *Electronic Journal of Human Sexuality*, *17*. Retrieved from http://mail.ejhs.org/volume17/BDSM.html.

Principle Five

EMPHASIZE CLIENTS' OWN WORDS, KNOWLEDGE, AND NARRATIVES

Introduction

Emphasizing clients' own words, knowledge, and narratives asks sex therapists to center the experience of erotically marginalized clients. Erotically marginalized clients may not have had many experiences where the knowledge that they have acquired through their experiences and internal understanding of themselves is valued. Sometimes they may specifically be looking for a sex therapist to be an expert and fix their problems. Although it is a common therapeutic tenant to value the experience of the client this feels even more important to us when working with clients whose narratives have continuously been dismissed, pathologized, or made invisible. The origins for Principle Five are found in Narrative therapy, Dialogic principles, and the Freedom Paradigm. Each of these approaches offer a different lens through which we value, understand, and enact Principle Five in our work as sex therapists.

Humans are storytellers, and that includes the process of telling stories about ourselves. The way that we see the world, the lens that we look through, is our narrative. Our narratives influence how we understand the world around us and our internal experiences. The tools that we use to write these unspoken narratives are vast. Our very first narratives are those told to us by our primary attachment figures, our parents, grandparents, or caregivers. These first narratives become our internal voice. Later we build on this personal narrative through our exposure to culture and community. Mainstream narratives, or dominant narratives, are created by those who have the most power and influence. These mainstream narratives are part of the cultural influence that impact how we write our own narratives. Dominant narratives do not center the voices of erotically marginalized clients. For example our culture typically uses the word "sex" to describe sexual intercourse between a male and a female, or more explicitly penetrative intercourse with a penis and a vagina. This definition of sex is a narrative based on the dominant culture. It creates a limited band of what is and what is not defined as sex, erasing anyone who is not in a cisgender male/cisgender female dyad or is not having penetrative sex with a penis and a vagina. The result is that when the word "sex" is casually mentioned in the media or conversations, the internal visual that is accessed is one that is exclusively heterosexual and heteronormative. All other sexual behavior becomes "other", "alternative", or "taboo." Through the lens of oppression mainstream narratives function as "mechanism of propaganda . . . to dull or diminish the perceptions of the oppressors by the oppressed" (Hanna, Talley, & Guindon, 2000, p. 431). Mainstream narratives aren't simply the "most popular" ones; not participating in these narratives, or participating in an alternative narrative, is actively punished. Oppression maintains itself through the power of these narratives. In the above example, a dominant narrative definition of sex gives power to those who practice that behavior, and creates a separation and judgment against those who don't.

Being othered is not simply semantics, it's a way to create a power hierarchy that ensure that those with the most power keep it. People who do not identify as heterosexual have historically been labeled as "deviant." Even up until 1973 homosexuality was in the Diagnostic and Statistical Manual as a mental illness (Jagose, 1996). This narrative, that being lesbian, gay, or bisexual (LGB) was deviant or a pathology effects the way that LGB people feel about themselves, including doubting whether they should receive the same rights and respect as heterosexuals. It is not uncommon today to work with LGB clients who are still battling with the internalization of this narrative that there is something essentially wrong with them.

The field of sex therapy offers an example of the power of narratives. The PLISSIT model was developed in 1976 by Jack Annon for medical providers and clinicians providing brief sex therapy. It provided a way for those providers who had first contact with someone experiencing sexual distress to triage the client and ensure that they received the care that they needed. The letters stand for Permission, Limited Information, Specific Suggestions, and Intensive Therapy. Permission is the first approach, "Sometimes, all that people want to know is that they are normal, that they are okay, that they are not 'perverted,' 'deviated,' or 'abnormal,' and that there is nothing wrong with them" (Annon, 1976, p. 50). Annon found that clients experienced distress when their personal narrative was different than the dominant narrative and attributed negative judgments to their behavior. In this example of an intervention, Annon, using his power as a "professional," directly addresses and allays this concern.

Narrative Therapy

Research on Narrative therapy has examined its application and effectiveness with specific populations including families (Morgan, 2000), survivors of traumatic experiences (Borden, 1992), clients of color (Semmler & Williams, 2000), clients diagnosed with eating disorders (Lock et al., 2005), and clients with Asperger's syndrome (Cashin, 2008). Narrative therapy has also been recommended as a tool for working for lesbian, gay, and bisexual clients (Tanner & Lyness, 2003) and their parents (Saltzburg, 2007). Although there has yet to be specific research regarding the use of narrative therapy with erotically marginalized clients, the importance of helping a client to tell their own story and to redefine it in a positive way has been noted repeatedly in the available literature (Burdge, 2007; Lev, 2004; Schrock & Reid, 2006). Narrative therapy provides a venue for erotically marginalized clients to redefine and understand themselves outside of the oppressive and constant stream of messages that come from mainstream society. Unlike a medical model which uses a client's past to reveal causes of "problems," a narrative approach utilizes personal storytelling (Schrock & Reid, 2006) and an empathetic environment (Saltzburg, 2007) as a way to support clients to build identity. Identity is not an abstract, psychological concept, but is something that exists only in the narrative we tell of our own lives (Halverson, 2005). By giving voice to the present and to the ongoing messages of the past, clients can counter misinformation and negative assumptions that have been internalized (Palma & Stanley, 2002).

Dialogic Principles

Dialogic principles center client's experiences and knowledge as an integral part of the therapeutic process. Our fourth principle, *practice a relational and dialogic approach to sex therapy*, provides dialogic tools for therapists to access to help clients build and understand their own narratives;

> *The therapist promotes dialogue by responding to the client's utterances commonly in three ways that invite a further response. This includes (A) using the client's own words; (B) engaging in responsive listening; and (C) sustaining attunement to nonverbal utterances, including silences.*
>
> *(Olson, Seikkula, & Ziedonis, 2014, p.6)*

Using a client's words and phrases in our own responses to the client demonstrates our interest in and respect for the client's experiences and worldview. It also provides a mirror in which clients can have their experiences reflected back to themselves. For clients with erotically marginalized identities who are isolated, this may be the first time hearing someone else talk about their experience the same way they understand it. There is an opportunity to help clients reflect on what it is like to hear their story, to be curious about meaning, and to deepen their understanding of themselves. Responsive listening sets the stage for clients to have the space that they need to understand their own complexities. Too often we are encouraged to distill ourselves down to a label or idea, which does not allow people to explore, contradict, and create meaning without assumptions or judgment. Responsive listening communicates to clients that they are valuable and their experiences are worth making time for, this process creates space for clients to create and understand their own narratives.

Freedom Paradigm

The Freedom Paradigm describes freedom as a psychological state wherein a person is not inhibited by emotional pain, obstructive thoughts or compulsion (Hanna & Cardona, 2013, p. 350). Hanna and Cardona conceptualize this move towards freedom as a move away from oppression. The experience of oppression has a direct impact on the narratives that people form and the maintenance of oppression requires the continued devaluation of oppressed narratives. As sex therapists we are called on to be curious about where our clients narratives come from, whose narratives are being prioritized, and how we can help erotically marginalized clients create and value their own narratives. Hanna states that oppressive narratives maintain oppression and believes that the oppressed need to end their belief in the oppressive message to achieve freedom. Helping clients shift the narrative allows them to not only stop participating in the maintenance of an oppressive message, but also create a new narrative that empowers them.

The field of sex therapy is not immune to the maintenance of oppressive narratives. Kleinplatz gives the definition of masculinity as an example,

> *Sexologists recognize that definitions of masculinity centered on the belief that a man's worth is to be measured by his last erection can only impair his sexual functioning, not to mention his enjoyment; but we mention this in passing, just before we treat his erectile dysfunction.*
>
> (2012, p. 105)

The narrative that masculinity is tied to sexual performance, and specifically an erection, is maintained by the definition of erectile difficulties being categorized, and treated as a dysfunction. What are alternative narratives about erections and sexuality? What are alternative narratives about masculinity and sexuality? Whose experiences do the dominant narratives privilege? Whose experiences do the dominant narratives erase?

Vignette

Barrett was a 37-year-old African-American transgender man who sought sex therapy to understand more about how his body was working sexually. He described experiencing erectile dysfunction explaining that he was having trouble getting off, which had never been an issue before. Barrett transitioned his gender when he was 35 years old, and prior to his transition anonymous sexual encounters had been a consistent and important part of his life. He had been taking masculinizing hormones (testosterone) for two years and though he experienced the initial increase in sexual desire that is often a side effect of testosterone, he experienced a significant

(continued)

(continued)

drop in the last six months. Barrett had not had any surgery to change his genitals. He typically experienced desire during sexual arousal, maintained desire throughout the sexual experience and experienced orgasm during the sexual experience. He came in asking the following questions:

- *Is there something wrong with me?*
- *Am I less of a man if I can't orgasm?*
- *Was I more of a man before I transitioned, since it was easier for me to participate in anonymous sex at that time?*

When we began our work together, he had no language to talk about his genitals and had actively avoided conversations about sex that might require him to discuss his body. He felt extreme dysphoria at the thought of having a clitoris or a vagina. By creating a safe space for Barrett to be curious about his body, his sexual desire, and the relationship between the two, Barrett was able to create language that did not feel dysphoric. Barrett identified strongly as having a penis, and after creating this language that felt affirming and accurate, he was more able to describe his feelings during his sexual encounters. We were then able to work together to identify the multitude of messages that Barrett has received about sex and gender that influenced his understanding of himself as both transgender and as a man.

Emphasizing client's own words, knowledge, and narratives honors our clients experience and validates the building of their own narrative. This helps clients prioritize and build narratives that are authentic to their own lived experience and is an act of healing. For work with erotically marginalized clients this approach is especially important because of the mainstream anti-sex, anti-pleasure, homophobic, transphobic, and heterosexist messages that we all receive about sex and sexuality. Erotically marginalized clients have the challenge of not just creating and understanding their own narratives of themselves, but doing it in opposition to messages that devalue their gender identity, sexual orientation, desirability, body, and even personhood.

Words, Knowledge, and Narratives

Words

Part of the inception of this book was creating the term *erotically marginalized* to describe something that did not yet have language. This is a parallel process to the experience that we have with clients who also do not have the language that they need to accurately describe their experience. In his qualitative research about the intersection between nonbinary gender identities, sexual behavior, and intimacy, Damon Constantinides found limited access to language to be a theme (2011). One participant described, "I sometimes feel like I don't fit anywhere . . . I wish I had something strong to hold onto that I can say, 'Yeah. I'm this'" (p. 163). Anecdotally, in our work with erotically marginalized clients we have found this sentiment to be true. Language has power, not only to make ourselves understood to others, but also in how we understand ourselves (Ritchie & Barker, 2006). Language legitimizes our experience.

The words that erotically marginalized clients use to describe themselves, their behaviors, their bodies, and their communities may also be specific and used in a way that is different than the therapist's own experience. For sex therapists who are themselves erotically marginalized, there can be a feeling of comradery between client and therapist knowing they share an experience. However, within shared experience there is always difference, and in these situations it becomes even more important to clarify use of language with clients. By assuming shared language we lose opportunities to further understand our clients' experiences and to build narratives together. When a clinician and a client share the same self identification, for example, if they both identify as queer, the clinician can ask, "What does being queer mean to you? How do you identify 'queer' for yourself? What is it like to talk to a queer therapist about your own queer identity?"

When an erotically marginalized client meets with a sex therapist who does not experience erotic marginalization, the client may use the therapist's understanding of language to determine if they feel the therapist is someone safe to talk to. This does not mean that a therapist needs to experience erotic marginalization themselves to understand the language that a client is using. However, it offers the therapist an opportunity to practice the principles by modeling transparency and the tolerance of uncertainty by clarifying meanings of words and identities with the client. Clients want to know if their therapist has the capacity to understand them, not that they already do understand them.

One way for a sex therapist to actively work on understanding erotically marginalized identities and the language and labels that clients might use is to participate in a Sexual Attitude Reassessment (SAR) training. SAR trainings offer an excellent opportunity for clinicians to clarify their own experiences and values regarding sexuality and sexual practices, before encountering them in the office with a client (Sitron & Dyson, 2009). SARs are regularly offered through the American Association of Sexuality Education, Counseling and Therapy. They are usually designed as a full-day intensive training that includes exposure to sexually explicit, and often provocative material followed by processing with a skilled facilitator.

Vignette

Jack identified as Latinx, nonbinary, and transgender. Ze first began working with me when ze was in hir final year at college. Ze was out on campus as nonbinary and transgender and was struggling with coming out to family. Ze also had a history of sexual trauma, and was not yet ready to talk about it. Building our clinical relationship was a long term process and although gender was on the table to talk about, sex and dating were kept private. It wasn't until two years of working together that Jack began talking openly about hir shame regarding sexuality and dating. It was then that I learned that Jack identified as "bisexual." I was surprised, knowing that ze identified as nonbinary hirself. I file the term "bisexual" away as a way for a binary identified person to describe an attraction to men and women and was interested to hear it used by hir. Curious, I asked more about what it meant to Jack to be bisexual. "Oh, I mean it in the very literal sense. I am attracted to two and only two genders. Transgender and female." Jack's definition and use of bisexual was not one I was familiar with, despite our shared identity.

Knowledge

We believe that clients are the experts on themselves and come to therapy full of knowledge of their own world and internal experience. This knowledge is not always clear to clients and sometimes it is disregarded based on years of oppressive messages that devalue the experience of erotically marginalized clients. The therapy office can be a place of safety and possibility, where clients have the opportunity to reconnect with these essential truths that have been lost to them.

Vignette

For as long as he could remember, Jared (white, cisgender, male) was told that he was caring and loving. As a child his parents valued kindness and noticed when Jared shared with other kids or took time to help others. Jared grew up believing that he was kind and caring. His internal monologue supported this as he found joy in helping others through babysitting and taking care of children. As he grew older and interacted more with mainstream media he began to internalize an alternative narrative. Television and movies taught him that real men were not caring and kind and that Jared's kindness was a weakness. His high school soccer coach used to call him a "girl" and a "fag", words attacking both his gender identity and his sexual orientation. Jared felt even more shame as he realized he was sexually attracted to both men and women. When Jared sought out a sex therapist at the age of 33 for help with dating and emotional closeness he carried these narratives with him. At times he felt proud of his essential kindness, and at the same time he felt shame and embarrassment.

People seek therapy when they find that they are living a story that is not their own (White & Epston, 1990, p. 28). When Jared came seeking sex therapy he was uncomfortable with himself, and this discomfort was especially palpable when it came to his sexuality. This was particularly confusing to him because his local knowledge, his lived experience, had taught him that living with kindness felt authentic and right. He experienced a cognitive dissonance between an internal story that being a good, strong, and attractive man also meant being a kind man, and a dominant narrative in which this strength was interpreted as weak. Dominant narratives are part of a complicated system of power and control that benefits those already in power and punishes those who go against that narrative (Foucault, 1977; White & Epston, 1990). In Jared's life, the dominant narrative, that men are strong and women are weak, therefore being kind and womanly is unmanly, maintains a system of misogyny and patriarchy. The enactment of masculinity has very clear rules that must be followed to maintain power and "pride."

When these rules are challenged, there are steep punishments. Jared experienced these punishments for the first time in high school, when it was no longer acceptable to be a kind and caring boy. This dominant narrative appeared repeatedly in Jared's life, leaving him feeling ashamed of who he was. The mainstream narrative also conflates gender and sexual orientation, assuming that if someone who is male identified expresses femininity (or a trait labeled feminine) he is therefore gay.

This dominant narrative is rooted in homophobia and enforces heteronormativity, the idea that being heterosexual is normal and anything else is abnormal. If women are viewed as equal to men and being gay, lesbian, bisexual or queer is equal to being heterosexual, this dominant narrative loses control and power. When we name something, we can see it, be curious about it, and change it (if that is what we decide to do). When Jared presented for therapy, he thought he was essentially flawed because he was a kind and caring man. The narrative that he had learned was that men who were kind and caring were not sexual or attractive. When Jared was able to identify this as a dominant and controlling narrative, instead of a truth, he could then begin to understand himself better and decide which parts of the narrative he wanted to keep, and which part he wanted to rewrite. He was able to access his knowledge, value it, and believe it.

Narratives in Sex Therapy

Our first narratives, the ones that we learn from our primary attachment figures, are the narratives that become our internal voice. These narratives are learned from how our families treat us and how they treat each other. As adults we all have individual narratives about our sexual identity, our sexual behavior, our bodies, and about relationships. Our narratives are the ways in which we understand our world. In the therapy office, our clients share their narratives with us both directly and indirectly. It is often a disconnect between the dominant narrative and the subordinate narrative that cause clients seek therapy.

Vignette

Dara was a 40-year-old, white, assigned male at birth person who came to therapy seeking help deciding whether or not to transition. Dara said that she always knew that she was different, but that as a child there was no way to explain or understand that difference. She had never heard about people being transgender until she saw a daytime talk show as a teenager. That television show depicted transgender people as mentally disturbed. Dara decided at that time that she was not transgender, because that was clearly not her experience. In her 30s, Dara encountered a more diverse group of people in media and literature who were all identifying as trans, transgender, and nonbinary. Dara's experience of being trans as an identity was no longer a single single story or narrative, and suddenly a new world seemed possible. Dara began to search for people in her community and through online networks who had a similar experience to her. She was clear that she was not a man, but she also was not a woman. Dara identified as a transwoman and began searching for mirrors that would help her create a narrative that matched her internal experience. As she built this narrative she also began to build the confidence that she needed to share her identity with her friends and family.

Many erotically marginalized clients have not had the privilege of writing their own narrative. They have grown up in a world in which their experiences have either been invisible or pathologized. As a young person Dara knew of no one like herself. When she first learned about trans people, the stories were pathologizing and she did not see herself in those narratives either. It was only later in life, when Dara had the tools that she needed to begin looking for other people who were similar to her, that she finally began to understand and describe her own truth. Dara's work was to find and give power to the subordinate narrative that more fully described her experience. Through this process of naming and understanding herself she was able to counter misinformation that she had internalized from the dominant narratives around her.

Clinical Tools

Building New Storylines with Unique Outcomes

The therapeutic relationship can be a place to help clients build new narratives that more clearly fit their experiences. It offers an opportunity for the therapist to empower their clients to claim their own narratives. This might be the first time that a client has been given the space to understand their own narrative through their experience. Narrative therapy offers tools for helping clients build new story lines by identifying unique outcomes. Unique outcomes describe the times that were not ordinary, standard, or more dominant in a person's struggle with something. Unique outcomes are the magical moments that stand outside of harder and more difficult storylines. Clinical contexts that incorporate narrative therapy approaches allow a client to tell their story and identify unique outcomes that can help them in understanding their story differently, externalizing the problem, and re-authoring their story. Through this process clients can integrate negative experiences in new ways that builds confidence and lead to a more empowered way of thinking (Semmler & Williams, 2000).

Speaking the Unspoken

Being a person who experiences erotic marginalization is a radical act. Our clients are living a truth that has not yet been written. Often, clients struggle to find support or comradery because no one else in their life has had the experience that they have, and sometimes the thing that needs to be said does not have words yet. There are times when we, as therapists, are called to use all of our skill and training to be creative and adaptive. Speaking the unspoken calls on us to notice when something is not being said, and find language when there might be none.

Vignette

Kim walked in the door, sat causally on the couch and said, "You were right." I wondered what it was I had been right about. Our last session was three weeks ago and I remembered talking at length about Kim's feelings about her housemates starting the process of trying to get pregnant. She looked at me and said, "When you said, 'But you are family.' I've been thinking a lot about it." Kim identified herself as a Korean-American fat queer polyamorous cisgender woman. She had worked hard to build a community with her housemates that felt unconditionally supportive and loving. She first came to see me because of her frustration in finding a sexual relationship that felt satisfying. Most recently we had been discussing the decision for her housemates to try to get pregnant and parent together. Kim did not want kids but she was fine with her housemates choosing that path. However, now her relationship with them felt complicated. What Kim was describing to me was her realization that her feelings towards this couple were similar to her angry feelings towards her mother. My words, "But you are family", were in response to Kim's feeling that she should not have a say or opinion in the decision of friends choosing to have a child. The couple however was clear that they were not just interested in having a kid but in building a queer family together and wanted to include Kim in a way that felt good to her. In that moment I said out loud an unspoken truth that was lying beneath the surface of Kim's feelings of discontentment. If Kim joined this new family, she risked the experience of sadness and heartache that she was currently healing from with her family of origin and possibly feeling more alienated from her cultural heritage.

In the example above, we reflect back her words, knowledge and narrative, providing a structure for her to understand this experience for which there are few models. Over the next few months Kim was able to build more and more language for her feelings and talk more clearly and openly with her housemates about the meanings and connections to her family of origin.

Co-Creating Language and Meaning

Clinicians can help clients create, maintain, and internalize a new and more authentic narrative through the co-creation of language and meaning. This intervention is based on a relational therapeutic stance in which the work in therapy is understood as happening between the client and the therapist. Dialogic practices encourage responding to clients' every utterance, this concept gives us a starting point for what this might look like in practice. For clients who do not have language to talk about their experiences, having a co-narrator can help them try different language on to clarify what meaning that are making through their experiences.

Vignette

Ash came to therapy seeking help because she was experiencing distance between herself and her family of origin. Ash was in her mid-30s and identified as African-American, polyamorous, cisgender woman, and queer. She was in a healthy, polyamorous, long term relationship with a cisgender man. Several themes continued to reoccur during our work together. As Ash neared her 40s, she became more and more unclear about her role and her place both in her community and her family. Her intersecting identities left her as an outsider in multiple communities. And although she had developed strategies for reconciling these experiences, there was something happening that she could not quite explain. Through our work together we discovered that Ash felt confused about her path. As a queer, polyamorous, African-American woman who didn't want children and was in a relationship with a man, she had very few role models of people who were traveling a similar path. Ash had a strong community of African-American women that she felt connected to both through her college sorority and through her work. However, she felt like she could not share her polyamorous relationship structure without alienating herself. She also had a strong group of polyamorous and queer friends who were mostly white, but spending time with them often felt exhausting as they turned to her to help them learn to be better anti-racist allies. In our sessions we talked about the limitations of the space and what it was like for Ash to work with a white therapist. We acknowledged that even this space did not feel completely safe. Ash and I had known language and meanings to talk about the experience of racism and homophobia that she experienced. But it was more difficult to talk about what it was like to feel invisible as a polyamorous person. She described assumptions that were made, offhanded jokes made in front of her, and the frustration of not knowing how to explain her reality in a way that would be understood. Together we joined around the monogamist assumption that all married people are monogamous and that you are monogamous unless proven otherwise. We discussed the difficulty in describing a consensual non-monogamous relationship to people who simply saw it as cheating. Through our work together Ash developed some language to talk more clearly about her experience and slowly began to make inroads of understanding with all her communities about the ways that she wanted to be able to be seen as her most authentic self in all her identities, in all her communities.

Externalizing

Externalizing is the process of moving an experience from a flaw to a problem. Problems are something we can look at, be curious about, and brainstorm solutions for; whereas a flaw is internal, terminal, and chronic. White and Epston describe externalizing as, "an approach to therapy that encourages persons to objectify and, at times, to personify the problems that they experience as oppressive" (White & Epston, 1990, p. 38).

The technique of externalization, which is core to Narrative therapy, also provides a tool with which erotically marginalized clients can examine and understand the outside forces of heterosexism, homophobia, transphobia, fatphobia, and racism. This technique has specifically been associated with successful work with other sexual minorities (Saltzburg, 2007). Externalizing the "problem" can create needed distance between difficult emotions and experiences, allowing a client to look at the situation from a less vulnerable position (Saltzburg, 2007). By building an understanding of the role that oppression and discrimination plays in their lives, clients can identify in what ways it has enlisted their participation and have more how agency to determine how they will interact with it in the future.

Countertransferential Check-In

We believe that when we are working with clients, our whole self comes with us. It is important for clinicians to have clear boundaries, and equally important be aware of what the therapist brings into the room and how it might be affecting their work. Research about heterosexism in the field of therapy found that therapists who are unaware of their own heterosexism often perpetuate this bias in their work with LGBTQ clients. This happens regardless of the sexual orientation of the therapist themselves (Giammattei & Green, 2012). It is critical that clinicians are aware of their own bias and discrimination in order to provide non-biased sex therapy to erotically marginalized clients. In Principle Four we share a sexual history form that can be used with erotically marginalized clients. We recommend that all therapists who are using this form with clients complete their own sexual history form. If possible, it is ideal to have someone else read the questions and the therapist can reply verbally. This gives the clinician the opportunity to assess their own history and to experience what it might be like to talk to someone else about these personal thoughts and feelings. Below are some further questions for clinicians to consider after completing the sexual history form.

Sexual History Sex Therapist Questions

1. What feelings came up for while completing the Sexual History?
2. Did any of your responses surprise you? Which ones? What did you find surprising?
3. What are three ways that your own experiences with gender and sexuality impact you as a therapist?
4. Are there client demographics similar to your own that you frequently work with? Which demographics? In what ways is your experience different than clients with those shared demographics? In what ways is it similar?

Key Points

- Emphasizing client's own words, knowledge, and narratives honors our clients' experience and validates the building of their own narrative. This helps clients prioritize and build narratives that are authentic to their own lived experience and is an act of healing.
- For work with erotically marginalized clients this approach is especially important because of the mainstream anti-sex, anti-pleasure, homophobic, transphobic, and heterosexist messages that we all receive about sex and sexuality. Erotically marginalized clients have the challenge of not just creating and understanding their own narratives of themselves, but doing it in opposition to messages that devalue their gender identity, sexual orientation, desirability, body, and even personhood.
- Erotically marginalized clients may not have had many experiences where the knowledge that they have acquired through their experiences and internal understanding of themselves has been valued, therefore, it is imperative for sex therapists to emphasizing clients' own words, knowledge and narratives.
- Although it is a common therapeutic tenant to value the experience of the client this feels even more important to us when working with clients whose narratives have continuously been dismissed, pathologized, or made invisible. The origins for principle five are found in narrative therapy, dialogic principles, and the freedom paradigm. Each of these approaches offer a different lens through which we value, understand, and enact principle five in our work as sex therapists.

References

Annon. J. S. (1976). *Behavioral treatment of sexual problems: Brief therapy*. New York: Harper & Row.

Borden, W. (1992). Narrative perspectives in psychosocial intervention following adverse life effects. *National Association of Social Workers, 37*(2), 135–141.

Burdge, B. J. (2007). Bending gender, ending gender: Theoretical foundations for social work practice with the transgender community. *Social Work, 52*(3), 243–250.

Cashin, A. (2008). Narrative therapy: A psychotherapeutic approach in the treatment of adolescents with Asperger's disorder. *Journal of Child and Adolescent Psychiatric Nursing, 21*(1), 48–56.

Constantinides, D. M. (2011). *Intersections of gender and intimacy in the lives of transgender people with non-binary gender identities* (Order No. 3456031). Available from Dissertations & Theses @ Widener University; ProQuest Dissertations & Theses A&I (871211349). Retrieved from http://0-search.proquestion.com.libcat.widener.edu/docview/871211349?accountid=29103.

Foucault, M. (1977). *The history of sexuality, Vol. I.* London: Routledge.

Giammattei, S. V & Green, R. (2012). LGBTQ couple and family therapy: History and future directions. In J. J. Bigner & J. L. Wetchler (Eds.), *Handbook of LGBT-affirmative couple and family therapy* (pp. 1–22). New York: Routledge.

Halverson, E. R. (2005) InsideOut: Facilitating gay youth identity development through a performance-based youth organization. *Identity, 5*(1), 67–90.

Hanna, F. J. & Cardona, B. (2013). Multicultural counseling beyond the relationship: Expanding the repertoire with techniques. *Journal of Counseling & Development, 91*, 349–357. doi 10.1002/j.1556-6676.2013.00104.x

Hanna, F. J., Talley, W. B. & Guindon, M. H. (2000). The power of perception: Toward a model of cultural oppression and liberation. *Journal of Counseling & Development, 78*, 430–441.

Jagose, A. (1996). *Queer theory: An introduction*. New York: New York University Press.

Kleinplatz, P. J. (2012). Is that all there is? A new critique of the goals of sex therapy. In. P. J. Kleinplatz (Ed.), *New directions in sex therapy: Innovations and alternatives* (pp. 101–118). New York: Routledge.

Lev, A. I. (2004). *Transgender emergence: Therapeutic guidelines for working with gender-variant people and their families*. Binghamton, NY: Haworth Clinical Practice Press.

Lock, A., Epston, D., Maisel, R., & deFaria, N. (2005). Resisting anorexia/bulimia: Foucauldian perspectives in narrative therapy. *British Journal of Guidance & Counseling, 33*(3), 315–332.

Morgan, A. (2000). *What is narrative therapy?* Adelaide: Dulwich Centre Publications.

Palma, T. V., & Stanley, J. L. (2002). Effective counseling with lesbian, gay, and bisexual clients. *Journal of College Counseling, 5*, 74–88.

Ritchie, A., & Barker, M. (2006). 'There Aren't Words for What We Do or How We Feel So We Have To Make Them Up': Constructing Polyamorous Languages in a Culture of Compulsory Monogamy. *Sexualities, 9*(5), 584–601. doi:10.1177/1363460706069987

Saltzburg, S. (2007). Narrative therapy pathways for re-authoring with parents of adolescents coming-out as lesbian, gay, and bisexual. *Contemporary Family Therapy, 29*, 57–69.

Schrock, D. P., & Reid, L. L. (2006). Transsexuals' sexual stories. *Archives of Sexual Behavior*, *35*(1), 75–86.

Semmler, P. L., & Williams, C. B. (2000). Narrative therapy: A storied context for multicultural counseling. *Journal of Multicultural Counseling & Development*, *28*(1), 51–62.

Sitron, J. A. & Dyson, D. A. (2009). Sexuality attitudes reassessment (SAR): Historical and new considerations for measuring its effectiveness. *American Journal of Sexuality Education*, *4*, 158–177. doi: 10.1080/15546120903001407

Steinmetz, K. (2016, January). This pronoun is the work of the year for 2015. *Time Magazine*. Retrieved from http://www.time.com/4173992/word-of-the-year-2015-they

Tanner, L. R., & Lyness, K. P. (2003). Out of the closet, still in the home: Providing queer affirmative therapy for youth and their families. *Journal of Feminist Family Therapy*, *15*(1), 21–35.

White, M. & Epston, D. (1990). *Narrative means to therapeutic ends*. New York: W.W. Norton & Company.

THE CASE OF V

Anastasia Fujii

Introduction

This case study will focus on common themes observed and addressed in therapy with erotically marginalized clients who hold similar intersecting oppressed identities (AMAB trans and/or nonbinary, queer, person of color), as well as past experiences with sexual trauma and current desire to engage and/or engagement in dominance during sex. The common presenting concern I will be exploring is severe anxiety connected to taking on a dominant role, related to (a) fear of identifying with and/or affirming the actions of their sexual assailant(s) and/or (b) being read as their sex assigned at birth due to the socially constructed connection between aggression and masculinity. For this purpose, I have developed a fictional client, "V," who exemplifies these themes in their identity, experiences, and presenting concerns. This case will highlight the utilization of narrative therapy techniques in this sex therapy context.

Location of Therapist

I am an individual, couples, and family psychodynamic psychotherapist in Philadelphia, PA. My practice is psychodynamic, relational, and at its core holistic, recognizing and integrating the biological, psychological, and social aspects of experience, as well as the individual, institutional, and cultural roots of issues as they arise. I am also an LGBTQ+ cultural humility consultant and trainer. I have practiced in a diverse range of settings, with the primary focus on my work being to provide a safer space of support and healing for erotically marginalized people, including queer, trans, gender nonconforming and nonbinary ("QTGNCNB") individuals, many of whom also identify as polyamorous ("poly"), non-monogamous, and/or BDSM-oriented. I prioritize serving clients who are disproportionately under or inadequately served, including in LGBTQ-focused mental health settings, including clients of color, QTGNCNB clients, and disabled and/or chronically ill clients. My approach to psychodynamic work is informed by transfeminist, relational and narrative theories.

To socially locate myself: I identify as a queer person of color. I am Asian American, mixed race, and have light skin. My gender identity has always been creative and nonbinary, and more recently I have felt that the designation "agender" best describes how I see and experience my gender identity. This identity and experience comes with nuanced experiences of privilege (I do identify with my sex assigned at birth to some degree, and therefor do benefit from cissexism) and oppression (while I am often able to pass as a cis woman, this has not been a consistent experience – as my gender expression varies – and when I do pass, my gender is being inaccurately assumed, therefore my true gender is erased.) I primarily use the pronouns assigned to me at birth, not because they feel affirming or particularly resonant, but rather, because I have yet to locate more self-affirming language, and using them has allowed me to move through the world more easily, albeit with my gender experience largely unseen. Likewise, I experience racism, while also benefiting from skin privilege. I was raised and am currently middle class. I am not currently, and have never been, religious. I also live with chronic illness and disability.

I identify as a person living with multiple minority stress and I also recognize that several of my primary identities are such that I simultaneously benefit from privilege and suffer from oppression. This reality is a major facet in my work and it also informs my clinical practice, particularly when working with clients who, like V, also experience oppression that is intersectional.

As therapists, we hold inherent power in the therapeutic space, which can heighten the oppressive capacity of any privileged identities that we hold. I commonly have QTGNCNB clients of color share that they sought me out specifically due to a desire to work with a QTGNCNB clinician of color. I am public about many of my own identities in my online presence and in early interactions with perspective clients because I think it is important for these clients to have awareness of and access to providers who hold resonant social locations and experiences, especially because many come to therapy apprehensively, due to mistreatment and/or harm in past psychotherapy experiences. At the same time, I work actively to be aware and to not overly identify with clients with whom I share some or many social locations. As a queer practitioner, the core of my therapeutic orientation is such that I see each client as the author and expert of their story and identities and believe that they must become known to and understood by me through a self-determined process.

Presenting Concern

V first contacted me by email, expressing concern about their "intense anxiety" following a series of recent sexual experiences. In our initial session, V described their relationship with a new partner, with whom they agreed to explore taking on a dominant role during dominance and submission (D/s) oriented sex. During their first experience domming, V reports feeling initially somewhat detached, and then suddenly unable to breathe. V had experienced panic attacks during adolescence and was able to use tools they had learned at that time to regulate.

Since that initial experience, however, V has experienced high levels of anxiety, and has continued to experience panic attacks when thinking about and engaging in D/s oriented sex. V fears that being aggressive and powerful during sex equates to their identifying with the aggressor (their father, their rapists, and perpetrators). V also feels increasing concern that their desire to be dominant will be perceived by current and future partners as a masculine trait, a possibility that triggers the trauma of pervasively having their gender identity denied.

Case History

V is a 27-year-old Latinx, queer, AMAB, nonbinary transfemme person who uses the pronouns they/them/theirs. V identifies as neurotypical and non-disabled. V currently identifies as middle class, though they were raised in poverty. V was born in the Dominican Republic and immigrated to the United States, along with their mother, father, and one-year-old sister when V was five. V's father was an alcoholic and struggled with chronic under- and unemployment. V believes that their mother struggled with post-traumatic stress disorder (PTSD) and postpartum depression (PPD), and shares that their mother has been depressed for as long as V can remember.

V was parentified from a young age, frequently caring for their younger sister while their mother was "too depressed to function" and their father was intermittently too intoxicated to provide adequate care. V's father was emotionally and physically abusive towards V and emotionally, physically and sexually abusive towards their mother. V's father would antagonize V by telling them to "be a man and defend [their] mother," but when V would do so, their father would become enraged and accuse them of trying to "take his place." He would also frequently refer to V as a "maricón" or "faggot." At that time, V describes a sick feeling they felt whenever their father would refer to them using these words, which at the time they did not entirely understand as being connected to early feelings of shame about their gender identity and sexual orientation.

V and their family moved frequently between New York, New Jersey, and Pennsylvania due to V's father's job instability, which made it difficult to develop a support system. Over time, V found support online, through social media and blogs. V describes seeking out queer and trans community on Facebook and Twitter, long before they felt capable of naming their own identities or orientations. V constantly felt torn between a sense of obligation to protect their mother and sister from their father, and needing to flee the family's home to protect themself.

V's father died in a car accident when V was a sophomore in high school. Soon after, V's maternal aunt, who had moved from the Dominican Republic more recently, began living with the family. V saw these two events as a window of opportunity. No longer feeling the deep obligation to protect and care for their mother and sister, they were able to center themself for the first time. V had heard rumors that this aunt was shunned from their family for being a lesbian, and V became very connected to her once she began living with the family. V came out to themself as trans and nonbinary at age seventeen, and soon after confided in their aunt. Their aunt was very supportive, but also cautioned V about not disclosing to their mother because of her "condition." Both V and their aunt were closeted in their home. V focused on their academics and moved to a large urban area at age eighteen, on a full academic scholarship.

College was a very tumultuous time for V. Being separated from their family of origin felt simultaneously freeing and overwhelming. V was able to find queer and trans community at college, but they also struggled with depression and anxiety, as well as intermittent periods of substance abuse. V describes feeling deeply conflicted about their gender identity and expression during college. V was sexually assaulted twice during college, both times by cis men. Both times, V was presenting as more femme and this further complicated their feelings about the fluidity of their gender. V describes a growing self hatred due to their realization that they equated femininity to victimization and masculinity to perpetration, despite their awareness that this thinking pattern reinforced a binary view of gender.

At the time of our first meeting, V was working as an administrative assistant where they felt pressure to present as masculine. In the advocacy community in which they were a part, they felt freedom to present more fluidly and/or femme, but they reported feeling burdened by a near constant fear of being misunderstood and/or misrepresented. V had also recently gotten sober, and without the ability to self-medicate with alcohol, V was struggling to manage their anxiety.

V met their new partner at a queer sober party. V felt excited to experience a romantic connection with a fellow sober person. V described feeling shocked by how safe and seen they felt in this relationship, given their typical challenge to build healthy connections with others because of their history of abuse. V and their partner, who identified as a black queer cis woman, were in a primary polyamorous partnership throughout the duration of our work together. V and I worked together for two years, until they moved cross country to attend graduate school.

Therapeutic Work

When V first came to see me, they described their level of anxiety as "crushing." As a therapist who draws frequently from narrative therapy techniques, V and I spent the first months of therapy exploring V's personal narrative, including articulating the roots of their anxiety. The primary components we identified included the shame they felt about their sexual desires, guilt about disengaging from their familial unit (their original narrative being that they had selfishly abandoned their mentally ill mother and traumatized sister), and shame about their struggle to articulate their true gender. Later in our work together, they also began to explore the confusion and loss they had long felt in relationship to their racial and ethnic identity, due to the frequent and often unexpected relocating they did as a young person, and later in relationship to connection with different partners and communities.

In the beginning, engagement and assessment intertwined, as V felt unknown and unknowable, and having opportunity to respond to personal identity and experience-based questions provided an opportunity to develop a strong base to our therapeutic relationship. V's self-identification and self-determination in our therapeutic process was at the forefront of my thoughts as we proceeded in treatment. I asked specific and detailed questions throughout to ensure that I was gaining a full and nuanced understanding of the significant identifications, systems, relationships, and experiences in V's life.

Together we created genograms of V's family of origin, chosen family, and romantic and sexual partners; and I utilized ecomapping techniques to incorporate the role of the significant influences on V's personal experiences and relationships (including racism, cissexism, and heterosexism). This was a slow process throughout which V and I frequently discussed its significance. We came to the collective understanding that while V felt somewhat impatient to dive into exploring the more present anxiety catalysts, that it was essential to first ensure that V felt seen and known by me, their therapist, for only then did it become possible for them to trust and feel able to dive deeper into their deep guilt and shame narratives. V maintained a therapy journal during treatment, which they described as a way to feel grounded and connected to our work outside of session. Because of the amount of gaslighting and invisibility that V had endured, they worried about being able to integrate their insight therapy into the fabric of their life.

V felt deeply misunderstood, having repeatedly received messaging from family of origin, society at large, as well as voices from within the queer and trans communities at their college that their identities and experience of the world are not real or unacceptable. To model self-acceptance and to provide mirroring, I did disclose some about my own complex self-identity. The only question that V asked me about myself during treatment was more of an observation. They observed and verbalized to me that they noticed that I only wear black clothing. For me personally, my choice in a monochromatic wardrobe is bound up in both my gender and racial identities, and ultimately I decided to share this with them. I described how for me, my gender identity felt possible to express with any specific combination of feminine or masculine clothing, and similarly, my racial identity is almost always read as ambiguous, so that having the coherence of a single color felt containing and like a representation of a whole self.

This appeared to resonate deeply with V and this conversation was one that sometimes they referenced as one of few times in their life when they had heard a narrative of gender, ethnicity, and race that made sense to them. I did, of course, consider any possible negative outcomes of this sharing, but ultimately decided that for V to experience mirroring and to hear that their experience of difference does not separate them from that of all others (a belief they held that they also linked to be proof of their inherent wrongness or badness) would be valuable.

Living as a Latinx, queer, nonbinary transperson whose gender identity, race, and ethnicity have often been misunderstood or denied was one factor that made V nervous about seeking treatment. As a mixed race, queer, nonbinary person who passes as cisgender, V's anxiety of not being seen resonated deeply for me personally. This was something I paid close attention to throughout our work, to ensure that my interpretations and interventions were centered around V's needs and experiences and not my own. While this was a potential area of challenge, the intersections and shared experiences between us were also a powerful component of our therapeutic relationship. V disclosed early on that a major component of their willingness to reach out to me had been the hope they had felt seeing my face – that of a queer-presenting person of color – on my website. In time, we also explored some of our shared experiences of being ambiguous in the eyes and minds of others. While this is certainly not a unique experience, to V or myself, it is one that is often overlooked, misunderstood, or made invisible in a majority binary gender, mono-racial society. In addition to their fear of being invalidated by a therapist, V had also never sought therapy previously due also to lack of access, and largely because of the stigma attached to seeking care for mental health within V's family and community of origin. We talked at length about the motivation and strength that had led V to confront this stigma by seeking treatment.

In the beginning stage of treatment, I made sure to regulate our pace, as V frequently became flooded, feeling desperate to be seen and heard, but finding themself paralyzed by vulnerability and fear of my judgment. V frequently would ask, "Do you know what I mean?" At the end of each story shared, which in time, we came to collectively understand was their way of checking to see if I was with them. They feared my abandonment and/or rejection constantly. V's gender identity and sexual orientation had been shamed by their father and erased by their mother. V's aunt had provided some mirroring, but her living closeted in the family's house appeared to further V's belief that being seen could only be a detriment. V had spent their entire life learning that who they are was not acceptable. V had also developed strong, binary associations between masculinity with perpetration and femininity with victimization, which caused great tumult and conflict in their experiencing of their gender fluidity.

I utilized narrative techniques to support V in using externalization to create space between identities (actual and perceived), behaviors, and desires that they viewed as sameness (and therefore "proof" of what they described as their "inherent badness") with their father. It appeared helpful to consider the difference between biologically predetermined and learned behavior. We deconstructed and rebuilt deeply rooted negative beliefs V held about themself. In particular, we explored alternate narratives to V's anxiety belief that their desire to be dominant and aggressive sexually was symbolic of their desire to be abusive. As we dove deeper into their connection to dominance, a new narrative emerged, in which V found great connection to being a powerful sexually while simultaneously maintaining awareness and sensitivity to the safety, needs, and desires of their partners. This unique outcome completely transformed the way that V perceived their own emerging identity as a domme. By reauthorizing their narrative about what it was that connected them to dominance, almost instantly V began reporting a diminishment of their anxiety and stress.

My work with V ended when V moved out of state to attend graduate school. During termination, I worked with V to establish individual therapy in their new home state, as well as couples therapy, as their partner planned to join them as soon as she obtained employment. We created a plan for ongoing strengthening of their new narrative, including limiting contact with the primary "gaslighters" in V's life (primarily their mother and extended family), as well as continuing therapy and journaling, a practice that V had found incredibly helpful during our work together.

Implications and Further Questions

A common and pervasive theme in my work with V, and many other erotically marginalized clients, is that in addition to chronically experiencing oppression, and in most cases surviving sexual harassment and assault(s), clients come to treatment burdened by the long term traumatic impact of living in a society that negates both their identities and experiences. The profound levels of anxiety I have witnessed in clients who have spent years caught between their own truth and the mistuned "reality" that is forced upon them by family of origin, colleagues, providers, and society at large is devastating. For those who are also survivors of sexual assault, in a sense, they have been violated and traumatized, not only by their assailant(s), but by society as a whole. Radically believing the truths a client shares can often, over time, diminish the impact of gaslighting. Creating a space where a client is not responsible for proving their narrative, nor solely responsible for providing an education, is certainly healing. Yet, the reality remains: clients leave my office to confront a culture that continues to perpetrate against them. What can we as providers do to confront and work to change that reality? Becoming a LGBTQ+ cultural humility consultant and trainer is one way that I have addressed this question, but I am also thinking about what more we can do to support our clients in creating this change for themselves in more areas and aspects of their lives.

Principle Six

LOCATE ONESELF AND RESPOND TO CLIENTS' META-COMMUNICATION

Locating oneself as a clinician with erotically marginalized clients is the keystone to the arc of meta-communication. When a clinician is able to locate themself within the therapeutic relationship they are building the scaffolding for a stance of preemptive radical inclusion (PRI). PRI in practice is intentionally assuming that a client is someone who experiences marginalization, whether it is visible or not. This practice allows clinicians to notice and name their own privileges and to be more attuned about these identities of privilege in the therapeutic relationship. PRI is a way of de-centering the therapist's own experiences in order to make space for their clients'. Location of self is the structure in which clinicians can practice PRI and attune themselves to client meta-communication.

Location-of-self is defined by Dee Watts-Jones as:

> *The name of a process in which the therapist initiates a conversation with a [client] about similarities and differences in their key identities, such as race, ethnicity, gender, class, sexual orientation, and religion, and how they may potentially influence the therapy process. Implicit in this communication is the idea that these identities are meaningful and embedded in the work. In extending this invitation to the [client] to reflect and discuss the intersection of their identities, the therapist lays the groundwork for these issues to be raised throughout the course of therapy. The therapist signals a measure of comfort with going into the experience of social location in relationship inside and outside of the therapy room. Location of self begins with the therapist engaging in self-disclosure, but the process goes far beyond what is typical in the use of therapist self-disclosure.*
>
> *(Watts-Jones, 2010, p. 405)*

Dee Watts-Jones articulates three assumptions related to location of self for a therapist. The base assumption is that the therapist needs to have a certain level of comfort about any identity or concern in order to feel they can go into more depth with the client and help them build meaning and language to address it. This foundational level of comfort has the secondary effect of creating a meta-communicated space of accountability for the client to feel safer exploring within.

The second assumption of location of self is that the identities of the therapist and the client matter in the therapeutic relationship, particularly identities of both social advantage and power, as well as identities of marginalization and oppression (Watts-Jones, 2010). The third assumption is that neither the clinician nor the client in a therapeutic context can avoid the impact of oppression because it is embedded into the larger social and cultural systems on both micro and macro levels. Specifically, concerns related to power and oppression are always relevant to the therapeutic work. "In this framework, good therapy includes a lens for seeing the legacy of wounds and entitlements that run underground as well as those that surface in relationships, and a space for witnessing and healing these" (Watts-Jones, 2010, p. 411).

Meta-communication in a sex therapy context with erotically marginalized clients has a few tributaries of meaning. It can be understood as the unspoken or the aspects of intimacy, desire, arousal, and identity that are still without language. Meta-communication is all the non-verbal cues (tone of voice, body language, gestures, facial expressions) that hold meaning, and either enhances or disallows what one might say with words. There is a dearth of knowledge in our culture to describe the diverse experiences of sexuality and gender identity. In practice this can result in clients having difficulty explaining their experience. For erotically marginalized clients often the difficulty is not necessarily due to resistance or shame, but is the result of simply not having created the language that is needed to expressed themselves. This requires therapists to be mindful of all of their clients' meta-communication and to work with them to make meaning with the language that is available. This also means that clinicians need to be aware of their own meta-communication. Watts-Jones is one of the first to notice that the

> *Therapist's demeanor – voice, body language, warmth, and ease – is another key influence in how this particular location of self comes across, and it has occurred to me that the use of the therapist's voice and body is a neglected area in training.*
>
> *(Watts-Jones, 2010, p. 412)*

Just as there is a lack of training on how to locate oneself as a clinician it is true that the therapist's meta-communication in their work with clients is neglected in larger training and supervisory settings.

Co-creating language that brings meaning to meta-communications is critical to the practice of sex therapy with erotically marginalized clients. Making meaning and giving language to meta-communication is a huge part of helping people in romantic and intimate relationships negotiate consensually non-monogamous agreements. In the next section of this chapter we will introduce a clinical approach that focuses on co-creating language and meaning for sexual desire and intimacy. The Alternative Family Structures Approach (AFSA), created by Shannon Sennott, is an eight-session foundational guide for clinicians who are working with clients who wish to be in consensually non-monogamous relationships or redefine their family structure to include other emotional, sexual, or intimate partnerships. In our clinical work we offer this approach to clients, describing the eight-session arc, as a way to build in structure to talk about things that have only existed in an unspoken form previously.

This approach is general enough that it can support all kinds of variations and constellations of relationship orientations and structures. This approach supports a partnership that is considering opening their relationship after years of being monogamous, or relationships that are having difficulty finding compromises within their polyamorous commitment that is already present, and all that lies in between and beyond. We remind clients that these are often not skills of communication that were learned as an early blueprint in families of origin for clients. Therefore, it can be helpful to have a therapist attune to the meta-communication of the partnership while working within a structured approach, to aid partnerships in finding language and agreements that meet everyone in the relationships' needs.

Alternative Family Structures Approach (AFSA)

AFSA is founded on transfeminist and feminist thought, social justice frameworks, and principles of allyship (Sennott, 2011; Sennott & Smith, 2011). AFSA can be understood as a lens for other therapeutic models and orientations (i.e., CBT, DBT, Individual, Group, or Family Treatment). AFSA is designed for *affirming* clinical treatment with polyamorous, consensually non-monogamous, and open relationship systems. We understand that this approach has limitations around the use of language related to "couples" and "partnerships" and may not fit the needs of a client who self-identifies as a relationship anarchist because in relationship anarchy there is not prioritization of any one intimate relationship over another, no matter if a connection is sexual, romantic, play, or platonic.

The Alternative Family Structures Approach has an assessment component and an agreement planning component, we tell clients that the initial commitment is eight sessions. We ask that all parties who are currently active in the relational system stay static while going through the process of assessment and agreement planning. This means that the relationship would not change until the eight sessions were complete and consensual agreements are created.

Assessment: Sessions one and two

Assessment sessions are ideally 90 minutes, this allows for the experience of information gathering about the relationship and family to be organic and responsibly paced.

First Session: The history of the relationship (including desired shift in structure) and the love story.

Is the Relationship in Crisis?

In the first session there are a number of important assessments that need to be considered. It is critical, before anything else, to assess for current relational crisis, namely, is the relationship in a stabilized committed context or is there a person at risk of leaving or ending the relationship? It is very common for clients to seek therapy to open their relationship after there has been a secret emotional or physical relationship by one partner that is discovered by the other partner. If the answer to this question is yes, this is the story that is most important to gather information about in order to aid the partnership in making meaning of the relational situation.

The way that one might ask the question about intimacy with others that is outside the current commitment agreement of the relationship, in a dialogic frame, is to give clients multiple possibilities or "voices" to hear, that could help them find the one that fits best for them. It is very common for people to not have a shared language for a relationship outside of the current relationship agreement. It is important to offer a wide variety of possibilities and acknowledge that even the language that the therapist is offering might not feel best or quite right. The key is to offer options and then ask if any of them resonate for each person. It is likely that one person will feel that one word describes their experience, while the other will pick a different way to illustrate it. It can be helpful to share with clients that they will likely have different language for their experiences and that there are multiple meanings that can be made from these experiences. If clients do not have their own language the clinician can offer ways that other people that they both know and work with have described this experience: cheating, affair, extra-marital relationship, an infidelity, a flirtation, having feelings for someone, acknowledging and acting on an attraction.

It is important to find out if there was a sense of betrayal around this relationship or if there was open communication. Do not make the assumption that if there was open communication that there is not a feeling of crisis alive within the relationship. It is very possible that all partners knew what was happening but it still feels disorganized, upsetting, unclear, and unstructured. However, it is a different foundation for opening the relationship because the partner who may be feeling scared or hurt by the decision to engage in connections outside of the relationship usually does not also feel betrayed by their partner, as they likely would have if there was not transparency or if the partner denied the relationship and then got caught after being suspected.

If the relationship was a secret, there are other nuances to consider in the therapeutic work with this relationship. There has been a rupture of trust in the relationship, which makes it difficult to navigate agreements needed to responsibly construct a consensually non-monogamous relationship. New agreements for an open relationship rely on being able to trust that one's partner is going to act with integrity and accountability in the process. If there has been a secret relationship there is often other unspoken dilemmas in the relationship, and much that is not discussed. Unspoken experiences can lead to more crisis as the partnership begins to create language to describe their feelings.

One important dynamic to be cautious of is if there is a desire to open up the relationship, based on or related to an affair, and the hope of the partner who had the affair is that they would continue to see the person that they cheated on their partner with, it is likely that this will feel extremely difficult, even triggering, for the other partner. It is not uncommon for that partner to still be willing to agree to this, even if it is triggering, because they do not want to lose their partner entirely, however, this is a moment where the clinician needs to fully assess for enthusiastic consent. There are always exceptions but what we see most commonly is that it can be processed in the partner's brain as a traumatic experience that is happening over and over again, which is not entirely consensual, it is driven by a fear of losing their partner, which needs to be illuminated in the therapeutic context. It is usually recommended that if a partnership is working to repair their relationship after an affair that they do not jump immediately into connections with other people, at least until they understand why the communication broke down initially, to lead to an affair. This can be done using the AFSA but it might be suggested that the clients dedicate a handful of sessions to the exploration of betrayal and trust, with a lens of radical acceptance and honesty, so that all partners feel like their truest needs are being articulated, considered, and incorporated into their new agreement.

More ideal circumstances for this type of relationship renegotiation is that all partners feel a desire to consensually open the relationship and no one has acted outside of the relational commitment. This includes not breaking agreements with one another, even when it is hard to keep them (i.e. coming home after a date at the agreed upon time, or, sticking to a plan that is made about intimate contact with a new person).

What is the Love Story of this Commitment/Couple?

If clients are not in a relational crisis the clinician can continue with the assessment. Many of the relational blueprints for clients working on consensual non-monogamy have their roots in the beginning of their love story. For this reason we will often ask clients to share their story of meeting and becoming romantically involved. This question aids a clinician in gathering information that is not just content. It also allows the clinician to learn a great deal about the current level of connectedness each person has to their historical foundations.

For example, clients who beam and giggle, smile and snuggle, from the moment that they hear the question asking about their love story. They might co-create the story, toggling back and forth between each of their memories, filling in details and descriptions. This type of co-constructed narrative could speak to both a resilience and limitations within the partnership that the clinician can keep in mind as they meet with their clients. The strength is the level of affection and love between the people, and the ability to be transported back to a time that brings them so much joy and excitement. In a dialogic sense, it is as if these memories and their vividness serve as another voice or perspective in each of them, that can be accessed and utilized to bring new images and resonances to the current moments of difficulty. The possible limitations that a clinician might watch for is that there could be details that were important but did not make it into the joint co-constructed narrative. This might indicate that there is a tradition within the relationship of avoiding discussions of difference between them, and there could be a habit of conceding to one another in order to not rock the boat about matters of the heart. Obviously these behaviors can be defenses that are built in childhood, to navigate concerns with family of origin dynamics. Avoidance of speaking to differences, because it could lead to conflict, is a common defense structure to develop in childhood. At one time when the person was young, this avoidance was likely quite essential to their survival within their family. However, it becomes less useful when beginning the process of opening up a relationship because that experience requires that clients individually do the work of uncovering their authentic relational desires. It is the hope that they would be different from one another, if they are not, the clinician might also be curious about this and reflect this observation back to their clients.

Another type of response to the question about a love story, though there are many that fall in between these two extremes, is one that is either told by only one partner, with very little input from the other, or, a description that lacks vibrancy and richness, and feels more like a distant or deadening report of the beginning of their relationship. It is important not to jump to conclusions about why this is the presentation, however, it can be a sign of being stuck in a negative dominant story (White, 2007) about their relationship that does not have many windows into the uncharted worlds with new possibilities. It can point to negative sentiment override (Gottman & Silver, 2014) and possibly a power imbalance between them that has led them to be more cautious about allowing for vulnerability and hopefulness in their interactions.

What is the Relational Foundation and Structure?

The next step is to gather information that can be helpful in understanding the strength of the clients' relational structure. People do not need to be together a long time to be a strong relationship, in fact, many partnerships have more openness to change and shifts within the relational context when they have not developed long standing patterns that become a blueprint for neural pathways of the relationship. This openness or flexibility can lead a partnership to actively co-creating a polyamorous agreement before there has been any relational trauma from an affair or emotional betrayal. When a consensually non-monogamous relationship agreement is co-constructed within a space of integrity and optimism there is a beginning point that is founded on trust, respect and accountability. It is helpful for the clinician to ask what brought the clients together at their beginning and how long they have been in a committed relationship. Was consensual non-monogamy a relational ethic from the beginning of the marriage or committed relationship? Some dialogic question to ask: What is the history of the idea behind the desire to enter into an alternative relationship structure? What has come from their commitment to one another? This allows for each person to describe what has been valuable to them about their commitment to one another and it gives the clinician a sense of what stands as the most important or prized areas of the relationship to each person.

Many people will say that their children are the most valuable part of their commitment. It is important for the therapist to find out how many children they have, what ages they are, if there were any traumatic births or experiences related to their children. The fear of losing a child is one of the most undeniably strong fears that exists, if clients are concerned about how their children might react to them having an alternative relationship structure then it is likely they have had an experience of feeling as though they could lose a child in another setting. We see that the more open and transparent with children clients can be, the more likely they are to see this new arrangement as a positive and supportive shift in their parents' relationship (more on this at a later point).

Do the clients in the partnership share a home together? It is important to assess how much time they actually spend together and then how much time they spend together alone, without children. If clients do not live together we find that they are usually skilled at creating intentional time to be together. If clients live together this intentional time is almost always harder for them to carve out and co-create. The one-to-one formula is very helpful in supporting clients to create intentional time with partners that they live with while also seeing other people. The one-to-one formula suggests that for every one on one time that a person spends with a new connection they would schedule one on one time with their partner that they live with and have children with.

What is the Quality of the Romantic and Intimate Connection in the Relationship?

How does the romantic and intimate connection feel for the partnership? It is valuable to explain that there will be a more extensive sexual and relationship history done of each person in the relational structure, but in the first session it is important to get a sense of the type of intimate relationships the partnership experiences and the level of satisfaction each person feels in the areas of romance, desire, and sexual and intimate connection to one another.

It is helpful to get a sense of the current romantic and intimate connection of the relationship. Asking clients to describe their current intimate and emotional connection can elicit information about the areas that they feel similarly about and the places that they feel differently (Lev & Sennott, 2011a). If there are little to no differences in their descriptions that is information about them as a partnership. It is possible that they are deeply and thoroughly attuned to one another, however, it could also mean that they tend to avoid conflict or difference because of a belief that one cannot handle the unspeakable dilemmas of the other.

Most importantly in this section, it is valuable to know what was the catalyst for restructuring the relationship or the precipitating factor that is bringing them into therapy at this moment. Was there an infidelity that brought the clients to the decision of consensually opening up the relationship? If not, was there a desire for intimacy with someone else by one of the partners? These details are critical to know as a clinician begins their work with partnerships interested in alternative relational structures. It is important to know if there has been a betrayal, a breach of trust, or a disruption in the attachment within the relationship. If they plan to move forward with opening their relationship and remaining in intimate partnership with each other, there will have to be a full exploration of the concerns related to trust, and an understanding reached about the longer term effects of broken trust on reactivity, jealousy, and negative imagining of the future of the relationship.

Second Session: Sexual and relational Genogram – children, family, friends, community supports and professional networks.

The second session is spent gather genogram information for each partner in the relationship (McGoldrick, Gerson, & Shellenberger, 2008). This includes important community and family supports and how each partner imagines that these important figures in their life would respond or react to learning of a structural shift in the relationship. In this session it should be shown, in sharp relief, which family and community members each partner is the most concerned about discussing the shift with, and why they have these concerns. Often there are people in their extended family and community that the couple does not want to know about this shift to an open relationship. This is one of the tricky pieces to the process of opening a relationship because it does not serve the relationship to hold a secret from loved ones and family, however, if there is a possibility of being mistreated or oppressed by family and community it is difficult to help clients negotiate their process of "coming out" (more on this in the following sections).

At the end of the second session clients are given an overview of the process of doing an extensive sexual history for each partner and why this is critical to the success of polyamorous and consensually non-monagamous relationships. Most areas of sensitivity in open relationships are present for each partner based on past experiences with love, desire, and intimacy – this includes, but is not limited to, relational contexts and messages that people received growing up, from their own parents, siblings, religious communities, peers, and others. The individual sexual history sessions are also where incidents of trauma, attachment concerns, early family neglect, and sexual coercion are given language and context, within a therapeutic setting. It is preferable, if clients feel they have the time and economic support, to meet with each partner twice individually, to complete the in-depth sexual history form in the context of a therapeutic interview. If the clinician is working for a group practice or agency where insurance is being accepted, the number of sessions can be even more, and the clinician and the clients can take their time with the form. If a partnership does not feel they can afford to wait four weeks before coming back together the clinician can offer to let them each complete the 16-page sexual history form at home, on their own, without sharing with the other person(s) in the relationship.

Sexual History Assessment

Sessions Three, Four, Five, Six: Sexual and Intimate History Sessions: During the completion of the sexual history for each person it is likely that the clinician will hear some things from clients that their partner(s) do not know about them. Clinicians need to know what their own stance is on differences between privacy and secrecy. It is up to the clinician to share at the beginning of gathering the sexual history information what their personal practices are about "secrets." Some clinicians feel that a secret of infidelity or an emotional affair should not be shared with the therapist if the client does not have any intention to tell their partner. Other clinicians believe that it is not realistic or supportive to tell people upfront not to share the things that they might feel the most shame about, as this sends the message that it *is* a shameful and unspeakable issue that cannot be understood or resolved. It doesn't matter so much which way a clinician goes with this, though it is recommended that in making this decision that the clinician explores their own relationship to infidelity and intimate secrets, so that they can make a countertransferentially informed choice. For example, if a clinician has been cheated on or betrayed themselves, there could be some important personal positions that could use examination before making the decision. It can also be helpful to imagine how one would advise a friend about an infidelity or emotional affair, because that tends to be how one feels on a more personal level and is more connected to their countertransference. How would one respond to hearing that their friend was cheated on, and how would they feel if their friend cheated on their partner?

One way to talk about this with clients before starting the sexual history sessions is to make clear that any information that is brought up in individual sessions or in the completion of the sexual history at home, are things that may or may not come up in therapy sessions further down the road but there cannot be any secrets kept by the therapist for either person, if that is the clinician's stance. They would need to make clear that all information must be something that the partner is willing to talk about within a therapy session, at some point and in some way, that they are happy to help clients think about ways to discuss difficult experiences and be a support to them in the process of communicating with their partner about them.

These sessions are individual sessions, usually two for each partner. Clinicians use these sessions to discuss and examine each person's sexual history (see Principle Four for details on how to take a sexual history of a client). The sexual history includes client's first memories of sensual or sexual feelings, when and how they first began to masturbate and self pleasure, and what kinds of messages they received growing up from their parents and siblings about sexuality and intimate practices. It covers a client's actual history of sexual relationships, including their ideas and notions of desire and love, as related to sexual practices and how they feel about their current sexual relationship with their current partner/s and what they would like to be enhanced or different, as well as, what they find erotic and sensual. Lastly, if there any concerns related to sexual or physical trauma that have not surfaced in the initial genogram sessions, this is a place to open up a conversations about how to integrate an awareness of specific trauma experiences into the therapeutic context.

Agreement Planning and Commitments

Session Seven: Agreement Planning

Why Should People "Come Out" as Consensually Non-monogamous and/or Polyamorous?

It is important for clients to understand that to live a polyamorous lifestyle there has to be some sense of pride about the relational configuration. There needs to be, just as in any sort of coming out process, an experience of community and familial pride. This can only really happen if all people involved feel like they are being treated respectfully and that everyone in the structure is acting and living with integrity. Often partnerships interested in opening up their relationship have been living with heterosexual, straight, white, monogamous privilege for their entire lives. This is commonly the first time that clients have had to think of themselves as marginalized, and even more stressful for them, erotically marginalized. They might need to be taught about the concept of pride (Sennott, 2011), which the clinician can do by discussing the parallels between someone coming out as LGBTQ. Even if clients do not want to tell their larger families, communities, or children, they are likely to move forward with an open relationship, whether they have a clinician's help or not, so it is recommended to meet the clients where they are at and give them as much support as possible while still trying to instill a sense of pride and excitement about their new family identity. Pride takes time to build, and there are many reasons why clients want to stay in the closet about their relationship status, the biggest one being that they do not want to lose the monogamous privilege that they have out in the world. This is a topic that needs to be visited and revisited, explored fully, but always meeting each person where they are within the process.

The relational nature of consensual non-monogamy also makes it difficult to come out because each person in the relationship is likely to fall at a different place on the continuum of pride about their identity. One person in a partnership could feel ready to start sharing this new identity with people while another might wish to continue keeping it private due to shame and fear of judgment by others. It is important to support the partner who is wishing to talk about it with people and help the partnership to negotiate a compromise (i.e. telling one trusted friend or family member as opposed to posted an announcement on social media). Frequently, the partner who is behind in the coming out process has family of origin and attachment fears that mire them in a dominant storyline (White, 2007) about the magnitude of rejection that they will experience throughout their family and communities. This causes them to have catastrophic thinking that their partner who does want to come out in some way wants to do it in an extreme way. To be fair, sometimes this is the case, however, usually it is not the expectation of the partner who wants to come out that they would tell everyone in their life immediately.

Telling Children about Polyamory and Consensual Non-Monogamy

Many clients in partnerships believe that it would be better for their children if they do not "find out" that their parents are opening up their relationship. This is an interesting position, and it is usually linked to a fear of being misunderstood or judged by the children, or, that the children would tell other people and put the parents or family at risk in some way. Not telling children about a relational restructuring is not a protection for children, rather it is an avoidant protection of the parents themselves (Lev & Sennott, 2011b). The sooner and the earlier that children know what their parents are doing the more able they are to internalize this decision as a positive and life enhancing choice. If parents wait to tell their children, the message that the children get is that there is something different and strange happening in their household and they have no language to describe it, but they can definitely feel that there are shifts and changes happening. If parents try to keep this information from their children they often find out about their parents having an open relationship accidentally. It usually comes out in an unintentional and unaccountable way, which can often feel traumatic and scary for children. It is better to encourage clients to develop a very intentional plan for how they are going to tell the children and when, so that the parents can be accountable to the entire family system and not just to each other.

Clients will often agree to the idea of telling their children in an intentional way but then want to have their children keep this information a secret. It is not appropriate to ask children to keep polyamory in the family a secret, because that puts too much responsibility on the child to keep their parents safe from social repercussions (Lev & Sennott, 2011c). A different approach for the partnership is the notion of privacy versus secrecy. If parents are able to share with their children that protecting the privacy of the family is different than keeping a secret, then they can discuss the social stigma that comes for restructuring a relational system and give their children tools for determining when or if they would want to keep this information private in certain situations. Just like any sort of coming out process thoughtfulness and planning are paramount. If children are interested in sharing with certain friends it can be useful to suggest that the parents do some role plays with their children so that they know what they would want to say and to whom. This is part of the intentionality of the plan and how parents can support their children in learning how to find allies. When a straight white monogamous heterosexual couple opens their relationship to the possibilities of polyamory they also engage in the identity shift into becoming erotically marginalized. When a couple is erotically marginalized and they have children, that means the entire system is at risk of being oppressed and mistreated. This is not something that parents would want to shelter their children from, rather, they want to empower them to learn the principles of allyship and social justice (Sennott & Smith, 2011), so that they can begin to determine who are safe people in their life to tell and who are not.

My Polyamory, Your Polyamory

Everyone comes to polyamory and consensually non-monogamous relationships with a different idea of what it could or should look like. This has to be explored comprehensively for each partner, ideally before agreements and consents are put into practice.

We often find that there are people who are relationally oriented to polyamory and then there are people who are open to practices of polyamory, consensual non-monogamy and alternative family structures. These are two very different experiences for partners, there needs to be co-created language that leads to shared understanding about where each partner might be located in this context. These three questions will help with the discussion of practices of openness in the context of each person's relational belief system.

- What are each partners' greatest hopes and visions about opening up their relationship? This question allows for an open and dialogic process. Asking people to envision their lives as a polyamorous partnership is helpful in learning what each of their ethical and relational values for the process might be.
- What are each partners' greatest fears about opening up their relationship? The same is true of this question, it will allow the clinician to learn how vulnerable each person feels and about what, and why.

- What (if any) obvious deal breakers does each partner have? Deal breakers are connected to a person's relational landscape, both early family of origin experiences and consequent attachment patterns. The answer to this question might change frequently or, it could shift meaning and importance as clients moves through their journey of openness. It is important to chart the deal breakers for people, and check in about them. It is most helpful for clients when they know each other's deal breakers but they have gone through the exploration, back to family of origin or other relational contexts with their partner, to know *why* they have that deal breaker. It is that which we are the most vulnerable to that we are the least flexible about, deal breakers are rigid for a reason, because they are protecting the most vulnerable parts of a person's intimate and sexual landscape. Excavation of the source of deal breakers can function as a support to creating a loom of woven understandings between partners of the most relationally vulnerable parts of themselves.

There is a belief by many people who are considering consensual non-monogamy that if they are "a jealous person" that they cannot successfully practice non-monogamy or polyamory. This is not necessarily the case. It is helpful to understand and discuss jealousy as a signal of something not feeling either accountable or familiar in the relationship. A lack of either accountability or familiarity can spark jealousy. Accountability is actualized through communication between partners about expectations with other partners and one another. Familiarity is created through lived experiences and the learned skill of tolerating the uncertainty of a new relational dynamic. Once a person can identify whether they are feeling jealous because something is new and feels scary to imagine and consider in the unknown world of a non-monogamous relationship, or because they feel their partner is not providing enough connection, communication, and consistency, then the clinician can support the process of moving through the jealousy in a productive way. Most importantly, it is not the feeling of jealousy that is a problem, it is the way that people behave as a response to the feeling that can be challenging. It is the clinician's work to give clients tools to discuss openly and parse out the function of jealousy in each case that it arises.

Hopes, fears, visions, desires, and deal breakers; all of these extremely personal threads weave together a loom of individual polyamorous identity for every person. It is the clinician's charge to create a therapeutic environment where each partner can explore and learn their own identity while figuring out how to match "mine with yours." No two people have the same identity, nor would we want them to, that is something to remind clients of when they feel they are at an impasse about an aspect of their agreement.

Session Eight: Agreement Contracting

When a partnership is new to consensual non-monogamy it is helpful to remind them that they can start slowly and add new agreements as they go.

This can help stave off the kind of jealousy connected with lack of familiarity. If a partnership takes it slow in their process of opening their relationship each has the chance to become more familiar and consolidate trust and belief in the other's consistency of behaviors. Moving slowly is particularly important if there is a vast difference within the partnership about what polyamory *feels like* and *is*. For example, a common difference within a partnership is that one person feels that they want to have less emotional and intimate attachment but more sexual possibilities and partnerships, while another person imagines finding one other person who they could have an emotional, intimate, and sexual relationship with. It is easy to imagine how each of these visions might threaten the other, if a couple is not well differentiated (Schnarch, 2011), therefore, taking it step by step in the agreement phase would be incredibly important. Every partnership is different but the aim of having co-created language and designed agreements, with a therapist as a support, is to create a contained, affirming relational environment that is in the interest of preserving the partnership and to enhance their intimate and romantic relationship.

In the process of laying out an agreement it is recommended that clients, at least initially, adopt the one-to-one rule. Many clients that have been together for multiple years and have children have not made spending time together alone a priority. It is common for clients to say that out of everyone in their lives they spend the *least* amount of quality time with their partner. If you ask a partnership like this if they can imagine not being jealous if their partner has a weekly date that is intentionally planned they commonly say no, because they don't have that kind of time with their partner so why should someone else. The one-to-one rule operationalizes the solution to this concern. For every one-on-one date that a partner has with another person in their life, they have a one-on-one date with their partner as well.

If clinicians are working with clients in a partnership or polyship (consensual non-monogamous relationship with multiple partners) that want to have open lines of communication and interaction between all partners, it can be very helpful to have all partners meet, after it has been established that there is a desire to move forward with a romantic practice with a new person. This is a way to avoid what is commonly seen, where a new person says that they are polyamorous because they want to date a polyamorous partner when in actuality, they are not entirely comfortable with the idea of being a part of a consensual non-monogamous open system. A full system meeting is a way to discern when a new person says that they want an open relationship but then, do not feel comfortable to meet their prospective new partner's other partner(s), which does not work well for a polyship that has open communications between partners. It is also a way for a polyship to present together with the prospective new person and get a sense of any red flags that might come up. A partner might be able to see things that the person who is falling for a new person might not see, and it can be helpful to talk through these possible red flags. This is a way of both sending a message of complete transparency to the new person, it is also a way of testing the person to make sure that they truly are completely comfortable with the idea of openness and polyamory. It is not usually recommended that people engage in romantic practices with people who do not honor and respect the importance of the polyship's commitments and agreements.

Relational components, such as time, locations, and frequency of seeing other partners or dating other people all need to be negotiated and be a part of the primary partnership agreement. These aspects are the most important in holding a frame of transparency and respect between the two primary partners. Clinicians ought to normalize for couples who are just beginning this journey that airing on the side of more conservative agreements is much easier to work with down the line, to open up more, than to try to "take back" something that felt like an emotional breach. When partnerships are first starting out it is helpful to discuss the idea of a co-created atmosphere of appreciation and exploration. This means that there might be missteps taken, but being open to repair and reevaluation is critical to finding lasting agreements and commitments in a polyamorous context. There will, inevitably, be painful moments of emotional stretching, but it does not mean that something should or would automatically become a deal breaker. It is the sex therapist's work to support their clients to move forward in a thoughtful, consensual, and deliberate way, with accountability and tenderness given equal importance in the therapeutic process.

Key Clinical Points

- When a clinician is able to locate themselves within the therapeutic relationship they are building the scaffolding for a stance of preemptive radical inclusion (PRI). PRI in practice is intentionally assuming that a client is someone who experiences marginalization, whether it is visible or not.
- Location of self allows clinicians to notice and name their own privileges and to be more attuned about these identities of privilege in the therapeutic relationship. PRI is a way of de-centering the therapist's own experiences in order to make space for their clients. Location of self is the structure in which clinicians can practice PRI and attune themselves to client meta-communication.
- Alternative Family Systems Approach (AFSA) is founded on transfeminist and feminist thought, social justice frameworks, and principles of allyship (Sennott, 2011; Sennott & Smith, 2011). AFSA can be understood as a lens for other therapeutic models and orientations (i.e., CBT, DBT, Individual, Group, or Family Treatment). AFSA is designed for *affirming* clinical treatment with polyamorous, consensually non-monogamous, and open relationship systems.

References

Gottman, J. & Silver, N. (2014). *What makes love last?: Now to build trust and avoid betrayal.* New York: Simon and Schuster.

Lev, A. I. & Sennott, S. L. (2011a). Understanding gender nonconformity and transgender identity: A sex positive approach. In P. J. Klienplatz (Ed.), *New directions in sex therapy: Innovations and alternatives* (2nd ed.), (pp. 321–366). New York: Taylor & Francis.

Lev, A. I. & Sennott, S. L. (2011b). Trans-sexual desire in differently gendered bodies. In J. J. Bigner & J. L. Wetchler (Eds.), *Handbook of LGBT-affirmative couple and family therapy* (2nd ed.), (pp. 113–130). New York: Routledge.

Lev, A. I. & Sennott, S. L. (2011c). Clinical work with LGBTQ parents and perspective parents. In A. E. Goldberg & K. E. Allen (Eds.). *LGBT parent families: Possibilities for new research and implications for practice* (pp. 241–260). New York: Springer.

McGoldrick, M., Gerson, R., & Shellenberger, S. (2008) *Genograms, assessment and intervention* (3rd Edition) New York: W.W. Norton & Company.

Schnarch, D. (2011) *Intimacy and desire: Awaken the passion in your relationship.* New York: Beaufort Books.

Sennott, S. L. (2011). Gender disorder as gender oppression: A transfeminist approach to rethinking the pathologization of gender non-conformity. *Women & Therapy, 34*, 93–113.

Sennott, S., & Smith, T. (2011). Translating the sex and gender continuums in mental health: A transfeminist approach to client and clinician fears. *Journal of Gay and Lesbian Mental Health, 15*, 218–234.

Watts-Jones, D. (2010). Location of self: Opening the door to dialogue on inter sectionality in the therapy process. *Family Process, 49*, 405–420. doi:10.1111/j.1545-5300.2010.01330.x

White, M. (2007) *Maps of narrative practice.* New York: W.W. Norton & Company.

THE CASE OF QUEERAN: WHEN SHARED INTERSECTIONALITY SUPPORTS BLACK, FAT, AND QUEER HEALING

Lexx Brown-James

Introduction

As a licensed marriage and family therapist working with marginalized populations, I find it necessary to deviate from some of the basic white-centric practices of the field. I identify as a Black, fat, woman with natural hair who is pansexual. In therapy these identities are very important, especially to the marginalized clientele I typically serve. Most of the people who seek me out choose me as their therapist for one of two reasons, and sometimes both. One, being that they want to work with a Black woman because they feel it will cut down on the amount that they have to change themselves or codeswitch to be what white society deems as "acceptable." Two, because they are dealing with trauma from existing in a white, male, heterosexual, Christian world. In my office, my Blackness sits in the room with my clients. This means that I use language and references that are typically universally understood by most Black people. My clients also ease into a language of their own, which often means letters are dropped, sentences are shortened, and a "YAS" might escape the lips in an exclaim of agreement. As unique as living in Blackness is in the room, there is also a benefit, especially for the following case, in my identity as a woman.

Being both Black and woman means that I am uniquely qualified to understand the oppressions that Black women face. The blatant oppression is racism, sexism, and classism, where Black women are discriminated against for their Blackness, for their sex assigned at birth and limited financially in their earning power and potential, because patriarchy, white supremacy, and colonialism made it so. Further, Black women also experience sizeism, where we are discriminated against for our body shape and size. Then, there is texturism, where Black women experience prejudice based on how our hair naturally grows out of our heads and how it is deemed unprofessional, unclean, or unkempt; which basically means outside the white standard of beauty. Lastly, Black women experience colorism, which is the oppression people of color based on their skin tone. Typically, the darker a person is, the less worthy they are deemed. Black women face these oppressions from birth, and being a Black woman therapist, I am able to identify with other Black women who have undoubtedly had experiences in at least one, if not all of these realms.

I also identify as pansexual, which I define as a person who is attracted to people outside of gender presentation or sex assigned at birth. For the following case, orientation, body size, race, gender, and hair texture were all shared and this was another parallel identity to my client. With all of our parallel identities, we found very quickly, that we existed in many of the same social circles – queer, Black, and political to name a few. Surprisingly, this helped us build rapport quickly because we spoke a common language that was all our own. In being able to relate to the atrocities, oppression, prejudice and the feelings that come along with being a Black woman, my client and I were able to trust each other in ways that I'm not sure would have made sense with another therapist. Rapport between client and therapist is a powerful indicator of success with clients.

Case Study

Queeran is a Black, fat, queer woman who sought therapy for unresolved depression. She initially came in because of discomfort with the amount of drinking she was doing following a break-up with her partner and a shift in her living situation. Depression was integral in her life for quite a few years and this was exacerbated by the loss of her grandmother, surviving sexual assault, and subpar romantic relationships throughout her life.

Queeran was cautious at first, she had previous therapists who had not been a good match for her. We took time at the beginning of our work to build rapport. Our similarities regarding Blackness, womanhood, body size and sexuality in place, helped to propel our therapy journey forward. With Queeran's sharing of her life, I noted that I not only visited similar places, but also knew some of the people she mentioned. I then felt that it was necessary to share with Queeran that I visit these places as well and in full disclosure if she wanted to continue therapy with our few degrees of separation. Despite our shared similarities, it took a little bit of time before we could address the hardest part of Queeran's depression. In the beginning we discussed her singlehood and desire to have a romantic relationship, but how there was residual trauma from past partners' emotional abuse. Queeran wears her hair in a range of natural styles, dyed a myriad of colors at any given time and has been criticized by her exes for it. Queeran was also in mourning from the loss of her grandmother, who was an important person in her life. She relied on her grandmother for leadership, love and guidance and following her death, she was now very alone in the world.

Queeran's goal for therapy was to not feel her grief so sharply and eventually to resolve past sexual trauma. As a therapist with many marginalized identities as mentioned above, I noted the need to be deliberately slow with Queeran. This was in part for her, I did not want to be another person in her community who let her down and I had to be aware of my own countertransference in seeing myself in some of her experiences. She lives in a world that consistently rejects her and I believed that solely using therapy interventions created by white men for white people might not be as helpful in this case. This meant that therapy would be Black and I would use common cultural factors and share certain aspects of myself – experiences of racism, sexism, sizeism, texturism, etc. to relate with her, while centering her stories.

With erotically marginalized people who are marginalized not only because of their attractions, but because of how they look and that they have the audacity to feel mostly good about themselves, I believe therapeutic rapport is everything. People who look like me, like Queeran, are often expected to be quiet. If we are not quiet, we are termed aggressive or intimidating and often have our painful experiences dismissed as exaggerations, falsehoods, or dismissed as "misunderstandings." I believe that taking the time to get to know Queeran and her experiences, and empathizing with what is needed for her to navigate the world, helped her to get to a point where she would share about her sexual abuse. It took six sessions for us to get to some of the hardest experiences she has had in her life and I think it was only because at times, I was vulnerable about experiencing some of those same oppressions.

As a sex therapist, I use the PLISSIT model (Annon, 1976) with all my clients. PLISSIT stands for Permission giving, Limited Information, Specific Suggestions, and Intensive Therapy. It was designed as a way to provide health care professionals a scaffold through which to address sexuality concerns. Getting and giving permission is the key when working with erotically marginalized folks because so much of their lives are directed without permission being asked or given. This is also true of sexualization – the use of sexual power to manipulate, coerce, and harm others. As Queeran shared the intimate information about her sexual assault experience, I knew we were on a precipice for her. My reaction and handling of this vulnerable and intimate experience would make or break our therapeutic relationship and possibly Queeran's decision to return to therapy. I thought to myself, she's been let down by her therapist and left before after sharing vulnerability, it could definitely happen again.

I have made it my specialization to work with people, specifically Black women, around sexual shame. Working with Queeran, it was clear there was sexual shame present, from the sexual abuse and exacerbated by the emotional abuse in later relationships; however, this work felt different. In starting to explore the sexual assault, Queeran was able to narrate the process with such a frankness that I was sure she had told others or done some extensive work previously. Typically, in recounting trauma, there is a lot of emotionality, pausing, hesitation, fear, sadness, and other complicated emotions. Queeran had some of those, but to a far lesser degree than I was used to experiencing; initially I wasn't sure what was happening. In practice I have found clients who are survivors usually hold sexual shame and negative thoughts regarding their belief that they deserved the abuse because they are "bad" in some way. As I learned more about her story, I prepared to shift this type of thinking through gentle reframing and even flat out correction. Marginalized folks, and specifically erotically marginalized folks, are often silenced, and therefore, told they are wrong, undeserving, and worthless. This can be in self-identity, orientation, biological representation of genitalia, self-expression, and in a myriad of other ways. I did not want to be a part of this larger psychotherapeutic system who told another erotically marginalized individual she was wrong. Yet, I was also nervous because some of the ideas that Queeran might hold could be unhelpful, as the narrative of survivors often are, until presented with another contrasting ideology. It was interesting however, because Queeran did not hold the ideas of badness or unworthiness because of the sexual assault.

When we reached the session finally to talk about her sexual abuse, I steadied myself. I put on my best listening ears and braced myself. [CW: Story about sexual assault of a child and suicide following in italics – story ends at end of paragraph].

Queeran reported that she was nine years old when it happened. She was playing through wrestling with her favorite uncle. It was innocent and easy at first, then turned into these sexual encounters of touching, groping, and rubbing. On the day that Queeran decided to end it, she told her uncle she was no longer interested in playing this way, walked out, and called her maternal grandmother who raised her. Telling her grandmother everything, her grandmother rushed to pick Queeran up from the uncle's home where she stayed while her grandmother was at work. Before her grandmother could get there however, Queeran's uncle killed himself. A single gunshot to the head – while Queeran was still in the house.

In telling the story, Queeran was overcome with grief. She got through the story, but then hesitated and struggled to find words when I asked about her feelings. She reported feeling safe that her grandmother would help her, believe her, and support her. She also felt that someone else would need to know and felt justified in telling. And yet, something was missing because in session Queeran was sure that it was not her fault and knew her uncle was wrong, and yet, she held onto the shame that manifested in her looking at the floor, not meeting my eyes, slumping her shoulders forward and leaking tears. Only a few would fall, like a faucet barely turned on. Throughout the processing of those four to six sessions I learned that Queeran had night terrors where she was paralyzed and experienced auditory hallucinations. The more we talked about this assault the more intense these night terrors became. In response, we sought consultations from her psychiatrist and medical doctor and Queeran decided to start an antidepressant. In session, we discussed spirituality and if this could be a manifestation of her dead uncle. Queeran thought about that and we decided that burning sage in her home to cleanse it and rid it of negative energy would be beneficial and give her peace of mind. We also discussed her belief in the use of crystals to manifest and amplify positive energy, and again, to cleanse her space. After few weeks when revisiting her abuse, I asked the question that is tough for all clinicians and all survivors: "What part of this, if any, did you enjoy?" This question, although hard, is necessary because many survivors feel shame for moments of pleasure, arousal, and even orgasm that can occur during sexually abusive experiences. When I asked, Queeran looked at me in horror, and I thought I made a mistake that would damage our rapport. As it turns out, she did not know she could share that piece of her story because no one had ever asked before. Queeran shared that she enjoyed the play most of the time and that on the day when her uncle took his life, she was just tired of the play and decided to end it. Queeran, with tears streaming down her face, felt like a murderer; she felt like she shot the gun that killed her uncle. Queeren felt she was responsible for his death because she could have ended it sooner, gentler, with another adult present. This was the secret that Queeran harbored, the part that was unsafe to share with others, and the part that she most desperately needed to share.

Black people are orators. The circumstances of us coming to the United States, losing our language, being forbidden to read and write and having to learn a new language meant that we had to find ways to pass down and share our histories and our stories. I use this value in therapy, where my clients share their stories to integrate them as part of themselves so that they can own their experiences instead of feeling like a bystander and powerless in any situation that happened to them. Queeran and I worked to integrate these story parts with the understanding of how various types of oppression affected her. Identifying the sheer fact that pleasure in bodies that are of color, fat, queer, and feminine is considered taboo. Marginalized bodies have literally been tortured for and rejected for not being white, thin, straight, and male for centuries in the U.S. Therefore, the idea that those same marginalized bodies have a right to pleasure helped Queeran to understand that she was not wrong to enjoy the sexual play despite the clear boundary crossing that took place. Further, by normalizing her pleasure and moving the narrative from culprit to advocate, we were able to build Queeran's self-efficacy and reduce the idea that she was the cause of her uncle's demise. Once we worked through all of these moving pieces, we rarely revisited this narrative for her. Instead, we found that the work and reshaping of her self-perception without the sexual shame benefited her in healing past relationship trauma, navigating future romantic encounters, friendships, work relationships, medical care providers, and with her therapist. Queeran set boundaries, avidly pursued romantic interests, and practiced sharing vulnerable emotions with others that she previously avoided for fear of perceived weakness and rejection.

Working with Queeran further solidified the need to decenter whiteness when working with those who are marginalized, especially as a therapist with multiple marginalized identities. This means that all the therapy modalities we use need to be applied with prudence because they can further ostracize and silence the voices of those who so desperately need to be heard. From this case, I hope others can value a therapist being their authentic self. I also hope that from this case, professionals working with survivors realize the importance of reaching beyond the typical representation of survivorhood to support the whole self of the client. I do contemplate what this case would have looked like if Queeran and I did not have such parallel social identities and how that would affect our working together. I also wonder, actually, hope that other therapists, like myself, are constantly working to help those who amplify the voices and experiences of those who erotically marginalized.

Reference

Annon, J. S. (1976). The PLISSIT model: A proposed conceptual scheme for the behavioral treatment of sexual problems. *Journal of Sex Education and Therapy*, *2*(1),1–15. doi: 10.1080/01614576.1976.11074483

THE CASE OF BETH

AndreAs Neumann Mascis

"There are different kinds of neglect you know. Some kinds of neglect mean you're not really a person. It's the biggest kind and no one can see it."

This is how Beth began to talk about ableism and its impact on her identity and sexuality. "It's sort of like the age I am changes depending on what someone wants from me - or really what they want to feel. Like if they want to feel like they're rescuing me, I am a five-year-old. If they want to feel inspired by me then I'm adult, but not really. It's more like I am Yoda and Wonder Woman all at once."

"What if they want to date you, then what?" I asked.

> *"Then I'm a thing. No, I don't know, not always, I guess but It's always hard to tell, ya'know? Like, not to be paranoid or anything, but I feel like I want to say like 'what is this about for you, ya'know. Like one time I was at this party and there was this girl and we made eye contact and I swear it was like the movies. She came over and we started dancing and she totally handled the wheelchair like it wasn't even there. I mean if your confident and creative and stuff the chair can be a total prop and a lot of fun, but a lot of people are scared of it, like it's catching or like its gonna suck them in or something. Anyway, so she was awesome, with me, like we were just two people dancing and with the chair like totally hot right and I'm thinking 'this is really happening' and we dance for a long time and she leans in and I'm thinking I might say something dirty. And then she says 'I'm here with my wife, see right over there? And we want you to know we think you're just amazing.' And just like that, I'm a thing again."*

This was the beginning of what would be challenging and powerful work. As I am a visibly disabled, queer, clinical psychologist, Beth had sought me out specifically. She identified that she hoped to work on the impact of ableism in her initial contact with me, but it was months into treatment before she initiated conversation related to Disabled identity. When I asked about disability, she disregarded the question or made a joke. With all of the identities we – visibly – shared, she still had no way of knowing for sure how her identity would be seen or met, no way of knowing how much of my lived experience of ableism and internalized ableism would inform my perception and experience of her. She was not wrong to be wary. At the beginning of my career, our shared identities would have derailed our work rather than supported it. Ultimately my own healing, activism, and scholarship afforded me the opportunity to provide expertise and what would now be a potent treatment, not afforded by shared identity alone. The complexity of our initial treatment relationship reflects the toxic and self-sustaining impact of systems of oppression. As is true of marginalized people, Beth and I were both enculturated to sustain ableism, simultaneously to deny its existence and to demonstrate our worth by adhering to its rules and parameters. Within that system Beth and I are conditioned to be wary of each other. Beth and I are not alone.

Disability is terrifying. It is at the core of all human experience. Yet, our ability and willingness to engage with, define or understand disability and its function in societies remains elusive. Disability evokes our fear of mortality, vulnerability, and the primitive and random gore of corporality. Disability challenges our myth of autonomy and control. Our fear of disabled sexualities is fueled in part by the need to deny our embodiment and thus renders the classification of disabled as one that is distanced from the experience of being human (https://ballastexistenz.wordpress.com/2014/05/01/love-fear-death-and-disability/) (Ray & Sabara, 2017).

Defining and understanding disability, and its function as a category, mirrors our struggle with embodiment. For Beth, the experience of feeling seen as a sexual being and a potential connection both integrates and denies disability. Her description of potential attraction vacillates between the hope that her able bodied interest has the capacity to both see and not see disability. Disability embodied, "can you dance with my wheelchair" and disembodied, "can you see me in spite of and because of my identity as disabled."

Finding articulation for Disability as embodiment, Disability as identity, Disability as social construct begins with a medical model that delineates disability against a body/mind norm and depends on function, limitation, and cure. The Disability Rights Movement challenged embodiment by locating disability as a limitation of environments and the social structure that systematically excludes a population of people from full participation in relationships, community and culture. Further disembodiment is explored in the models of human variability and universal design that seek to generalize disability as a reflection of body/mind diversity. That attempt to neutralize disability has been met with resistance in the Disability Justice Movement, which asserts the re-embodiment of disability and intersecting identities. It underscores the ways in which the experience of disability cannot be equalized in a culture in which all identities are rendered hierarchical in their access to structural and relational resources. Ambivalence about defining disability as embodied or disembodied, as medical, societal, relational or identity is ongoing. However, the fuel of that struggle is a reflection of hierarchical access to participation in the human community (Clare, 2017; Shapiro, 1993).

Beth

Beth is a 31-year-old Latinx cisgender, female identified, queer, disabled person who came into therapy with symptoms of anxiety and depression that had begun to impact her relationship and work. Beth has cerebral palsy and uses a wheelchair. She works as an administrative assistant in a community college.

She lives alone in subsidized accessible housing. Beth has been in a relationship with a white, able bodied, gender non-conforming partner for just over a year. Beth reports that her symptoms of anxiety have been increasing over the last few months. She cites conflict in her relationship and job insecurity as her primary stressors. Beth describes conflict in her relationship centering around the question of living together. Beth is not permitted by her current apartment management to have extended overnight guests. Therefore, Beth's partner would not be allowed to move into the current subsidized apartment. Finding another wheelchair accessible apartment that they can afford is equally out of reach. While Beth has a lifetime of experience making use of profoundly inadequate and unjust resources, her able bodied partner is distressed enough by these limitations that it is undermining the strength of the relationship. While their sexual relationship has continued to be strong, their emotional intimacy has suffered.

Beth is the youngest of three children. Her siblings are nine and twelve years older. She reports that unlike her siblings, she had been unplanned and was conceived at a point at which her mother had thought she was no longer able to conceive. Her parents divorced shortly after she was born and while her siblings continued to see their father, her contact with him was sparse. In her childhood, the reason Beth was given for lack of contact was that her father lived in a third floor walkup and she was not able to access his apartment. Later, Beth was told by her mother that her father's family was very religious and that her disability was a punishment for her parents' divorce. Beth notes that while her mother did not believe this, she did blame Beth and the expenses associated with her disability for the family's financial insecurities.

Beth reports a history of sexual abuse, beginning at the age of six. She had difficulty identifying with or understanding her experiences as abusive in part because it happened in the presence of others, disguised in the context of care or treatment intervention. She did not report these incidences for both fear of not being believed and for fear of further burdening her mother's resources in needing to find new providers. Beth also describes a series of surgical interventions associated with her disability that, while not inherently traumatic, included the emotional experiences of trauma including powerlessness, pain, feelings of being trapped and fear of death. During one of those surgeries, her father lost his job and the family lost his health insurance and financial support. She, her mother and her siblings were forced to move into an apartment that was inaccessible. This meant that she could not come into or leave the apartment independently and, because the bathroom was too small for her wheelchair, Beth could no longer use the bathroom without significant help. When left alone in the apartment or fearing her mother's anger, Beth would wait to use the restroom until she was in significant pain.

Beth began having her first consensual sexual experiences at 14 with a female classmate. She describes the relationship as overwhelmingly positive until they were caught "making out" at school. Despite the fact that the encounter was no more significant than many of the encounters she witnessed with her peers, the responses of the school and her parents were severe. A determination was made that because of her disability, she could not have wanted or consented to sexual activity and had therefore been victimized. Her girlfriend was expelled and Beth was given an extended suspension. This created a series of resource challenges, not the least of which was that she was left home alone, unable to access food or the bathroom for hours until her mother or siblings returned home. After that experience, she reports having largely withdrawn from social activities at school or with her friends. "You just never knew who might be watching and what they could do."

Her relational world improved when she went to college. Through Women's Studies and anti-racism work on campus, she reports having "come into my identities as a disabled queer Latinx." She recalls a particularly emotional moment in one of her classes in which she was moved to "come out as disabled. I mean I use a wheelchair right? So it's not like it was news but it was like all the sudden mine, not like something that I had done to someone and not like something done to me but all of the sudden it was mine. It was me ya' know?" Beth also describes an active social and sexual life during that time. It was then that she also encountered kink community and began exploring power and sensation play in ways that challenged and changed her relationship to her body. She describes having realized how much of her social, emotional and sexual activity and choices had been about managing the other person's needs and feelings related to her body. "Like if I could make myself into what I thought they wanted maybe they wouldn't notice that big wheelchair over there or the fact that I'd accidentally gotten myself into a position on the bed that I couldn't physically get out of". Despite the emerging and empowering experiences she was having relationally and intrapsychically, the limitations imposed by her environment continued to shape and, at times, dominate access to a rich relational world and the social and emotional resources in those relationships that are the elements of affect management/regulation and resiliency.

Our work together began after Beth's first panic attack. I am a white, queer masculine identified, disabled psychologist with cerebral palsy, which has been present since birth. I am currently a crutch user but have, at other times in my life, been a full time wheelchair user. Our work together is both informed by the differences in our social location and uniquely embodied in the identities we share. As a white middle class person, I grew up in the knowledge that, on some level, the systems that determine access to resources were designed to work for me. This not only shaped my skills and abilities in advocating for myself, it also fundamentally changed how that advocacy would be received and responded to. As a white person, I was also taught to value autonomy and independence above all. Though we have not yet explored it in depth, it is evident that for Beth, structural and emotional estrangement from particularly her father's family has meant loss of access to cultural experiences that would nourish her Latinx identity. Beth notes that her older siblings have memories and experiences with her paternal grandmother that she does not and that, unlike Beth, they are able to speak basic Spanish.

Cerebral palsy, itself, is essentially a brain injury that has a wide and diverse range of impacts and a complex symptom picture that is not entirely understood and rarely, if ever, explored or discussed. Having a range of those embodied experiences in common has provided what can be profound mirroring in being able to name or describe a mind/body sensation or experience that no one else in Beth's life has shared or been able to name. This unique and embodied element of the transference has provided opportunities for concrete support, and has, more profoundly accelerated aspects of the work through what might be described as enriched self-object experiences of validation (mirroring), belonging (twinship), and safety and aspiration (idealization). Our work will also continue to reflect the complexity of our differences in power and access to material, social, and emotional resources.

Social location is at the foundation of every definition of health or illness. Disability, as both an identity category and a diagnostic category, is profoundly changed by social location. Differences in access to resources define the quality of someone's life as well as the prognostic trajectory of their experience. For Beth, the impact of social location is material, corporeal, interpersonal and intrapsychic.

> *"I mean when we are fighting about the living situation, sometimes it's almost funny. They (the partner) look at me and say things like – 'well I mean they can't just do that, they can't just tell you who you can live with' and I'm like dude what planet do you live on? Must be nice there right? Except like I can't really say that. Plus there are all these things they either don't know or aren't thinking about. Like for real if we got an apartment that I couldn't get into by myself or pee by myself, they think they wouldn't care but it would change everything. I mean our whole dynamic. And then I end up feeling like maybe I'm not trying or I have trust issues or something. But then like really it's a million things, they have no idea and I'm not even sure I want them to know all of it"*
>
> *"What is it like for you when they say things like that?"*
>
> *"I mean it's weird right like they are totally convinced that I have all the choices that they have if I were just doing it right. But it also makes them sort of seem like a little kid. Like isn't that cute that you think that? But I am the holder of the reality of the situation but kind of in secret, like a parent. And then I think of all the work of getting them to understand and it sort of ends up feeling like I have to convince them of everything I can't do which makes me the kid – except I can do all the things I want in the relationship if I have the set up that I need, which I do now – but see? It's hard for able bodied people to imagine that a door frame or a step or something can really make or break you."*
>
> *"Can you talk to them about how you need things set up to maximize your movement?"*
>
> *"A little – usually, I guess. I try and make it about other things. Like when we were first dating I couldn't really do stuff at their house because, you know the set up was all wrong. But I wasn't ready for them to get all that so I made it about how my space was more private and stuff. That was before all*

> *the drama started with the apartment management regulating sleepovers – which to this day they totally can't get their head around. It's totally a white thing too like 'what do you mean I can't just have what I want' I mean no offense right, but for real."*
>
> *"What's that like for you and me do you think? Is there stuff you feel that I'm not going to get but having to explain it would just change things between us?"*
>
> *"I mean you get it right? Mostly. I mean I know you know and that's cool. I guess I wonder if you think I'm not advocating for myself right or trying hard enough."*

For Beth the interplay of structural access, institutionalized ableism, and white supremacy become defining forces in the power dynamics and intimacy possible in relationships. Beyond that, they echo Beth's familial experiences of attachment and trauma. The challenge of the therapy becomes integrating systemic oppression into a dimensional understanding of the intrapsychic work.

Self-psychology provides a framework through which the intrapsychic impact of social location and access to social and emotional resources can be described. Simplistically put, at the core of the psyche is the Self. The Self, not unlike the brain, gets constructed and reconstructed in the context of its relational environment. Emotionally significant encounters in that environment meet the needs of the Self and include feeling seen or validated (mirroring), feeling a sense of alikeness and belonging (twinship) and feeling a sense of safety and aspiration (idealization). An adequate relational environment strengthens resiliency, affect management, and further connection at the center of psychological well-being.

Berzoff (2012) articulates the interplay of social location and psychological well-being by identifying the way in which societal structures themselves create social and emotional agreements that serve Self Object functions. As societal structures shape and stratify access to housing, employment, transportation, education, health care and social supports, they also structure and inform access to the relational world. Beyond that, Berzoff (2012) asserts that the institutions themselves serve Self Object needs. Within systems of oppression, the degree to which people access safety, belonging, validation or aspiration is the undercurrent of marginalization. Systemic ableism has determined a relational context for Beth in which the arc of her intimate relationship is pitted against housing, mobility physical safety, and the intrapsychic experiences of attachment and self-efficacy.

Intimacy, sex, and sexuality are integral to social location as a resource for social control. Societal structures further systems of oppression in the categories of relationship structures that are supported or inhibited. Sexuality as a resource of social control is evidenced by contrast not only in a change in attitudes (Gay Marriage) but also in change in diagnosis -from illness to identity (homosexuality removed from DSM II).

Disability challenges our ambivalence about being embodied. Sexuality as a resource of oppression defines itself in the mythical homogeneity of body functions and experiences. That myth is shaped by culturally dependent standards of beauty and a hierarchy of sexual attractiveness. Disabled people's sexualities have been subject to that social control. Disability confronts human embodiment in ways that both intrigue and horrify. Managing the challenge of that body can be seen through the rendering of disabled sexualities as asexual or fetishized (Kafer, 2013; McRuer, 2006). Sexuality and disability as parameters of social control were reflected in debates related to the passage of the Americans with Disabilities Act. Fueled by the promise of capitalism, (access adds to the available workforce), the ADA nevertheless found itself defining sexuality and disability in its relationship to the human community by deeming that HIV, although it manifested disabling conditions, did not merit protection (Davis, 2015). Beth, having come into majority under the aspirations of the ADA has benefited from, and withstood the distance between that aspiration and current cultural will. Beth has benefited from an ADA fueled expectation of having a life that is at the very least deinstitutionalized and at best a system of equity to facilitate autonomy. Beth's place in history further reflects the distance between aspirational legislation and cultural will. The equity of accessible housing neutralized by the regulation of sexuality and intimacy imposed by housing policy.

Beth's sexuality as both queer and disabled is inherently subversive. Her experiences explicitly in her high school and implicitly in her current housing policies reflect institutionalized regulation of intimacy. Ableism functions to both infantilize and sexually neutralize people with disabilities. The legacy of that oppression is evidenced in past and present manifestations of eugenics as well as institutional housing policies that implicitly or explicitly limit or prohibit the sexualities of residents. For Beth, the housing that maximizes the mobility of her disabled body exercises social control over her Queer Disabled identity. A reflection of her earlier experience at the party, oppression generates the need for embodied disability rendered both seen and unseen, valid and invalid (McRuer, 2006).

Sexuality, beauty, and attraction have been defined not only with compulsory heterosexuality but compulsory able bodiedness at its core. Beth's identities impose sexuality on an identity that has been rendered asexual. Beth's Latinx identity and catholic family offer complex messages regarding the providence of her disability as a punishment in the face of failed institutionalized heterosexual intimacy. Expressions of her family's Latinx culture related to gender identity and gender role distance Beth not only from her queer identity, but at present distance Beth from an opportunity to share her intimate relationship with her family. The impact of that distance is to further limit the ways in which Beth can be regarded as an adult within her family of origin.

Beth's sexuality has been shaped in the intersection of queer, disabled and Latinx identities and cultures. She describes having been rendered asexual within her family. "Like, no one was really planning my wedding day ya'know and then I turned out to be queer . . . well no one talks about that." In the context of her current relationship Beth acknowledges a reflection of her early loss of cultural connection. "There's no way to really bring my partner to my mom's. I don't even think it would be a problem as much as like – no one would get each other, like at all."

While marginalization and oppression can serve to isolate, a sense of community (twinship) and reflections of identity (mirroring) serve a compensatory function in the face of stigma. Beth describes more opportunities in queer community to be affirmed in her sexuality. "Queers are used to different kinds of bodies, different kinds of sex, lots of talking." She describes feeling validation and belonging in aspects of queer community. "Sometimes it's hard when I can't get in places or it's like super white but like I find my folks mostly."

In a culture that depends on the hierarchy of social location, structural and psychosocial barriers to disabled sexualities are vital to keeping disabled people at the margins of the human community. Clinically we are challenged to locate the problem not with the psychiatric vulnerabilities of the people we serve, but with the systems that are designed to distance marginalized people from the social, emotional, structural and community resources that cultivate the capacity for intimacy, resiliency and well-being. In the ongoing work with Beth, symptom management and relief will be achieved by locating the problem within the systems of oppression that inform her experience, and fortifying the intersection of her identities and relationships that reflect and affirm her Self.

The marginalization of people who, either by self-identification or perception, are disabled are rendered asexual or fetishized in the larger society culture. We have increasingly understood that identity categories shape and structure the systems of oppression that determine access to the material, social and emotional resources that, in turn, become the resources for and determinants of wellness. Ableism that renders disabled people separate from human-ness and sexuality.

The clinical implications of that imposed separateness are vast.

References

Berzoff, J. (Ed.). (2012). *Falling through the cracks: Psychodynamic practice with vulnerable and oppressed populations*. New York: Columbia University Press.

Clare, E. (2017). *Brilliant Imperfection: Grappling with Cure*. Durham, NC: Duke University Press.

Davis, L. J. (2015). *Enabling acts: the hidden story of how the Americans with Disabilities Act gave the largest US minority its rights*. Boston, MA: Beacon Press.

Kafer, A. (2013). *Feminist, queer, crip*. Bloomington, IN: Indiana University Press.

Lorde, A. (2017). *Your silence will not protect you*. London: Silver Press.

McRuer, R. (2006). *Crip theory: cultural signs of queerness and disability*. New York: New York University Press.

Ray, S. J., Sibara, J., & Alaimo, S. (2017). *Disability studies and the environmental humanities: toward an eco-crip theory*. Lincoln, NE: University of Nebraska Press.

Shapiro, J. (1993). *No pity: People with disabilities forging a new civil rights movement*. New York: Times Books.

PART III
Systemic

Principle Seven

SUPPORT PARTICIPATION OF FAMILY AND COMMUNITIES

Introduction

The experience of erotic marginalization can be scary, lonely, and isolating. The experience of discrimination and oppression can be systemic (job, school, church) or personal (family, friends) and losses can be high. Clients who are exploring an identity or experience that is marginalized may have never spoken to another person about it before they walk into your office. There can be a feeling of cognitive dissonance as clients' feel a sense of liberation and joy while at the same time experiencing shame and fear. Supporting participation of family and communities in your clinical work helps clients create a space in which they feel good about themselves. Being a part of a community that either shares a client's experience of erotic marginalization or provides radical acceptance reflects a client's reality as normal and valuable.

Building Mirrors

We build our identity based on the reflections of those around us, most often our primary caregivers. So what happens with a client doesn't have access to an accurate reflection? When they know no one in their life who shares their experience or identity? When those closest to them fail to be able to hold their whole self? The clients we work with are often coming in looking for a reflection; they want to know themselves.

Involving Existing Communities

A client's current communities are a good place to start helping them find the support that they need. Where are the places that they feel safe and whole? Is there a family member who will be more likely to understand their experience and be supportive? We can work with our clients to identify the resources that they already have available to them.

Coming Out to Family and Friends

Some clients may be seeking support from a therapist to come out to family and friends, or that may be the unexpected result of other work together. 'Coming out' historically referred to the experience of telling people that you were gay or lesbian. We think of it as the act of sharing an erotically marginalized identity. Coming out is only necessary if there is an assumption already being made about a person's sexual orientation/gender identity/sexual preference/relationship. These assumptions are one way that heterosexism and cissexism operate. In this way, coming out automatically puts a person in a position of vulnerability. For example, a cisgender heterosexual couple who is in an open marriage may find that they need to come out about their relationship structure when an elderly parent comes to live with them. Or, a cisgender man in a long term relationship seeking help for "erectile dysfunction" may need to come out to his partner as having a sexual script that involves bondage and discipline in order to shift his experience with sex.

Clinicians can join clients in the process of coming out, help them assess for safety, make a plan, or provide education and resources. For example, a client coming to terms with a nonbinary identity might feel like they have no one in their life who truly understands them. Explaining their identity to others, including parents or partners, can feel overwhelming. If the client would like support speaking with family and friends, as clinicians we have the opportunity to act as both therapist, ally, and educator. We can prepare a client's support system to become a protective factor and strong allies to our client by providing education about the gender binary, nonbinary identities, and how to support someone living with transphobia, as examples.

Vignette

Russell and Olivia came to for sex therapy because they had been discussing opening up their marriage for some time but felt that it would be helpful to have another opinion before they acted on anything. Olivia was white, cisgender and identified as bisexual; she had relationships with assigned-female-at-birth (AFAB) people when she was in college but had only partnered with men since. Russell, a white, cisgender, heterosexual man; he identified himself as a "serial cheater" and he had cheated on almost every woman he had ever been with until Olivia. Together, they came to the realization that he had been trying to fit himself into a monogamous relationship structure that didn't feel authentic. Olivia believed and helped him see that he was not a bad person for having attractions outside of their marriage, that it was perfectly natural, just not common in his family of origin or in the world around them.

Olivia and Russell were a delight to work with, they had a robust romantic and sexual connection and excellent communication, they were a couple who were well situated to navigate the complexity of transitioning a relationship from monogamous to polyamorous. We worked collaboratively to come to a mutual understanding of each other's positions, to establish their agreements and how they wanted to communicate moving forward. After that was established I asked them who from their families and community they were planning on involving in this process, essentially who they were going to come out to. It quickly became clear that they had a stark difference in who they were comfortable telling. Olivia wanted to tell people freely, her parents would potentially be supportive, she felt like their friends would get on board and their two children (ages six and ten) would need to know what was happening so they could live their lives freely and openly. Russell, having been ostracized at times by his family and friends for his various affairs over the years, did not want anyone to know. He was certain everyone in their lives, with the exception of a few friends, would judge them and he felt that their children did not need to know, nor would they be able to comprehend the situation.

I worked with them to come to mutual understanding and respect of each other's positions and to navigate how to bring their families and community along. Clients who have had little to no experience of marginalization have rarely had to sort out when and how to come out and to help their communities understand their position. I told them that we are "queering their nuclear family," and it might take time for people to catch up but that they will need support now more than ever. We wound up bringing each of their parents and siblings into sessions, followed by a separate session with their children. I worked with them to help explain to their children that this is not a secret, there is nothing to be ashamed of, but they could choose to keep it private unless they feel comfortable sharing it with someone.

Their coming out sessions went well overall, Olivia's parents had a lot of thoughtful questions, but held the position that it isn't really their business or place to judge their relationship. Russell's parents predictably had a harder time, they referenced the past a good deal, his mother tried repeatedly to align with and take care of Olivia, thinking she was being victimized. Olivia remained steadfast in her enthusiasm for the situation and held her position that this was as much her decision as it was Russell's. After the session, I emailed with his parents some and shared a good deal of literature for them to educate themselves about consensual non-monogamy as a concept and to read stories of other families with parents in an open marriage, and they worked hard to move away from a framework of

(continued)

(continued)

pathology towards one of acceptance and understanding. Russell and Olivia's kids came in for multiple sessions over the months that followed. They had one session as a family to begin to discuss this new configuration and begin to understand what would change and what would stay the same. They also came in without their parents to ask all the questions they were holding and share their fears and concerns. Over time, the whole family began to shift their identity towards a family who honors independence, connection, honesty and the ability for everyone to get to be their truest fullest selves.

Coming Out to Children

Our culture, despite often sexualizing our children, is also terrified of talking to children about sex or sexuality (Levine, 2002). This area often feels the most difficult for our clients. The Sexuality Information and Education Counsel of the United States (SIECUS)'s Guidelines for Comprehensive Sexuality Education: Kindergarten through 12th Grade (National Guidelines Task Force, 2004) are an excellent resource for clinicians and clients and can demystify what age-appropriate comprehensive sexuality education looks like in practice. In the case of Russell and Olivia, it was important for them to share with their children the family's alternative relationship structure. By sharing it with their children they are normalizing polyamory as just another relationship choice and minimizing the possibility of shame. If their children do experience stigma from other people in their lives, having their family for support and language to talk about will increase their resilience.

Recently on an online group a parent asked, "How do I talk to my three-year-old about gender?" Our response based on our work and our own parenting is that it is appropriate tell a three-year-old that it's how one feels on the inside. We've seen this work with kids, and it works better when trans identities are presented as an option all of the time, "boys, girls, nonbinary and trans kids," We also regularly change the language in children's books to be more inclusive including adding "nonbinary and trans" to "boys and girls" and using gender inclusive pronouns. For kids, what is around them is just normal – it is more often adults who feel uncomfortable or unsure how to talk to a kid about the wide range of human sexuality in an age appropriate way. When working with clients it is important to help them identify their cultural and personal values about sexuality and find a way to share with their family that feels authentic to their beliefs. For more of a discussion about this check out *Harmful to Minors: The Perils of Protecting Our Children* from Sex by Judith Levine and Deborah M. Roffman's books *The Thinking Parent's Guide to Talking Sense About Sex and Talk to Me First: Everything You Need to Know to Become Your Kids' "Go-To" Person About Sex.*

As clinicians we also sometimes sit with clients who are making the hard decision to not come out about a part of their lives. As noted, coming out involves vulnerability. We help clients assess their physical safety and emotional safety before coming out. Clients are encouraged to look to family members who are likely to be most supportive first. By getting supportive family members on board clients can begin to build their support system. Sometimes, the safest thing is to not come out, which can be a difficult decision to help clients make.

Building Community

Another tool of resilience for erotically marginalized clients is helping them build new community. When clients are feeling othered, on the outside, or like there is something wrong with them, it means that they are not getting mirrored enough in their daily life. As discussed, erotically marginalized clients may have grown up either without people like them (mirrors) or not been fully seen by the important family members in their lives. This affects the development of a sense of self. Helping clients build a community that sees their full self can be a powerful intervention.

Not everyone feels comfortable or safe sharing every part of their identity with many people in their lives, we don't want anyone to sacrifice their privacy or values. However, we have seen over time that it is vital to a healthy sense of self that people who are erotically marginalized to have some people in their life outside of a romantic relationship to be able to hold their experience with seriousness and sensitivity.

Using Online Communities

Many clients are resistant to building new community. For many people, making new friends can be challenging. Some clients may also be struggling with internalized homophobia/transphobia/erotophobia or hatred of themselves that they have to voice aloud. Sometimes erotically marginalized clients feel safer building and establishing relationships online, as it provides a certain level of anonymity. For these clients, or clients who do not have access to support groups based on location of ability, online communities can be a lifeline.

Not all online communities are created equal, clients may need help vetting a resource to determine if it is a safe space for them to connect with others. Online communities like FetLife provide social networking opportunities. Other things to look for are online communities that are closed and have moderators.

In Person

Connecting with people in real life provides client's a relational experience, but can be difficult based on their location or experience. Many cities have support groups, meet-ups, or munches (a social gathering for people interested or involved in kink or BDSM community or practices), where a client can get support or socialize. Volunteer opportunities at conferences or other events can also offer clients a way to build their community and support network.

As therapists working with this population, we feel that it is imperative that we stay up to date on local resources to share with our clients. Sometimes if the resources don't exist, we create them ourselves or empower our clients to. Forming support or affinity groups can be a powerful and transformative experience, it is one of the best tools we have as healers in our communities. Seeing oneself or one's relationship mirrored in a community of people can help those who are erotically marginalized solidify and build pride around their own experience.

Vignette

Shannon and Davis facilitate a couples group together and the vignette that follows focuses on that work.

Shannon had been working in private practice for a number of years and a significant portion of her caseload involved couples where one person in the couple was cisgender and the other partner was already trans or gender nonconforming identified or exploring a new identity outside the gender binary. She found herself thinking in session with each couple how similar some of their struggles were and how amazing it would be if she could somehow connect the couples and help them to create community with each other. Each couple seemed to feel like their problems were specific to their situation, they felt a sense of isolation and it became increasingly challenging for them to discuss their struggles and excitement with the people in their lives who identified differently. She decided to begin asking them if there were a couples group in existence (there wasn't currently one in the area) if they would be interested in attending, each couple responded with an enthusiastic "Yes!" The couples group was born and has been running now for over four years at the time of publication.

The group has gelled beautifully, even though the membership of the group has changed over time and the members have held significantly different identities from one another over the years. Most of the couples would have never met each other if not for the group. The trans/gender nonconforming partners' identities have included transfeminine, transmasculine, nonbinary, genderfluid, "solidly on the fence" and beyond. The group members have seen each other through pregnancies and new babies, new jobs, miscarriages, deaths of parents, children leaving the home, becoming grandparents, surgeries, relationship disruptions, couples leaving the group because they separated, couples leaving the group because they feel they don't need the support in the same way, home renovations, moving, and so much more. Couples have joined the group because someone is newly exploring their gender identity or when a person has identified as trans for over a decade and the couple is wanting more support for their relationship. Over and over, we hear from group members that it is incredible to have a place where they can get support where they don't have to explain things in the same way, where there is some sort of common experience inherent in group membership.

This group is a closed group, we are very thoughtful about inviting new membership and always have extended discussions with the group members prior to considering expanding. We, the facilitators, mirror the identities of the couples in the group, in that Shannon identifies as cisgender and Davis identifies as trans and nonbinary. The participants know that we are a couple and what identities we hold, and we share personal experiences and challenges as appropriate. We have remarked many times to each other how powerful the experience of facilitating this group is for us both personally and professionally, both because the group members themselves are so thoughtful and engaged and also because the conversations and the territories the group is willing to explore stretches the limits of our thinking as individuals, as a couple and as therapists.

About 3 years into the group, one of our longest participating couples in the group, Seb and Parker, had reached a crisis point in their relationship. Seb was in their mid 40s, was white, designated male at birth and identifies as nonbinary, had been partnered with Parker, a white, cis, femme identified person also in her mid 40s, for over 20 years. They had fallen in love just after college when they both had recently come out as queer and had essentially only ever dated each other. Seb had done some casual dating in the couple of years before they met with folks of various genders, but had never been in love with anyone else before falling in love with Parker. They had recently started an apprenticeship at a local tattoo parlor and had found themself crushing on their mentor, a transmasculine person 15 years their senior. Seb and Parker had always had a "monogamish" relationship, they had a policy early in their relationship that they could both make out with people when they were out at parties, they used to go out dancing a lot in their 20s and early 30s before they had children. Neither of them had ever wanted more than a make-out with another person and the practice of openness had fallen away since their twins were born 10 years prior. Seb began talking to Parker about their crush on their mentor as soon as it happened, discussing crushes had always been a part of the culture of their relationship, but Seb was realizing that it was much more than just a casual crush like they had had in the past and realized that they needed to tell Parker, as their feelings for this person began to threaten the stability of their relationship, Seb had begun to have fantasies of leaving and starting a new life with their mentor, a fantasy that they didn't actually want to entertain. They decided to tell Parker that they had something big to talk about, and asked her consent to share it with her in the next couples group and she agreed.

(continued)

(continued)

Our group is structured so that one month the couples all come together and in the subsequent month we divide the group into trans/nonbinary partners one night and cis partners another, then the following week they all come back together again. At the start of each group, we do a go-around, where we ask each person to talk a bit about how they are doing, anything that they want to bring to the group about their personal life, and also how things are feeling in their relationship. In the group where Seb wanted to talk to Parker, they asked if they could go last as the group moved around, they shared that they had something they wanted to read to Parker and didn't want to derail the rest of the check-ins with their process. The rest of the group members agreed, in accordance with the norms of the group, to respect anything that the other members might be needing for any particular group meeting. When their turn came around, they asked Parker and the rest of the group if they would be open to them reading something they had written, and received consent; one of the members offered in support of Seb sharing, "when one of us goes deep, it helps all of us." Seb was usually a pretty funny and gregarious member of the group, often extending support to other members when they were in any distress, so everyone sat rapt with attention as they pulled out a folded paper from their pocket, hands shaking, voice quiet and low. They read a breathtaking letter to Parker, sharing the depth of their love for her, their commitment to their life, marriage and children, while also revealing the ways in which their queerness, their nonbinary identity had gone underground in the process of prioritizing other aspects of their life and identity. They shared, "now that that the roots of my identity, long dormant under the fertile soil of our life have received some sustenance and nutrients, the sprout is longing, begging, to break the surface of the earth, to find water and sunlight, to be seen and loved."

By the time Seb reached the end of the letter, both Seb and Parker, as well as several other group members were crying, everyone's focus was on the two of them, as they hugged and cried. Parker shared her appreciation for the letter and her fear that their feelings for their mentor would tear them apart, and that she felt selfish for feeling this way. Slowly, the group members began to speak up, one shared "I am so proud of both of you, you are modeling bravery for the rest of us," another said "there are no monsters in this room." Shannon asked, "would it feel helpful to hear if there is any resonance with either of you or your predicament in the room?" They both nodded enthusiastically. One member of the group, Shell (a white, cis woman in her early 60s) spoke up, and said "I feel like I am Parker in this situation and Maggie is Seb." Shell and Maggie (who was white, AMAB and had identified as a transwoman for the past 10 years) had been together for 35 years, and had been in a nonsexual relationship for the past 25. Shell explained that Maggie had been broaching the topic of opening their marriage for some time, and that Shell had consistently said no to that possibility, and that she was the one who had originally closed the door on sexual contact so many years before. Maggie said "when you have been married this long, there are things that bind you more than sex." She turned to Shell and said "I love you and I am sorry I took your husband away." Maggie replied, with tears in her eyes, "I love you and I took your wife away long before that." Everyone in the group had a sense that this was a conversation that was long avoided and took unimaginable courage to broach.

This group meeting illuminated for Shannon and Davis why they do this group, why they have remained faithfully committed to it for the past four years. The couples in this group are able to support each other in ways that are deeper and more profound than could ever come from couples therapy, by seeing themselves mirrored in each other, they are each able to come to new realizations about themselves and their relationships. The couples lean on and support each other in ways that are rich and powerful, they have had the honor and the privilege of watching them all grow and transform through their connections to one another.

This vignette from the couples group shows a glimpse of what it can mean for erotically marginalized people to have access to a community that practices radical acceptance. Within a layered experience that includes an exploration of gender identity, sexual desire, commitment, love, and family, Parker and Seb were able to find mirrors that revealed an experience that others in the group could relate to. During a revelation that could have felt isolating and trapped they were able to have a different experience of growth and connection.

In Session

Including participation of family and communities can take many clinical forms. The above vignette utilized a support group format to help clients form and maintain connections. Working with individual clients including family and communities can mean holding the possibility for clients during individual work or including clients' support people in session. Working from this kind of systemic approach that recognizes the client in the context of their environment is for many clinicians a familiar stance. Applying this to sex therapy recognizes that the root of many sexual problems or challenges, although often manifested through the body, have their roots in the broader context of our clients' lives.

As with all clinical interventions the inclusion of participation of family and communities needs to happen in a way and at a pace that feel authentic for each client. Coming out as a person with an identity or experience that is erotically marginalized can be scary and sometimes unsafe. Our office can be a safe space for clients to discover for themselves when and how to include or build their support systems.

Key Clinical Points

- The experience of discrimination and oppression for erotically marginalized clients can be systemic or personal and having access to or building a community of support builds a client's resilience.
- Clinicians can support clients by helping them identify current supports within their family or communities or help them build new system of supports.
- Clients must lead the process in a way that feels safe and authentic to them.

References

Levine, J. (2002). *Harmful to minors: The perils of protecting children from sex.* Minneapolis, MN: University of Minnesota Press.

Ortmann, D & Sprott, R. (2013). *Sexual outsiders: Understanding BDSM sexualities and communities.* New York: Rowman & Littlefield.

Roffman, D. (2012). *Talk to me first: Everything you need to know to become your kids' "go-to" person about sex.* Boston, MA: Da Capo Lifelong Books.

Roffman, D. (2001). *Sex and sensibility: The thinking parent's guide to talking sense about sex.* Cambridge, MA: Perseus Publishing.

SIECUS National Guidelines Task Force, (2004). *Guidelines for comprehensive sexuality education: Kindergarten through 12th grade.* Retrieved from https://siecus.org/wpcontent/uploads/2018/07/Guidelines-CSE.pdf.

THE CASE OF CHLOE: IDENTITY EXPLORATION USING A BLACK FEMINIST/SYSTEMIC APPROACH FOR WORKING WITH EROTICALLY MARGINALIZED CLIENTS

Erika Evans-Weaver

Introduction of Therapist

As both a clinician and a person in the world, my identities have evolved and will continue to evolve as I live and experience all that life has to offer. My identities are not fixed or stagnated, they change as I change and as I grow. Understanding my identities (personal and professional) helps inform who I am right now as well as who and how I want to be in the future. This is the foundation of my work with others. My role professionally is to help people understand where **they** are in **their** life's journey, determine if they are ok with it and if there are any changes they would like to make to improve their situation. Chloe came to therapy with this as her request; something was missing in her life and she was seeking support to figure out what that meant.

To locate myself and who I am can be long and convoluted. First, I am a Woman of Color. This identity is equally as important to me as my second identity; I am a mother. If I think about my identities as a hierarchy, those two are at the top. Moving down my hierarchy I am a doctor of Human Sexuality Education and a licensed Marriage and Family therapist. These identities are very important for they are my livelihood and help me provide as a Mother. My socio-economic status (SES) is on the cusp of upper middle class. As we move down my hierarchy I identify my sexual orientation as queer (pansexual to be specific) and also identify as polyamorous and as part of kink community. Finally, I identify as being close to middle aged. While I don't shy away from disclosure in therapy when there is an identified clinical intent and purpose, I choose to make my disclosures more about life's journey than the outcome (my identities). My rationale is to help clients learn, understand and appreciate that life is a journey and a process and that it is not the same for any of us despite the overlapping identities that we might share. This was an important approach to take in this case because Chloe was ready to take the journey to figure out her identities.

When I explore identities with clients (and I believe it is critical to ask all clients about their respective identities), I offer examples if clients are unfamiliar but I insist that my questions remain open ended to affirm the language and identities the client holds and not put limits to what the identities can be. Creating this space gives clients permission to take whatever identities or personas that are important to them and bring them into a judgement free clinical space. In this case, Chloe used African American as her primary identifier. Additionally, she identified her gender as female and asked me to use female pronouns when being referred to or for writing clinical notes. Another important identifier for her was her body shape which she described as full figured.

Chloe was a 46 years old and married to Norman; they have been married 13 years, together for 16 years and have 2 children, ages 10 and 12.

Chloe initially sought treatment because of a reported feeling of "discontent with life." She acknowledged that her life was full of professional and personal responsibilities that for the most part she enjoyed but felt like something was missing and she was not living an authentic life. She used to go out more frequently and as she put it, she had a "joie de vivre" that she doesn't possess now. Chloe was explicitly clear about not being unhappy, but that she just felt incomplete, Chloe also reported having a great love and respect for her husband and wanted him to be her happily ever after but felt a yearning to return to who she was prior to her relationship with Norman. She described their sexual life as "rote, safe, loving, traditional". Her communication of these characteristics was not disparaging or even disappointed. It was communicated as simply characteristics. Prior to her relationship with Norman, Chloe identified herself as being sexually adventurous and had a fondness for some forms of bondage and discipline with her past partners. However, when she met Norman, a cisgender African American male, she relinquished her adventurous sexual nature for what she believed to be a more stable and appropriate approach to relationships (sexual and emotional) and eventually marriage.

As we discussed why she felt the need to give up her adventurous sexual nature for this relationship, Chloe quickly recalled two experiences she had within the first couple of years of dating Norman. The first incident occurred when she took him to a BDSM (Bondage and Discipline/Dominance and Submission/Sadism and Masochism) club. She said he was both curious and uninterested at the same time. He would watch a scene and would make comments on how he appreciated the interactions or the chemistry of the people, but at the same time he was not fazed or interested in personally trying out anything. At the end of the evening they had memorable sex but they had to go home to accomplish that; he was affectionate at the club but not sexual. Chloe interpreted his response as bad decision making on her part, that maybe she had taken him into the deep end without trying out something smaller in their privacy of her apartment. So, a few months later, she brought a few items like handcuffs and a small flogger that she thought might be fun to try with him. He tried using the items with her but it was awkward and uncomfortable. It was at that moment she knew that Norman was simply not into the things she enjoyed sexually. Her interpretation was that this was really something abnormal and she put this aspect of herself aside believing it would never need to be fulfilled.

Genograms are an assessment tool used to gather information about the lived experiences of a client, a graphic means of gathering family information and organizing it in a way that can show familial patterns, relationships, strengths, challenges and more (McGoldrick & Gerson 2008). It is a tool that can be used throughout therapy and enhanced upon when used in combination with a relationship map. We did a genogram to gather information about her family. She was raised by two heterosexual and well-educated parents in the outskirts of a city. She remembers her family in a loving way that included her grandparents. Both of her parents were educators in the public school system. Her grandmother was educated as a nurse but was a stay-at-home wife and her grandfather had a management position in a factory. Since both of her parents worked, she spent a fair amount of time with her grandparents. They all lived together until she went away to college. Chloe identified her family as being middle-class. She discussed that her primary network of community (friends, family and neighborhood) were Black, primarily African American. Her early developing years were filled with African American culture and that did not change for her until high school when she was exposed to other communities. While she was not raised in a particularly religious household, they were a Christian identifying family.

The primary messages that she recalled from her childhood included the following: (1) College was mandatory. The only thing optional was graduate school. Everyone in this family from the north to the south is required to be educated and nothing less was going to be accepted. (2) You have to get married before you have children. It was ok to have premarital sex but not before at least your senior year of high school but having sex without condoms was not an option. No babies were to be brought into the home without a husband. It was also important to be discrete because a highly sexual negative reputation would have lifelong consequences. So much of Chloe's familial information was explored and discussed by creating a genogram in session. Then we transitioned into a relationship map for a more descriptive analysis of her identified important relationships that were both familial and friendly.

Relationship History

My version of a relationship map allows clients to communicate about all the members of their network, familial and non-familial, as we explore and discuss the impact that the relationship has on the individual. I use descriptive language in my relationship maps to help categorize or identify meanings of relationships, such as primary relationship (significant amount of energy financially, emotionally, sexually or in any other way), secondary relationship (moderate amount of energy financially, emotionally, sexually or in any other way), and tertiary relationship (least amount of energy financially, emotionally, sexually or in any other way). Clients are given permission to denote what type of relationships they have, how they feel about it, the benefit or challenge to maintain the relationship and more. These relationship maps give clients an opportunity to explore their overall network, not just their family

When Chloe reflected on her beliefs about intimacy and romance, she recalled never believing in monogamy but not knowing another way to live. She described feeling an attraction for both men and masculine presenting women. Chloe primarily dated men but had had a couple of flings with women. She didn't have long term relationships mostly because she didn't believe in the idea of "one person till death do you part." Chloe felt that was an antiquated way of thinking but did not know anyone who shared her perspectives. She could remember saying that she wanted a lover at each port in the world but her family and friends assumed that she just had a fear of commitment. However, that was never the case, she just knew that she loved people for different reasons and didn't believe one person could be everything to her, nor did she believe that she could be everything for someone else. Chloe kept these perspectives to herself to avoid potential isolation or consequence from family or friends. She recalled how her friends and family would ask questions about her relationship decision making because they rarely saw her dating the same person, and she would avoid giving a straight answer or simply reply that she hasn't found the best partner yet. As she aged and made professional strides, family would communicate their expectation that she should "settle down."

We spent some time discussing relationship constructs and the ways society upholds monogamy as a gold standard. This also provided me with an opportunity to discuss how language, labels and identities can be used to either oppress or liberate someone depending on the context of the situation. By being seen as incapable of commitment or an ability to maintain a healthy relationship Chloe was being pathologized by those around her. While it may or may not have been intentional, it was still impactful and painted monogamy as the only way to have a healthy relationship. However, Chloe had experienced many healthy and happy consensually non-monogamous relationships. But because of the impact of the narratives, she didn't give validation or credence to those relationships. Chloe and I discussed how she believed something was wrong with the way she wanted to love. In some ways, she considered it an affront to her parents' marriage, which she idealized, but at the same time recognized it wasn't for her. We discussed how often society likes to present life options in this very dichotomous way but in truth there's much more expanse to life experiences. We discussed ways to appreciate and see the beauty in both monogamy and polyamory, and the importance in recognizing how society attempts to pit one against the other and how to figure out where she might fit (if at all) on this specific continuum.

The discussion on how she loved was a natural transition to discussing her marriage and relationship with Norman including the origin. When she met Norman, she felt a stronger attraction for him than she had felt for any other. In discussing what attracted her to Norman her first response was his smile and sense of humor. She also loved his eyes and said there was a warmth and genuineness about them that proved to be true. His kindness and openness overwhelmed her. She smiled as she recalled their first kiss and how he was thoughtful enough to ask to kiss her rather than assume she just wanted to be kissed. It was evident that there was just so much she loved about him. She said he came into her life when she was questioning everything and everyone and he accepted all of her in a way that nobody else ever had. Chloe and Norman dated for three years before they married. She described their relationship as feeling very safe and while she enjoyed his company in so many ways, she was also aware that he didn't have the sexual knowledge or experiences that she had. During the early years of their relationship Chloe attempted to introduce him to the kinkier aspects of herself by taking him to play parties. While he didn't scoff at it, he didn't appear tremendously interested either and because of his other positive attributes and her overall attraction to him, she decided to overlook his disinterest and give her all to the relationship. It was no coincidence that at this time her parents and friends would frequently discuss the importance of finding "the one" and how challenging it was for a successful Black woman to find a decent husband, especially one to be considered "the one". Chloe described poignant and detailed memories of her inner struggle. She vacillated between wanting the security of this relationship with someone that she loved, feeling like she was conforming to the pressures of those around her and questioning whether her desires were simply unrealistic fantasies. The outcome of her struggle was her decision to take the next steps with Norman.

When speaking about Norman, Chloe conveyed care and thoughtfulness. She maintained that her decision to marry him was still one of her best life decisions. She reported loving and respecting Norman very much but initially felt unfulfilled emotionally and sexually in their relationship. She fondly recalled how she enjoyed his company and who he was as a co-parent. She didn't believe she could go on the parenting journey without him. Additionally, she appreciated how they shared a common background racially and their core beliefs as a family. He was raised similarly to her which always felt so familiar to her. Chloe's guilt and shame manifested as she discussed Norman. She felt guilt that she wasn't 100% in when they first got married and she felt guilt for not always being as appreciative for the abundance in her life (her words) that she believed she should have.

For the past year, Chloe had felt an unrest. She found herself yearning to experience something and had been having BDSM (Bondage and Discipline/Dominance and Submission/Sadism and Masochism) fantasies about a variety of different people. She said that the onset of these emotions was not sudden but was something that she had to work very hard to suppress. Chloe said the only reason she was addressing it now was because she had read an article about being Black and Kinky roughly four months ago. The article felt like someone was in her soul and talking about it. Chloe reported that this was a part of her past and she never pursued it because of Norman's lack of interest. However, this article left her feeling alive because there was finally a validation and acknowledgement that she is not abnormal. She was feeling a combination of satisfaction at the prospects and confusion about where this has been her whole life. This internal conflict is what brought Chloe into therapy and where our clinical journey had begun.

An initial concern that Chloe had was with her full figure body. She said she never had a small frame but she was at the time we began working together she was at her heaviest and that made her very uncomfortable. While her partner never made disparaging remarks she was making them about herself. In part this disappointed her because she knew she was falling into the trap of mainstream societal beliefs about standards of beauty. She self-identified as having attractive qualities but used the language "I've just let myself go." She felt that all her energy went into keeping up her home and her family, that she was last on the list. Three months into our work Chloe had really begun to make her Self a priority. The S in self is capitalized here because part of the clinical work was getting Chloe to understand that her Self was an entity inside of her that was just as important as Norman and her children. To accomplish this, we had to externalize the Self in order to create a new narrative of importance. My strategy for helping Chloe externalize her Self was to take a tour of the many versions of her that have existed through the years. Again, who we are as humans changes with the experiences we've had, the roles or responsibilities we have to fulfill, the interests we have and the people in our lives. So, Chloe and I discussed who she was, what brought her joy, what she took pride in, what she missed about herself and what she valued about life. With fondness, one aspect of herself she could recall as a common element that always existed was her love of dancing. Whether it was going to nightclubs, trying to learn the choreography from music videos, or taking dance classes, she just loved to dance. She used language like "lightness, euphoria, silly, playful, and skillful" when she discussed the different types of dance she enjoyed. We discussed the possibility of taking different dance classes because dance as an art form is something that makes people feel the tension and strength in their limbs. Many people use dancing to find grounding and centeredness (Leseho & McMaster, 2011). Additionally, since she already possessed such an enjoyment for dance, it was likely this would be a homework assignment she could and would accomplish. Obviously, as clinicians, we always want to help set our clients up for success and not failure but here this was especially as I was trying to get her to see the S in Self as important and necessary. The dance classes that were specifically recommended were ballet, belly dancing and jazz. Chloe would experience her body in three different ways, find out more about herself and be able to determine which (if not all or none) of these dance forms made her feel good in her skin. During these classes she discovered that she enjoyed belly dance the most. Chloe reported feeling sensual and empowered as she learned to isolate and accentuate different parts of her body. She added that it was also a dance that embraced and exalted various body types and that made her feel good. The focus was not in losing weight but being and feeling positive about her body. Chloe began taking two classes per week and this became a treasured time for her. She also began to invest in generating a space and opportunity to express this part of herself outside of class by attending local events or meetups where her identity expanded beyond Mom, Wife, and Professional. She discovered that she did not have a steady regimen of self-care and the consequence was that she gave up on herself. However, by being consistent in taking care of her Self, a number of things began to change for her. Chloe's sexual energy increased, he began to feel good in her body a little more, he changed her style of dress a little to reflect her mood, and she began making more sexual advances towards her husband.

During her recent sexual advances toward her husband, their normal sexual dance did not reach the level of excitement she was seeking. A number of different sexual encounters passed and in discussing how she felt about them, Chloe hesitantly admitted that sex with Norman was filled with love and care but not passion. Chloe identified Norman as a caring lover but not a passionate one and that was something she missed. We discussed how it felt for her to not love every part of her relationship with Norman or appreciate every aspect of him even though they might not be perceived as faults to others, and she admitted that it was very uncomfortable to her.

She cried as she discussed how this felt like an ungrateful concern or issue that for most people wouldn't even be an issue. This became a point for discussion. We explored whether she had to conform and enjoy the same things as everyone else and the origin of that narrative. Chloe recalled experiences with past lovers and what elements were similar and different from sex with Norman. The passion, hunger, roughness, and lastly the submissive side it would elicit from her were what she missed. The care and loving attention is what she identified as being the same. Additionally, Chloe confided that she had always missed those things during sex with Norman which was fine initially because she believed it was not an important aspect, "It was time to settle down and if this was the one thing, the only thing missing I could live with that." But Chloe wasn't sure it was something she could ignore any longer. She possessed a deep intense desire to re-experience the sexual escapades of her earlier years and a concern for what this meant for her future.

Through our therapeutic exploration of Chloe's Self and sexual needs, she uncovered that her enjoyment of kink was not a passing fancy but a very real part of her identity that has gone ignored for too long. While she wanted to maintain her relationship with her husband, she also felt a longing for more and didn't believe it would go away, Chloe had a desire to open her marriage. She had thought about what it would mean to open their marriage off and on for years but never believed that Norman would support such an action and did not want to betray him. This prompted additional examination of her belief system about relationships including trust, communication, intimacy, and sex as a behavior.

It is not uncommon for there to be a shift of clinical focus. In this situation I would argue that this was really the concentration of the work all along but that we had to explore the other aspects of her to get to this moment. In therapy, a client may come in with a presenting issue that needs to be addressed and as the layers of that onion are revealed, so too are the other issues that need to come to the surface to be addressed (Pipes & Davenport, 1999). In externalizing the Self and learning the importance of taking care of her, it gave permission to Chloe to examine other ways she needed care, attention and fulfillment that had gone ignored for too long. In working with erotically marginalized clients, it is critical to name these systems of oppression, bring it into the clinical space, provide clients with permission to confront it and the influence these systems may hold on the individual and their decision making. An examination of respectability politics and the oppressive states that Black women experience was essential as these systems were interwoven into Chloe's narrative and decision making, it would have been clinically negligent to ignore the role it played in her life. This conversation could not happen without confronting the norms that are not self-created but become self-imposed or self-policed and how that can create a barrier to happiness and authenticity (Hill-Collins, 2005).

Breaking the Shell

In the four months that followed she explored what it would mean to disclose her identity of being polyamorous and kinky to her community, to open her marriage with her husband, and her accompanying emotions about all of it. In experiential therapy, the type of Marriage and Family therapist I identify as, one of the primary goals to treatment is for clients to gain a deeper awareness of their lived experience and the impact this may have on their journey of self-fulfillment. In exploring what self-fulfillment would mean for Chloe she discovered that many of her decisions were influenced by her family and the politics of respectability. She also began to identify with the label of polyamorous. This was challenging language for her to own because of her belief system and the potential consequences she believed would occur as a result. The question was "If I am polyamorous, how do I maintain a marriage with someone who is monogamous?" She assumed that consequences would not only be rendered by Norman, but also by their respective families and friends. While she maintained a love for Norman, she wished that she had been more honest with him and with herself about her identity as polyamorous.

Chloe expressed great shame and disappointment in herself for not disclosing her identity to Norman and for not living authentically. Chloe's attempt to live a monogamous life was rooted in the narrative that she should find one man to live out life happily ever after. However, she never felt this was true or fitting for her but didn't feel she had space or agency to be something outside of monogamous. When I challenged Chloe to envision what life could look like as something other than monogamous, it created a mixture of feelings, including anxiety, excitement, and shame. The anxiety was connected to her concern for how Norman might respond to her and what she might be asking of him and their marriage. The excitement was connected to the opportunity to be honest and true about herself. However, the expression of shame was connected to both the possibility of hurting Norman and to her desire to have more than one partner in her life when her friends were experiencing challenges in finding just one. The question she asked was "How do I deserve more than one love when so many can't find the first one?" This evolved into a discussion on how she conceptualized what it means to be polyamorous.

I provided her with suggested readings such as *Ethical Slut* by Janet Hardy and *Opening Up* by Tristan Taormino and we discussed how these books are simply guides and don't take into consideration the experience of a Black Woman in the United States. When providing book, article, or film suggestions I believe it's critical to note how the cultural identities of the client may not be an exact match to what the authors are presenting which is going to shape the lens of the narrative being shared. That doesn't devalue the resource, it helps to conceptualize the experience or resource for the client so they have more control getting out of it what they need rather than trying to get out of it what the author or source is positing. In working with erotically marginalized clients I find this to be especially important as representations of self in the media may look more like caricatures, stereotypes, or at the minimum just be absent all together. For Chloe this explanation was particularly important because the narratives of others had already been such a major influence in her life; it was critical to give her permission to create a new narrative based on her needs and ideas.

Next Stages

Creating this new narrative meant a conversation had to occur with her husband. One of the questions that loomed was whether Chloe would continue to embrace this aspect of herself if it meant the end of her marriage. Without reservation, her response was a resounding yes. Chloe said she could not return to living in untruths and needed to come clean with Norman. Her ideal outcome was for them to stay together as a couple and negotiate through the logistics of what that would mean for them both. Chloe decided it would be more beneficial to come out to her husband in session. For two months we prepared coming out to Norman. This included role playing potential conversations to have with Norman in session until she was comfortable. We also worked to identify support groups to join such as Black and Poly, which has a local chapter in order to add to her network of support and broaden her experience of community.

When the time finally came for Norman to join our sessions, I situated the chairs ahead of time for them to mostly be facing one another. I made sure there were books about polyamory readily available and on the coffee table for ease of use in the session. Chloe did a great job forging ahead and claiming her truth. Norman was clearly nervous but very attentive to what Chloe had to say. As she welled up, he reached out a hand of support. As she finished coming out, his primary question was "Does this mean you no longer want to be married to me?" She reassured him that she wanted to still be married but see other people as well. She also gave him permission to see other people as well and he was curious whether he had to date others. Her answer was a confused reply of "no?" Norman took a very deep breath and calmly said "You've never been like any other woman . . . why would you start now? How do we make this work?" This prompted a sigh of relief with a combination of laughter and tears from Chloe.

Clinical Implications

Once Chloe and I started on our clinical journey, it became apparent that the presenting problem was simply the beginning and we needed to peel back the layers. Each layer revealed more about Chloe and where she wanted to go. So much of our time was spent unpacking the emotion of shame, affirming her preferred direction and giving her permission to live life authentically. At the beginning of therapy, I was confronting some deeply ingrained dualistic perspectives. There was a right perspective, a right way to do things and to live along with complementing wrong perspectives, or a wrong way to do things. Ultimately, Chloe's internal script said that everything she truly wanted in life had been wrong. During our time together, Chloe was able to see that the messages she had received weren't intended to make life miserable for her. These messages were connected to long standing ideologies about life, marriage and sexuality that might be very helpful for some people, but were simply wrong for Chloe. As a result, we were able to expand her continuum and her right vs. wrong thinking evolved into becoming more non-dualist in nature.

References

Dergel, S. (2014). Guide to CFO success: *Leadership strategies for corporate financial professionals*. Hoboken, NJ: Wiley & Sons.

Greenberg, L., Watson, J., Lietaer, G. (1998). *Handbook of experiential therapy*. New York: Guilford.

Hill-Collins, P. (2005). *Black sexual politics: African Americans, gender, and the new racism*. New York: Routledge.

Kenen, R. & Peters, J. (2001). The colored, eco-genetic relationship map (CEGRM): A conceptual approach and tool for genetic counseling research. *Journal of Genetic Counseling, 10*(4), 289–309.

Leseho, J. & McMaster, S. (2011). *Dancing on the earth: Women's stories of healing and dance*. Forres: Findhorn Press.

McGoldrick, M., Gerson, R., & Petry, S. (2008). *Genograms: Assessment and intervention* (3rd ed.). New York: W. W. Norton & Company.

Pipes, R. B., & Davenport, D. S. (1999). *Introduction to psychotherapy: Common clinical wisdom*. Boston, MA: Allyn & Bacon.

Principle Eight

PRACTICE ACTIVE ALLYSHIP

It is our belief that when a therapist is working with erotically marginalized clients, they should have a clear view of where they stand in relationship to allyship, advocacy and outreach. Clinicians need to be able to network with other providers in the area where they are located to aid their clients in finding other affirming providers. What is the practice of allyship in the context of being a therapist who works with erotically marginalized clients? We define the practice of allyship as the participation in the creation of a network for clients, and to see oneself as an active participant in the social support, emotional scaffolding, and larger network of affirming provider care for a client. Active allyship also means that when a therapist commits to working ethically with erotically marginalized clients, they must see themselves as having both privilege and power that they acknowledge and harness and do not take for granted or ignore.

We use the framing of *practicing allyship* as opposed to *being an ally* with intentionality, stemming from radical queer politics. Allyship is an active process, not an identity that a person can claim, claiming this particular identity for oneself is problematic, as one identity rests on, and potentially subsumes, a marginalized identity. A marginalized person can identify another person as their ally, but we caution anyone in a position of power or privilege to identify themselves as an ally to a marginalized person or group of people. Additionally, in more recent years in communities fighting for racial justice, there has been a movement to encourage people in positions of power to be an accomplice, rather than an ally, as acting as an accomplice is an active process, one that implicates the person in power and demonstrates their stake in the fight for justice and liberation.

A principal tenet of allyship in working with erotically marginalized people is that the clinician is not an expert on their client's experience of gender, sexuality, relationships, or sexual practices. We believe that the work of allyship as a therapist is not to be the expert on a client's experience, but rather, to nurture and support the unique and individual process of each person who is looking for support, affirmation, and increased access to resources. A clear stance of both allyship and preemptive radical inclusion is to believe that every person is the expert of their own identity and experience. Unfortunately, many clinicians who go through specialized training for working with people who are erotically marginalized, specifically with LGBTQAI folks, have the experience of both feeling like an expert and having clients believe them to be an expert. This false perception of expertise can be magnified within the therapeutic relationship when a client needs a letter of recommendation for gender affirming hormones or surgeries. More insurance companies are claiming to cover medical transitions for erotically marginalized people, however, it appears that more often than not clients have to jump through outrageous gatekeeping hoops to get their insurance carriers to cover these medically necessary treatments and surgeries.

The gatekeeping role a therapist might inhabit can be extensive. Often insurance companies will require that erotically marginalized people obtain a letter of referral from their therapist to begin gender affirming treatments. The letter that the clinician writes for insurance coverage is used to "confirm and verify" the client's medical necessity and psychological readiness to begin gender affirming treatments. In the best cases, a letter requirement by insurers is oppressive and intrusive for a client, because it illuminates that their identity is subject to pathologization and requirements of authentication by a professional. In the worst cases, due to factors of socio-economic status, geography, mental health status, or other concerns related to resources for a client, it is not possible for an erotically marginalized person to access these services at all, and they are never able to medically transition, if that is their desire. This, of course, leads to increased risks of suicidal ideation, self-harm, and debilitating depression and anxiety related to gender dysphoria and larger systemic oppressions that impact erotically marginalized clients.

In an effort to support clinicians who want to practice allyship with their erotically marginalized clients we have included a sample letter that we suggest clinicians use as a template for writing letters for clients (Appendix A). We have also included a form called The Self-Determined Gender Psychosocial Form (SGPF) (Appendix B), which was adapted by Shannon Sennott, from a gender psychosocial form created in 2009 by Arlene Istar Lev, the director of Choices Counseling and Consulting, in Albany, NY. The major changes that Shannon made from the original form created by Arlene Istar Lev relate to wording of questions and client consent, with a sharp focus on wanting the clinician to be extremely thoughtful about how they ask questions about a client's gender and family history. The SGPF is meant to be a guide for clinicians who are new to therapeutic work related to gender journeys and transitions and would like to have ideas for areas of exploration that can be helpful for some clients in their therapeutic work. This form is also useful in the process of gathering important information for writing letters for clients, as we will often quote a client in their letter to illuminate the unique perspective that each person has about their own experience of their gender transition. Quotes in personalized letters can come from answers to some of these questions on the SGPF.

The Self-Determined Gender Psychosocial Form is meant to be a supplement to other training and supervision that a clinician would have in the therapeutic specialization of gender identity and expression, as it can be a helpful tool in preparing to work with someone who is looking for therapeutic support in beginning a gender journey or transition. We highly encourage any clinician who has a client who is beginning the process of a gender exploration to seek supervision with someone who is known in the field. AASECT and WPATH have many resources for supervision and local trainings for therapists who are looking for ongoing support in working with gender nonconforming, nonbinary and trans clients. This form is a way to create scaffolding for a therapist to better understand the ways that gender identity has developed for an individual client. There are no right or wrong answers to any of these questions, they are meant to be jumping off points of exploration.

Allyship Practice Model for Transfeminist Therapeutic Approach

A critical part of the practice of allyship for clinicians working with erotically marginalized clients is to conceptualize their work using a transfeminist lens. Through the process of developing a tranfeminist therapeutic approach (Sennott, 2011) Shannon Sennott created an allyship practice model (APM) (Appendix C) for clinicians to utilize and draw from in the work of being a transfeminist therapist. The following practices are aspects of the APM with more in-depth explanations to support clinicians in integrating these concepts into their therapeutic work with gender nonconforming, trans, and nonbinary clients. Many of these practices, when applied expansively, can to be relevant in working with all clients who are erotically marginalized, not just people who are erotically marginalized based on gender identity or expression.

1. Transfeminst therapists understand that everyone, regardless of their gender identity or expression, can be an activist and ally in the movement to resist gender oppression.

   It is common for clinicians who do not self-identify as an erotically marginalized, to believe that they would be in some way stepping over a line or intruding on a community of people if they were to specialize in working with clients who identified as erotically marginalized. Often clinicians will want to provide accountable therapeutic spaces for clients but not know how to do this in a non-oppressive way. What these clinicians do not realized is that erotically marginalized clients need allies and activists working for them, when they, as the target identity, cannot manage to advocate or fight for their own rights, because they are fearful or frozen from an oppressive or micro-aggressive experience.
2. Transfeminist therapists recognize the intersections of trans/gender justice with reproductive justice, the women's movement, and other justice movements.

   The ability to understand the intersection of the gender justice movement with reproductive justice is critical to understanding that everyone is oppressed by the binaries that enforce the policing of gender roles and identities, as well as bodies and human rights related to bodily autonomy. The example that we often give about this intersection is to imagine if when a person wanted to have a child they first were forced to find a therapist who specialized in "procreation readiness." They would then be required to attend a certain amount of sessions over the course of one full year with this specialized therapist. After a year of consistently feeling and proving to this therapist that they wanted to have a child the therapist would write them a letter of recommendation for a medical doctor to prescribe the needed hormonal supplement in order for them to get pregnant. This type of gatekeeping is exactly what trans, gender nonconforming, and nonbinary people have been subjected to since the beginning of their experience of hormonal and medical transition. Similarly, this is exactly the kind of gatekeeping that used to prohibit people from being able to access birth control if they were not asking for it within the context of "family planning."

From the perspective of a person who identifies as erotically marginalized, for example, a person engaged in BDSM sexual practices, how would they navigate obtaining a primary care provider who is knowledgeable about BDSM practices and consensual bondage and control? One way to be an ally for clients who are trying to find affirming health care in the face of their multiple intersecting identities of oppression is to offer to make calls and connections with other providers for the client. This can look many different ways, but what is important to understand is that it is so much more difficult to be the target of oppression and seek competent care, than to be a provider calling another provider to see if they can offer affirming care for someone that you work with who is erotically marginalized. This conversation might include asking the provider if they feel comfortable treating a person who is actively involved in sexual practices related to a BDSM lifestyle, where they could be presenting with consensually obtained lacerations, piercings, burns, bruises, and wounds. It would also be important to ask the provider if they feel they could treat this person medically without pathologizing or policing their practices.

3. Transfeminist therapists recognize the intersections of gender with other systems of oppression (including, but not limited to: racism, classism, sexism, ageism, ableism, cissexism, heterosexism, misogyny, homophobia, transphobia).

This is another way to understand what it means to have a stance of preemptive radical inclusion in working with clients who are erotically marginalized. Clinicians need to keep in the forefront of their awareness that important intersections between multiple systems of oppression exist within a person's identity constellation. Some examples of these types of intersections might be: Sex therapy with a polyship that includes four sexual partners. The first partner identifies as multi-racial, transmasculine nonbinary, and queer. The second partner identifies as fat, femme, queer, cisgender, white, and an elder. The third partner identifies as being disabled, cisgender, person of color (POC), and pansexual aromantic. The fourth partner identifies as transfeminine, first generation first generation Korean immigrant, and queer. These identities are all intricately interwoven into each person's experience and into their larger relationship structure and cannot be understood in isolation.

4. Transfeminist therapists acknowledge how gender privilege and oppression have and continue to operate in their own lives.

   This practice might be the single most important element of allyship as a clinician working with erotically marginalized clients. The notion of understanding one's own location in the wheel of privileged and oppressed identities is critical. Identifying one's own privileged and targeted identities is accomplished through a process of self and group accountability. We encourage clinicians to create a peer supervision group that would act as a processing station for questions and concerns related to intersecting identities within each clinician. If a group of therapists were able, it would be ideal to have a facilitator who could lead the group process and who has experience in working intersectionally and using a social justice framework. This person does not have to be a clinician, they could be in social justice education or part of a non-profit that provides trainings on issues related to oppression and privilege. This could bring up questions of confidentially and adherence to different codes of ethics, however, there are ways of addressing confidentiality to protect client identities and the cross-pollenization of disciplines is part of what makes the practice of allyship stronger. With a transfeminst approach clinicians develop an instinct for identifying and naming the experiences that can happen within themselves and also, within the room, therapeutically. This skill comes from practice, through training, and by collegial collaboration and peer group supervision.

5. Transfeminist therapists recognize that trans and/or gender nonconforming people need allies, just as all oppressed and marginalized people need allies.

   There are many situations that can arise in a therapeutic context that might suggest that a clinician will need to take active steps to advocate for their clients in the context of being erotically marginalized. When listening to a client's concerns about areas of their life that they feel oppressed it is important for the clinician to acknowledge that as the therapist, they are in a position to be a protective factor for the client. If a client does not know a primary care doctor, a dentist or a massage therapist who will be affirming to them in their identity, whether that is about race, size, gender, sexuality, age, or disability, you can make initial information gathering calls for the client to find out the level of competency places that the client is considering going to can provide for them. Historically, physical health providers are often a source of traumatic experiences in relationship to erotically marginalized identities. Knowing that, a clinician can offer to cold call offices, doctors, and even other therapists, to inquire if they have an anti-discrimination commitment or policy. We have called restaurants that our clients wanted to go to for a first date to find out if they are able to accommodate people of size in their seating and table arrangement. When the host asked what we meant by this, we asked if the chairs at the tables had arms or if they were open, and they understood better what information we were looking to get. This conversation might be challenging for the person who is planning to go into the restaurant but is not as difficult for a clinician who is practicing active allyship.

6. Provide space for people to self-identify their gender and provide space for people to self-identify the pronouns they use to describe or identify themselves.
7. Use gender inclusive/all-gender language until the pronouns a person uses are established. This sometimes means asking what pronoun(s) and/or name a person uses (e.g. "What name do you use?" or, "What pronouns do you use?"). It is also important to receive consent to use this name/pronoun in some, or all, settings and to respect this confidentially. Some people might prefer you use a certain pronoun in session, but not when talking to them on the phone when they are home, etc.

   It is important to use gender inclusive language and pronouns until a client is able to establish a sense of safety and comfort with you. After you have built a relational connection it will feel less intrusive to ask them about pronouns, and there will be a therapeutic relationship to act as a support for the conversation. When talking about a client in a supervisory or group supervision setting it is critical that clinicians use the identity and pronouns that the client uses. This might mean that the therapist needs to explain certain pronoun uses and identities to colleagues in order for everyone who is discussing the client to be properly affirming to them by using their correct name, identity, and pronoun.
8. Mirror back language, especially self-identification.

   Mirroring back language is a key practice in active allyship with erotically marginalized clients. This is an essential part of sex therapy and helping erotically marginalized clients feel safer to share their authentic experiences. It is critical to ask clients how they self-identify about anything that could be related to an identity of oppression. This is particularly important when navigating intersecting identities of oppression. The therapist does not have to fully understand the choices and use of language and labels that their erotically marginalized clients use, however, they must mirror back to their clients the language that they use to self-identify. A transfeminist therapist takes a position of preemptive radical inclusion, a stance of radical acceptance, and they do not have an opinion or judgment about any way that an erotically marginalized client might self-identify, or sexual practices that an erotically marginalized client might engage in, or the gender identity(ies) or presentation(s) that they may embody and express.
9. Expect to make some mistakes – but never use this as an excuse for not acting.
10. Acknowledge having made a mistake (e.g. mis-pronouning someone), apologize, correct themselves, and move on.

One of the most critical positions of a transfeminist therapist is that they expect to make mistakes in the process of their work, and they do not allow this to be a reason to not act in the capacity of being an ally to erotically marginalized clients. If an erotically marginalized client has shifted pronouns from he/him or she/her, they/them, or ze/hir, this can often feel like a difficult change for everyone around this person to make. It is extremely important that the therapist be able to begin using the client's new pronouns in all the contexts that the client would like them to, including in their session notes, in clinical supervision, and in the context of sessions with partners, friends, and family.

Making mistakes with pronoun shifts is common, it is important for a clinician to let their client know that they are working on it, however, it is critical that if the therapist makes a mistake that they catch it and correct themselves, so that the client does not have to correct the therapist. When a therapist does not catch and correct themselves, they are communicating many things to their client, the most painful of which is that their client's identity is not important enough to the therapist to remember and incorporate it into the therapist's larger conception the client as an authentic person. When the therapist does catch and correct themselves it is important not to be overly apologetic or make a scene about the situation because this can lead the client to feel as though they have to emotionally care for the therapist, and this puts the burden back on the client.

Another way that a transfeminist therapist might make mistakes is during the process of supporting an erotically marginalized client naming or labeling a sexual identity or practice and giving language to how this identity impacts their life. When the landscape of identity is shifting and expanding it is possible, in the process of holding different identity possibilities for clients, that things can shift quickly. For example, if a client is beginning an exploration of BDSM and attending play parties they might come to session with multiple experiences of things that can fit for them as erotic, arousing, scary, unfamiliar, and all of these at once. Often, over time, the things that fit into each of these categories can move and shift, from experience to experience. It is not uncommon for the therapist to have forgotten that something was no longer part of a client's identity. These are the moments where it is important for the therapist to be transparent and point out that though they might not remember every detail, there is so much beauty in the complexity and nuance of their experiences and identity. If a client knows that their therapist deeply honors their process of exploration, they will be able to hold that the clinician may not recall all the specifics moment to moment.

11. Ask questions respectfully, and understand when someone elects not to respond if the question makes them feel uncomfortable.

Giving erotically marginalized clients the space to fully consent to answering questions related to sexual identities and practices, fantasies, desires, attractions, and anything that has to do with their body is critical to the process of respecting their identity. All of these areas of inquiry, as a

sex therapist, are places where there might not yet be language to describe a client's experience if the client is erotically marginalized. Narratives and systems of understanding are not part of the fabric of society for erotically marginalized clients the way they are for those who inhabit a more privileged and socially condoned sexual identity landscape (i.e. heterosexual, white, cisgender, non-kinky, middle class, able-bodied).
12. Work to create inclusive non-discrimination policies in their institutions, organizations, agencies and communities.
13. Challenge oppressive language and behaviors in themselves and those around them.
14. Avoid and challenge gender assumptions and stereotyping.

Creating a system in one's clinical practice that includes the process of making explicit that which is often unspoken is a key to being an active ally in a therapeutic context. This can take many forms, but we recommend considering using one's self as the model and also being clear about what you see your work including. When we get a new client, no matter who they are or how they appear, at the end of the first session we will usually ask them if they have any questions for us. After they ask their questions, or say that they don't have any, we say something like,

> *Well, I usually share with folks no matter who they are, if they are a new client, that I use she/her pronouns, and that I use a social justice lens in my work. This means that I work very hard not to discriminate against people based on race, ethnicity, gender identity or expression, sexuality, disability, size, citizenship, religion, and age.*

This type of overview offered by the clinician to a client is a perfect way to enact allyship in a setting where the therapist is new to the field and is working in community mental health or larger agency settings. In community mental health settings, where any person that a therapist might be meeting with could privately identify as erotically marginalized, this can be a radical act of social justice because those who need to hear that the clinician is an accountable and safe person to talk to about their identity will hear it, and those who do not need to hear it will likely not take it in. This type of statement also allows a therapist to have something to refer back to, if clients are saying racist, homophobic, transphobic, or sexist things and the clinician wants to address this. If a client (who is not erotically marginalized) says something oppressive we might say,

> *So remember how I said in our first meeting that I use a social justice lens and work really hard not to discriminate based on all sorts of identities of oppression? Well, the thing is, I also feel like it is part of that work to talk about these identities if someone is saying something against them. So I am wondering if we could talk a bit about the thing you just said about ______ and we can try to come to a place that works for both of us around that comment.*

This foundation of allyship is more of an action, and it is one of the ways that clients feel and see that their therapist is doing their own work on a larger systemic scale. The process of investigating where prejudices might arise in the therapeutic work for the therapist is critical to being able to honor erotically marginalized clients in their fullest and most authentic experience. It is most important to secure regular supervision, in order to navigate challenges related to aspects of countertransference. Most sex therapy supervision can be obtained remotely giving clinicians a wide range of supervisors to choose from, this also allows for clinicians to look for supervision based on areas of needed support.

Key Clinical Points

- We define the practice of allyship as the participation in the creation of a network for clients, and to see oneself as an active participant in the social support, emotional scaffolding, and larger network of affirming provider care for a client.
- We use the framing of *practicing allyship* as opposed to *being an ally* with intentionality, stemming from radical queer politics. Allyship is an active process, not an identity that a person can claim, claiming this particular identity for oneself is problematic, as one identity rests on, and potentially subsumes, a marginalized identity.
- A principal tenet of allyship in working with erotically marginalized people is that the clinician is not an expert on their client's experience of gender, sexuality, relationships or sexual practices. The work of allyship as a therapist is not to be the expert on a client's experience, but rather, to nurture and support the unique and individual process of each person who is looking for support, affirmation, and increased access to resources.
- The practice of allyship for clinicians working with erotically marginalized clients is to conceptualize their work using a transfeminist lens. Through the process of developing a tranfeminist therapeutic approach (Sennott, 2011) Shannon Sennott created an allyship practice model (APM) (Appendix C) for clinicians to utilize and draw from in the work of being a transfeminist therapist.

Reference

Sennott, S. L. (2011). Gender disorder as gender oppression: A transfeminist approach to rethinking the pathologization of gender non-conformity. *Women & Therapy*, *34*, 93–113.

THE CASE OF B, W, & G: MULTIPLICITY IN POSITIONALITIES OF THERAPY WITH A POLY TRIAD

Rachel Keller

Intro

This case summary presents a composite case of three clients involved in a triad relationship, all three of whom identify as queer and polyamorous in their sexual identity, and are between 23–28 years of age. All three clients presented are fictional composites, incorporating facets of clients I have worked with, that have similar positionalities and presenting problems of relational issues between them. The three clients are B; a 28-year-old queer, genderqueer identified, poly, disabled/wheelchair user, white, middle class, union organizer, W; a 23-year-old queer, nonbinary, poly, white, upper middle class, musician, and G; a 25-year-old, queer, female identified, poly, black, middle class, writer.

Presenting Problems

These three clients came to work with me because there had been a breakdown in the relationship between B and G, which was causing distress among all clients in the triad.

Clinician Positionality

I am in full support of the authors of this book's stated need for the lens of intersectionality, and the importance of being able to hold all identities together, to not have to isolate them in order to look at or discuss them. It is not the easiest practice, especially at the beginning, but so vital for clients, especially erotically marginalized ones, to be able to be seen in all their complexity. I believe that our predominant culture in the U.S. continually tries to reduce these identities, to isolate them, in order to maintain the existing power structures. Many of my erotically marginalized clients have expressed relief at not having to be reduced to one or two identities, that they can allow their full selves to be present in the room without experiencing further marginalization. I believe that not only does this allow for a much more nuanced view of the client, but the safety that is afforded to them by the permission to be themselves creates a much greater capacity for insight and healing. This does not eliminate the careful thought process a clinician may have around their own identity disclosure to a client. Purpose and intent must still always be considered, and I do feel there are many ways that disclosure of these identities can enrich the process, in addition to continually pushing back against the idea of what makes up a "normal" identity. I also feel that it is a valuable political statement to make these identity statements, to "show up to be counted," especially when there are positionalities that not only contradict the dominant paradigm, but would be hidden otherwise, and therefore modeling this takes on its own importance.

And so, with the intention of that modeling, I disclose that I identify as a white, disabled/dwarf, Jewish, middle class, femme/queer, poly, cis woman ("cis" meaning my gender presentation matches the sex I was assigned at birth). I am a clinical social worker, a licensed psychotherapist, who primarily works at Northampton Sex Therapy Associates, LLC, a sex therapy group practice in Northampton, Massachusetts. In addition to being a clinician, I am also an activist and a parent. My experience of being the only disabled/dwarf person in my family led to being marginalized within that structure, and affected my identity formation. Having even more impact is my experiencing the ongoing marginalization of having a physical disability that is both immediately identified as having an 'atypical' body by casual gaze, and the oppression of living in a society/culture that is not generally physically accessible to me. Since I am white, have always identified with the gender that was assigned to me, and grew up comfortably middle class, the only other major marginalization that I have experienced on any structural level is that of being a woman. The other identities are ones that are "passable," meaning that I have the privilege of passing for being a straight, Christian, strictly monogamous woman should I choose to.

Case Summary

The first sessions with these three clients began with the clients each presenting their perspective on what brought them in to therapy. These sessions were held with all three of them present, which allowed me a view into the dynamics that existed between them. I was immediately struck by their apparent priority of good communication with each other, that despite being obvious that there was clearly a lot of distress between them, that each was having a lot of difficulty holding onto themselves in these moments, they remained consistently able to conduct themselves in a way that was respectful and considerate of each other. Having experienced that communication and ability to process issues collaboratively is often a Poly hallmark of relationships, I asked them to share with me what work they had done as a group thus far together. I feel that this is illustrative of this book's second principle; of challenging binary thinking, in that I was framing them as their triad, holding them collectively in their relationship construct that they themselves used, which is very atypical of the ones our society typically uses. Further nonbinary thinking was displayed in the construction of their genograms. In addition to creating genograms for each of them in their past nuclear family structures, we also created together a genogram that contained each of them in their relationship, as well as the relationships they had with others, and important members of their communities, and all the interrelational ties that existed between them. One of them mentioned during this process that they had not previously had the experience of being able to "see" themselves and their relationships and community held in this way, and there was a lot of positive sentiment expressed at the importance and understanding that was given.

After these initial sessions, I met with each of the members of the triad to both get a sense of the individual meanings they have attached to sex and relationships, and to give them an opportunity to speak with me without needing to take into consideration the other members of their relationship, which was so prevalently demonstrated previously. During one of these sessions with G, she revealed that she felt that her interactions over the past few months with B could be considered emotional abuse from B, and that she felt some trauma as a result. This led to an extensive conversation around what that meant and looked like for her. I feel that during this session my mode of being with G could be framed as emulating the fifth principle of this book; using and giving priority to the client's own words, narrative and knowledge. That by my "being with" her in those moments instead of projecting my own interpretations of what trauma might mean, by maintaining a curiosity of that term, instead of solely accepting it in its diagnostic implications, I allowed for G to provide her own definition.

When we came back together as a group after these initial sessions, some collective goals with the triad were set. The major theme of the goals that we developed together was the seeming contradiction of each of them being able to articulate and act upon their own wants, needs and desires, while still participating in their relationships and structure of the triad. I proposed using the concepts of differentiation for the basis of the development of this skill set, so we used many of the tenets in *Passionate Marriage*, by David Schnarch, but expanded them into a less binary form for this relationship structure. The third principle of this book, support willingness and readiness to experience the anxiety of uncertainty, came into play many times during these sessions, as I encouraged each of their growing ability to express themselves to each other with topics they found difficult.

During all of these sessions there were many opportunities to use the first principle of this book: maintain transparency and name individual and systemic oppressions. Some examples of this included my noting to them that while my office was set up with accessibility for B and their wheelchair, that many spaces, including the door to get into my office building were not, and offering support around making that more accessible by meeting them outside the building before the appointment, as opposed to putting the onus on them to ask for it. This is further modeled by my asking at any initial appointment that I have with any client, visibly disabled or not, if there are accommodations they need for the therapeutic process.

The eighth principle, practice active allyship, was displayed during one session where W vocalized frustration at G's choosing to go to a weekend long workshop for people of color instead of spending time with them, and I expressed that while I understood W's feelings around the limited resources of time, this was an unusual opportunity for G, in that these spaces are not the norm, and the importance of chances to access them, and how easy it is for white people to feel access to almost every space. This resulted in a conversation in which G felt the agency to talk about how her marginalization around race sometimes took place even within the triad.

In further sessions, G was able to articulate her desire to leave the triad structure, that she felt the interactions with B had left her unable to continue with that relationship part of the triad. Through some grief work and their newly gained insight creating ability to let go of their original dream to continue in this format, the relationship reformed into a dyadic V, with W at the center. After ensuring that all three of them felt they had had the process they needed, counseling in this particular configuration was terminated.

THE CASE OF BENNY: MISOGYNY AND THE DISSOCIATED FEMALE SELVES

Eve Bogdanove

Client Introduction

I am presenting this case with the permission of an ongoing client, making sure to disguise his identity by adding composite details from related cases, as well as changing his name, identifying characteristics and details to protect his confidentiality. He is currently uninterested in co-authoring or reading this case contribution, however I anticipate there will be opportunities to revisit the possibility in the future, ideally to reflect on his progress over time and to deepen his exploration of his developing kink identity.

Benny is a 56-year-old, cisgender, olive skinned, white, second generation, non-European originating, heterosexual, working class man with severe trauma history. He has an above average intelligence, was raised Catholic, has a history of polysubstance abuse (including IV heroin), 23 psychiatric admissions, a long history of outpatient psychotherapy in clinic settings, a history of significant self-harm (cutting, burning, punching his head, genital abrasions) and multiple suicide attempts. As is the case with anyone with significant involvement in the mental health system, he received multiple psychiatric diagnosis throughout his adulthood. I diagnosed him with with Dissociative Identity Disorder (DID) and Polysubstance Abuse in remission and he is prescribed Wellbutrin and Haldol prn. He is six years sober, active in Alcoholics Anonymous and Narcotics Anonymous, works full-time as a case manager in the mental health field, lives alone, and his primary support system is a dedicated sponsor and a couple of sober friends. Benny's presenting problems were distress related to what he described as a "sick relationship to his sexuality," including compulsive masturbation to violent porn, intense shame and fear of relationships with women, and a history of long term molestation by a sibling and repeated violent rapes by his father. Benny's presenting symptoms were dissociative episodes, self-harm, suicidal ideation, intrusive violent sexual fantasies, hyperarousal, and emotional dysregulation.

I am presenting this case study from the perspective of contemporary sex therapy which offers treatment of a variety of disorders (mental and sexual) with specific training as it relates to sex, sexuality and gender. The underpinning of contemporary sex therapy is the explicit valuation of sex and sexuality as one of many cornerstones to mental health, but certainly one that is most often sublimated and repressed in service to greater ego functioning. I will be examining two major themes in this case: (1) repetition compulsion as a way for the client to access his well of pain from the abuse he suffered and (2) dissociated female parts as a way to remain loyal to his family of origin by avoiding rage (secondary emotion) from not just the abuse, but the betrayal of his traumatized and addicted mother who was unable to provide him adequate comfort and protection. Both positions allow the Benny to maintain loyalty to his family of origin allowing him to avoid confronting the attachment ruptures and consequent disappointment, terror, betrayal, grief, and shame that have prevented him until now to heal his sexual abuse. The reader will see as trust develops with this female therapist, the client is able to begin to heal the dissociated selves which releases him from the tyranny of shame and guilt embedded not just in his catholic upbringing, but the social stigma of being kinky. He comes to peaceful terms with a loving god and is able to consider what is possible for him as he redefines the narrative of his life and his recovery. Whether he chooses integration or negotiated cooperation among the alters in his system, he can begin to consider what and how he wants to define his sexuality. The client understands that alters refers to the fixed emotional parts related to the traumas he experienced and in his case, there are several alters, each of whom developed in response to the trauma to meet a need for the larger system. In cases of structural dissociation, the term "system" refers to the internal psychological landscape in which the client experiences and also presents to others externally. As he tells the truth of his abuse, he dismantles the previously related debilitating and paralyzing emotions he has long suppressed and delegated to his female alters, then he can begin to dismantle and rebuild the sexual script he carries linking pleasure and pain and decide for himself if and how he wants to pursue a sober, recovered adult relationship to his kink sexuality.

Clinician Positionality

This case offered an opportunity for me to combine my clinical skills from working with dually diagnosed (Serious and Persistent Mental Illness (SPMI) and Substance Use) homeless adults in NYC, supervision and training of peer specialists who are consumer/survivors/ex-patients of the mental health system (CSXs) in a progressive mental health agency, severely traumatized children and adolescents in foster care, domestic violence intervention for both perpetrators and survivors, previous long term work with two DID clients and most recently sex therapy with erotically marginalized people in a small, rural, mostly white working class New England town.

I came of age in New York City as a young, white, fat-positive, feminist lesbian and was involved in the gay and lesbian liberation movement of the mid-late 1980s, as well as AIDS and pro-choice activism. It was during this time that I discovered my own kinky, non-monogamous queer self and began to understand the privilege I carried as a white middle class person, in contrast with the targeted identities of being a kinky fat dyke. I received my MSW from Hunter College and went on to work with children and youth after the Columbine Massacre. I also started working with batterers and began to understand the psychology of the perpetration of violence. I had the privilege of working with leaders in the pro-feminist male movement which sharpened my lens for what could be possible for men's psychologies. This is where I brought together my understanding of mental health oppression and intersectional feminism with interpersonal violence and systemic oppression.

In 2008, I began my sex therapy training and as I matured professionally, I gradually grew more comfortable coming out as an erotically marginalized professional. Living in a small New England town, I was accustomed to seeing clients in the world, so making the leap to come out about my personal life professionally made sense. Having heard too many stories from peers about the paucity of kink competent therapists, I felt called to bring my skills and to bring all of my selves to the table to improve the quality of life for my own communities. This has not been without its challenges, as excellence in clinical work and commitment to ethical practice is both my professional responsibility and my personal value. Through reviewing the NASW Code of Ethics, seeking out peer supervision and reading the controversial work of Ofur Zur, PhD, I have developed my own "Professional Ethics Statement: Policy on Dual Relationships" (Appendix C) for any client with whom I might share social space. I have found this document to be necessary and helpful working in a small town, but also navigating the implications of work with erotically marginalized clients as an erotically marginalized person myself.

Goals for Treatment

It is important to note that most people diagnosed with DID are often misdiagnosed and over-medicated after years and even decades of involvement in the mental health system until they receive an accurate diagnosis and appropriate treatment. Benny has a long history of both inpatient and outpatient involvement and is now working in the field as a paraprofessional, so when he initially contacted me he was very clear about his goals for treatment and his ideal therapist. In fact, when he initially called, he indicated he picked me because of my experience with "sexual abuse, kink, psych, and recovery." His goals for treatment were: "someone to remind me that all of the me's are good," "to finally be honest with a therapist about everything," to work through his "sick relationship with sexual excitement," and "a roadmap for what healing from Childhood Sexual Abuse (CSA) looks like."

Within the first three sessions, I learned he had a harsh judgment towards his sexual desire, could not cry, was terrified that he would act out his sexual fantasies and actually hurt someone, dissociate when asked to be present in his body, and had intrusive thoughts of significant violence and sexual humiliation of women. He reported that he was fearful of his own capacity for violence and carries significant remorse for having attacked his mother when he was a teenager. Upon further exploration, it became evident this "attack" was self-defense, and was the singular event that curtailed years of her physically abusing him. He detailed significant events throughout childhood that can be summarized fairly as having been repeatedly tortured by every adult caregiver and a sibling throughout his youth. He was raised Catholic under the shadow of his father who devalued and mocked his mother's devotion and religious practice. He was deeply conflicted about his religion until he became sober and has since developed a meaningful and active practice. Since beginning treatment, he has begun to reconcile and heal the psychological split among the female and male alters within his system, whereby the female alters are the ones who hold and express emotion and pain and the role of victim and the male alters are the ones who hold the aggression and fear of and desire for sexual violence.

Treatment Context

In working with C/S/X's (consumers/survivors and ex-patients of the mental health system), it is important to acknowledge the number of times they have been asked to tell their story and to recognize that their disclosures of early trauma often go undocumented. The erasure and invalidation experienced by this for clients adds to the resistance and distrust of professionals. With any marginalized social group (e.g. People of Color [PoC], queer, working class, and/or erotically marginalized folks, etc.), it is important to anticipate a certain distrust of professionals because of the sensitivity to and impact of systemic inequities each group experiences. Consequently, history taking is often experienced as an enactment of a power dynamic. Benny confirmed this in his exasperation as he recounted stories of evaluations where he would share intimate details of his abuse only to end up feeling re-traumatized by the repetition without intervention he experienced. It was clear to me, given the level of sophistication of his presentation at intake and his histories as a trauma survivor, a C/S/X and as a possibly erotically marginalized person that to do an extensive historical biopsychosocial history could re-enact this familiar power dynamic. Instead, I chose to follow his lead, tracking his presentation as part of my assessment, with the goal to rule out diagnoses he historically had been given. I made explicit to Benny my decision not to do a formal intake as a way of setting a different tone for the therapeutic engagement that centered and prioritized his narrative, highlighting his capacities and strengths organically and authentically, and lastly, validating and responding to the gains he had previously made in prior treatment relationships and external supports (e.g. 12 step traditions, sponsor, church, and employment) which were evident in his presentation. Additionally, trauma informed practice dictates awareness of and mechanisms to safeguard re-enacting a quid pro quo dynamic that mimics abusive dynamics that these kinds of clients routinely experience (e.g. not requiring anything of Benny in order to get help). Furthermore, trauma informed practice requires the clinician to allow the client to maintain control and set pace of disclosure as a contradiction to the powerlessness they experienced at the time of the initial trauma, which empowers them and builds trust developmentally. This choice does require the therapist to have capacity to tolerate not knowing, to listen carefully for what is and is not verbalized and to be able to track the narrative how and as it unfolds. It also requires the clinician to be able to identify, connect and make meaning of discreet disclosures and to use informed consent consistently throughout treatment.

My experience working with erotically marginalized folks includes many young adults who live their lives embedded in social media and a variety of electronic communications. In our current world, relationships transcend real time. Biopsychosocial histories now include inquiry into client's online relationships in addition to their real-time relationships. Especially with neurodivergent young people and those who are aromantic and asexual, who seek online affinity as a lifesaving intervention, online relationships gain greater value. People morph with technology and technology morphs people. Certainly, there is a plethora of new theories and analysis of how all of this is changing humanity, psychology, and relationships. My experience working in this population is that it is necessary to have both HIPPA compliant platforms for these communications, as well as informed consent and appropriate written authorizations to allow for the kind of communications many of these clients are asking for.

In working with Benny, it became clear quickly that he needed to be able to communicate outside of session. Initially I suggested he carry a journal or log so that he could track who is communicating what with me, but he expressed distrust of himself to keep track of a notebook and also reported significant reliance on his phone for all of his other communications. I reviewed my Policy and Procedures with him, sharing the HIPPA compliant platforms I use for e-mail, as well as talking with him about potential risks with e-mailing me. He understood from our conversation that my responses to him would be encrypted by my e-mail provider, but his e-mails to me could not be protected.

Assessment

Initially Benny indicated that he had altered states, that he heard voices and that they were outside his head. He said, "I hate the word hallucination because it makes it sound like you are not telling the truth." This made me suspect that like most SPMI adults, his trauma history had not been identified and he likely experienced dissociative symptoms which would take time to discover. It is important to note, that while he had many gains from past treatment, he reported that he never told any one therapist everything. Initially, I did not know if this was because he was highly compartmentalized, dissociative, or just treatment savvy from years of being in the mental health system and successfully manipulating treatment providers to avoid dealing with the primary emotions of pain and grief from his sexual abuse. He reported deep distrust for women, growing up in a family where sex role stereotypes dictated men were expected to hurt you, but women's work was to protect you.

His mother, who was a victim of his father's severe domestic violence and spent Benny's first 14 years in and out of mental health institutions and alcohol and drug rehabilitation, was unable to protect him and would also beat him.

He reported he always had a part of him "that understood her," which I suspected was the part of him who, like her, was also being victimized by his father. I suspected that part of her physical abuse of Benny was because she identified with him, as a co-victim; but because he was male, she may have seen his father in him and felt some sense of empowerment or reparation by abusing him.

Within the system, Benny identified two alters: a 6 year old girl (Princess) and a 14 year old boy (Frankie). Princess holds the sexual abuse memories and keeps Benny connected to his dad and siblings. She often takes over driving and he loses time and finds himself at his Dad's house and in a conflict. Frankie will come out to deal with conflicts, he is able to show anger, but was also the one who discovered drugs as a way of keeping Princess quiet. Frankie hates Princess and is sometimes the one who starts watching violent porn as a way of making her go away. Mostly, Benny will show up pretty quickly and kick Frankie out because he is concerned Frankie will cause trouble and make him relapse. Relapsing is not an option now that Benny is 6 years sober and has done all his step work. Benny feels shame and guilt over the pleasure he gets from imagining himself as the Dominant. He reports he cannot orgasm until the female submissive is crying. He reports when Princess has been out a lot, he will masturbate compulsively to make her go away, sometimes lending to genital abrasions.

Treatment Themes

Dissociated Female Selves

When memories started to surface for Benny about the violent rapes by his father, he struggled with persistent arousal and his emotional reaction to it. He reported increase in self-harm during this time, as his best effort to manage the guilt and betrayal he experienced due to the physiological arousal.

Initially, Benny reported significant distress related to being in Princess "when things get too real or too personal Princess calls the shots. I can put down that part of myself when inflicting physical (and maybe emotional pain)." Getting Benny to develop a protective stance towards Princess was critical to stopping the repetition compulsion which was fueling the emotional dysregulation. Benny writes, "[Frankie]... wants to pound and gag her into submission." As Benny was able to recognize that harming Princess was re-enacting the abuse dynamics, he became horrified and struggled with how to inhabit a more protective stance towards her. Initially, his impulse was to make her go away by self-harm or watching BDSM porn which caused him significant guilt given his religion.

The work became helping him to understand why Princess was born, what her function was to the system and how to respond to her when she is distressed without re-enacting abuse. I learned that Princess is the first (known to date) alter who was born to hold and manage the feelings and memories of the sexual abuse. She was silent in the system until a few months into treatment when Benny experienced an "enhanced patdown with TSA" (likely targeted because of his olive complexion) and he began having intrusive memories, hyperarousal and emotional dysregulation. Benny reported seven incidents during this phase of treatment of superficial cutting, many incidents of head punching, and genital abrasions from compulsive masturbation. I worked with him on containment, self-soothing, distraction, redirection, and grounding techniques from DBT skills work he had done in the past. It became clear though that in order to manage the self-harm, I needed to help Benny see how the way he dissociated was replicating the misogynistic culture of his family and that the way he would begin to learn to manage Princess's emotional dysregulation would be to develop a protective and compassionate role towards her rather than blaming and punishing her when she came out and took over. Both Benny and Frankie blame Princess for the sexual abuse, they report she kept seeking it out because she is "weak and needy." When Frankie masturbates she comes out and he reports the only way to make her go back in so he can get the release the system needs is to scare her. I knew Benny was making progress when Princess e-mailed me directly to ask me to help make Benny stop being mean to her. As Princess develops strong maternal transference to me, Benny grows more conflicted. Princess reports she wants to be physically close to me, but this terrifies Benny because he finds that threatening and scary to be so physically close to a woman. Benny and Princess start bringing more conflict into treatment, Benny feels Princess is pushing him before he is ready. This period of treatment is marked by Benny testing boundaries, frequent crisis calls, need for enhanced DBT skill building, and installation of hope as I earned his trust. Success occurs as Benny is able to develop more compassion for Princess from a dissociated female self to viewing her as the part of him who was sexually abused.

Communication, Consent, and Boundaries with Therapist and between Alters

Correspondence outside of session has been instrumental in tracking communication between alters, but also in allowing for different kinds of disclosures, some of which are only possible through a less intimate forum like e-mails, text or letter writing. It has been very helpful for Benny to be able to refer back to my responses over time, especially when the need for repetition is required, as is the case with the treatment of complex trauma and structural dissociation because alters can act independent and without the knowledge of each other. A common symptom of DID is "lost time." The frequent e-mailing has allowed Benny to track his own disclosures and those of his alters to me.

In one e-mail Benny writes, "I am going to get better at taking your suggestions. I would like to be able to lie down on the floor and or be able not to have to look at you to do some of this work." In addition to introducing the importance of ongoing feedback to me at the beginning of treatment, I let him know how much I appreciated his feedback when he did start to give it to me. Additionally, I let him know that one measure of progress would be when he could give me feedback in the moment in person as he was feeling it. This permission made it possible for Princess to introduce herself. She writes, "I am happy I can talk with you. I was afraid, but it was good." A few days later, Benny writes, "So I don't know how I feel about Princess part emailing you . . . maybe she will give me less trouble if she can talk to you." These two communications helped to establish (1) a vehicle to introduce alters who otherwise were not yet ready to meet me in person, but who had been watching, (2) a way to develop intimacy and trust with a female caretaker by measuring how I responded to each of the alters in writing to see if that was consistent with in-person communications, (3) a way for Benny to give me feedback and direction as to best ways to help him manage Princess, and (4) begin to establish a way for the alters to track and review who has shared what with this therapist which is instrumental in the early treatment of DID.

Repetition Compulsion vs. Harm Reduction

Benny spoke about his use of violent pornography where a male Dominant is being sexually sadistic to a female submissive and that he can orgasm by seeing the female submissive cry. He expressed deep shame about this and fear that he was "sick." After assessing that he was watching fictionalized representations of consensual non-consent with adult women and not surfing the dark web or watching porn involving minors, I offered the re-frame for him that any way he could reclaim his sexuality, in ways that felt good, were acceptable. I told him that if he was watching porn that made him feel more shame or guilt or that frightened him that I discouraged him not to watch that so as not to exacerbate those feelings. When I offered the permission that the PLISSIT model directs us to use, he cried in relief.

Benny's alter, Frankie, reported significant sexual acting out prior to getting sober and Benny announced early in treatment he was not going to "even go near dating" because he was concerned about acting out. In evaluating his concern about acting out on his sexual sadism, I assessed that he had sufficient involvement of his super-ego and few indicators of psychological sadism – both of which were evident and consistent in his self-reports that he was concerned about ever acting out his sexual fantasies. He reported that when he is with younger female relatives, that he will not hug them or be physically affectionate because he is frightened of his fantasies and that he is not comfortable explaining why. He laughs saying that he can "just chalk it up to the distant male figures in his family" and the way sexism is performed, always demarcating the gender differences in terms of sex role stereotyping (e.g. men work outside the home, women work inside the home). He writes, "I end up hating myself for these feelings – all of these things – hating my mom and the way I have been used made me sick in confusing sex, violence and power and what is arousing and satisfying."

Initially, Benny wanted to stop all negative behaviors (e.g. self-harm, suicidality, and sexual sadism) and it was important to help him not deny, block or resist these behaviors but to accept them as parts of him that he can learn to channel in consensual and the least harmful ways over time. He writes to me that he is worried that Princess sought out the sexual abuse as comfort in a tortured world and as a result, it "makes me feel like I invited evil in and it has become a part of me." The idea of embracing the hated parts as a way of integrating and then managing them was a familiar concept from his early recovery years when he had to find appreciation for why he used in the first place. Making peace with these negative parts of himself was crucial in building awareness of how he was repeating harmful patterns of behavior and developing cooperation among the alters.

He talked about all the "fucked up sex" he had as a young adult, when Frankie was using and selling drugs and how many regrets he had about how he avoided intimacy and sought out anonymous sex, I suggested in time we could unpack the parts where he needed to make amends. He laughed saying "those people are long gone," and I offered that use of narrative therapy might be helpful (much like he may have done in early substance abuse recovery) that he could write a letter to his younger self or to the people he remembers with the frame that he was trying to make sense of his complicated history, a history he was decades away from understanding and to forgive himself, as anything he did to survive, to literally stay alive, was good, because he is still here to finally do this work. Though he is still many months away from doing this piece of the work, he was relieved by the alternate framing I offered and cried in discovering this option.

Contradicting the Gender Role Stereotypes and Confronting the Internalized Misogyny as Repair for Dissociation

Both Frankie and Benny saw Princess as the trouble maker, the manipulative needy dissociated female part and they joined each other in devaluing her vulnerability, blaming her for eliciting the sexual abuse Benny's body suffered. Splitting off the victimized self into a female alter was what made it possible for Benny to survive. By seeing female as the bad one, the one who seduced or provoked the abuse, the male parts could see themselves as superior, needing to control the female parts, a model that Benny grew up with watching his father's toxic masculinity and his domestic violence against Benny's mother.

Benny began to develop compassion for Princess as more difficult feelings emerged, "It is hard for me not to get mad or resentful of how debilitating it is to be subject to my princess childlike fears and dreams and reasoning." I introduced the idea of how he can choose to be "a good man" and that he didn't have to participate in the toxic masculinity his dad and maternal grandfather modeled for him, that he could respect women and girls and maybe one day tolerate being loved by one. He began to unpack the gender role stereotypes his family was so immersed in, blaming women and girls for having difficult emotions, whilst secretly harming them which generated the difficult emotions originally. He writes "how do I embrace this princess while I hate what happened to her? I don't want to be so fucked up – to be that princess is so fucked up. To be me is so fucked up."

Communication with Support (e.g. Sponsor)

Benny came to treatment at the support, direction and insistence of his NA sponsor, who in many ways, is quite exceptional. It was evident early on that Benny was experiencing a reparative relationship with his male sponsor because of how the sponsor inhabited his own masculinity. The sponsor led with vulnerability, compassion and also shared the same Catholic upbringing and spirituality that is so important to Benny in his recovery. Furthermore, the male sponsor, unlike Benny's father, embraced the concept of the loving, compassionate and forgiving god. It became clear that it was possible for Benny to work with a female therapist after he had re-worked a paternal relationship with his sponsor.

Benny reported the sponsor was pushing him to work on his sexual abuse and to work with a female therapist to help him heal his distrust of women. Benny was clearly heterosexual, without evidence of internalized homophobia, which I would expect more likely possible for many male survivors of molestation and rape. Benny indicated that his mother was a devout Catholic, prayed the rosary and taught Benny how to believe in God, but through the years of his abuse, he lost faith in God. He reported his father always mocked God. This split between his mother and father in their religious and spiritual orientations is also expressed in dissociated male and female parts that comprised Benny. He delegated the vulnerable, affect-filled regressed aspects to the female alter and the sadistic, impulsive, independent, devaluing aspects to the male alter. As Benny healed, telling the truth of his experience and beginning to integrate with Princess, one of the single most important acts was for Benny to find his way back to his belief in a loving God, which in many ways set the stage for repair with his mother or the female caretaker he experienced in the female therapist. For Benny, having a strong alliance and necessary communication and coordination between myself and his Sponsor allowed him to begin to master the developmental tasks as it related to his male and female parental figures. Benny wrote to myself and his Sponsor often, reporting deep gratitude for our help, "thank you both for caring about me, for knowing me and not hating me, and being able to help me."

Summary of Treatment

I have gratitude to the editors for giving me the opportunity to begin to articulate the complexity and success of the work I have done with this client. It has been very challenging, because the case has evolved so rapidly. When I first contracted to write about this case, it was not yet clear that Benny's diagnosis was DID and the disclosures of alters and introduction of Princess and Frankie happened within the first month of writing. Benny reported, "I am not forcing this stuff – it is like it is forcing me . . . As of today, Princess and Benny are starting to integrate, Princess needing to grow up and Benny needing to love that little girl. It is not something I was looking for to happen and have had very mixed feelings, but have decided to quit trying to block it and to instead embrace it."

As Benny began to allow the alters more in person contact, acknowledging the switching and beginning to map out the system, he presented with more affect regulation and stability, as well as more reported communication between the alters and more reflection about our work together. In particular, he begins to set limits that indicate his new skill of pacing and improved impulse control. His ability to put the sexual issues on hold indicates that he is getting closer to mastering the work on integration around the alters and is also tracking content better. "I just want to give masturbation a rest, it is too complicated. I would like to work on telling, pieces and the anger more so than the sex." Being able to accept his newly forming boundaries and support him in pacing the acceptance of his sexual script and reclaim and redefine meaning of what turns him on is key to developing his adult sober sexual self. It is not yet clear at the time of writing this case study if or when it might be useful to consider talking with him about "consensual non consent kinky sexual behavior." I think more needs to be understood at this time about the alters and the extent of integration he will accomplish. It is certainly noted as an option if and when Benny is feeling more finished with the active sexual abuse recovery phase.

As I reflect on the work with Benny, I can see clearly why it made sense to attempt to articulate it. For me, this offered a culmination and application of my own professional experiences over the past 27 years. This was the kind of client I worked for almost three decades to learn to help.

Principle Nine

BUILD A COMMUNITY OF COLLEAGUES

Introduction

When working with erotically marginalized clients, we are working with people who are often on the fringes of society, which can reproduce an experience of feeling or being professionally marginalized. As already outlined in this text, some clinicians who work with erotically marginalized clients may also identify as erotically marginalized themselves, and those identities might overlap or diverge from those of our clients. It feels critical to our clinical work to have safe spaces both personally and professionally to get support, supervision, affirmation, and be understood without extensive explanation or scrutiny.

As outlined in Principle Seven, we encourage and support our clients to incorporate existing families and communities in their process and to actively cultivate new supports. In this principle, we are asking clinicians to enact this principle for themselves, to centralize seeking their own supports to not only bolster us personally, but also professionally. Clients can sense our experience whether it is named or not and being isolated ourselves reproduces the isolation our clients might be experiencing in the clinical context. Conversely, if we have an extended network of providers with whom we have a relationship and trust, clients can benefit from that both overtly and subtly.

Therapeutic Networks

Many of our colleagues who work with erotically marginalized clients describe themselves as "the only one." Sometimes this is the only one doing that work in their agency and sometimes they are the only one doing that work in their town. In our own work we noticed a parallel process between our experiences as therapists working with erotically marginalized clients and our client's experiences. Similarities included being tokenized and asked to provide education or other free labor, a feeling of isolation, and a pressure to perform as a model minority to justify and prove worth (either professionally or personally). Principle Nine is an invitation for us, as therapists who work with erotically marginalized clients, to step out of this dynamic and model another possibility for our clients. If we are feeling like it is us against the world, our clients will feel that as well. If we feel connected and grounded in our professional and personal communities, we embody a vision for what is possible.

Creating a community of colleague who work with erotically marginalized clients is work, and we believe that it is important to name that this is in itself additional labor that is necessary for us to do the important work that we do. It can be more difficult to connect with other clinicians and providers based on geographical location as well. Some suggestions for building your community of colleagues:

- Join a professional organization that feels consistent with your work.
- Find and reach out to individual sex therapists who are doing similar work. (Damon and Shannon met after Damon heard Shannon present at a conference and thought to himself, "That is someone I need to know. We think about our work the same way.")
- Use social media to connect with other clinicians nationally.
- Participate in a training or educational program that provides opportunities to build connections with others.
- Use your personal networks to identify other sex therapists doing similar work.
- Read blogs or books that affirm your positionality and work.
- Seek out a supervisor who supports your positionality and work. (This could even be someone in another city or country.)
- Reach out to the authors of the articles that you've read that you feel connected and aligned with.
- Start a LinkedIn, Facebook, or Google Group, or some other social media connecting modality for other sex therapists who are working with erotically marginalized clients.
- Attend a sexuality or sex therapy related conference.

Interdisciplinary Collaboration

In addition to seeking out support and cultivating networks of fellow sex therapists who are working with erotically marginalized clients, it is also imperative to have an extended network of support and referral sources of interdisciplinary providers. This can include medical professionals, body workers, alternative health practitioners, lawyers, personal trainers, gyms, spiritual communities, and 12-step meetings. Our clients' experience of erotic marginalization extends outside of our therapy office and having a knowledge of what referrals in your community will feel safer is a way we can support our clients. It also offers us other providers to connect with who we know are going to be affirming about the work we are doing.

Vignette

Harper was a 33-year-old, Native American, cisgender, queer and kinky identified male. He was involved in BDSM, and enjoyed being dominated and engaging in needle play with his various play partners. We had been working together in individual therapy for about 6 months, mostly working on his anxiety management. His sexual practices come up in context in our work, but they were not the center of his concerns, he sought me out because it felt vital for him to see a therapist who would neither pathologize him based on his sexual practices, or assume that his identity or practices had anything to do with his current concerns. We had been working on his anxiety related to the traumatic loss of his mother and unpacking the fear he had that was associated with the current political climate, especially the voracious racism that had exploded nationally and acutely in our rural area. We began to discuss the possibility of medications, which he had been hesitant to explore because he felt like he should be able to "rationalize his way out of this." We worked together to create a narrative that it can be just as courageous to ask for support when you need it, as it can be to overcome hardship. I asked him if he currently had a medical provider that he could talk to about anti-anxiety medications, because I thought that working with someone that he had a relationship with might ease the encounter. He replied, "Oh no, I haven't seen a doctor in over five years." This opened up new territory, he shared that he hadn't seen a medical professional since about a year after he got involved in BDSM because he had had a disturbing experience. He explained that he went to see a new doctor in the metropolitan area he was living in at the time, who required that he have a physical before engaging in treatment. During the physical, the doctor saw his bruises and needle marks from a recent play party he had attended and questioned him extensively about where they had come from. The doctor's tone was clear, he did not approve and did not think that Harper was being honest that these markings had come from a consensual experience. He was so disturbed by the doctor's treatment of his body that he left the office and swore off doctors except in the case of an emergency. We spent the rest of the session unpacking this event, and creating language for the fact that he felt marginalized and pathologized by this provider. I mentioned at the end of session that I had names of several providers that we could discuss next time, if he felt open to it. In between that session and the next, I called one provider whose personal cell phone number I had, and emailed another to ask them both for their explicit stance on working with folks who identify as kinky and engaged in BDSM, specifically needle play and domination, and both reassured me that they used full consent models in their practice and would be highly respectful of any individual in their care. The next session, Harper returned and shared that he would like to discuss "those doctors" that I had mentioned, but that he was not at all sure he would follow through. I shared the research I had done and the feedback I had received and he was visibly surprised that I had done

(continued)

(continued)

that work on his behalf and that they had both responded in the way that they did. This instance of being able to advocate and act on behalf of my client was a relief for him, but it also provided support for my own clinical work. Being able to easily and comfortably connect with colleagues that I trust makes my work not only more effective, but also more satisfying.

The following organizations can be helpful resources. This is not meant to be an exhaustive list. We encourage clinicians to do further research to find organizations in your area.

The American Association of Sex Educators, Counselors and Therapists (AASECT)

www.aasect.org

AASECT is the certifying body for all sex therapists and counselors. They offer an annual conference.

Altsex Conference

altsexnycconference.org

Annual conference focused on work with erotically marginalized clients.

The Asexual Visibility and Education Network (AVEN)

www.asexuality.org/

Online community and resources about asexuality.

The Eulenspiegel Society (TES)

www.tes.org/

Nonprofit BDSM/Leather/Fetish group dedicated to social interaction, educational exchange and ever-changing diversity of that community.

FetLife

https://fetlife.com/

Online Social Network for the BDSM, Fetish and Kinky Community.

Manhattan Alternative

www.manhattanalternative.com/

Network of therapists in NYC who work with Erotically Marginalized Clients.

National Coalition for Sexual Freedom (NCSF)

www.ncsfreedom.org

Organization protecting the rights of erotically marginalized people – houses the Kink Aware Professionals (KAP) Directory.

National Queer & Trans Therapists of Color Network

www.nqttcn.com

Network of therapists working with erotically marginalized clients of color.

Philadelphia Trans Wellness Conference

www.mazzonicenter.org/trans-wellness

Annual conference focused on trans wellness, includes a professional track for therapists.

Sex Down South Conference

www.sexdownsouth.com

Annual conference focused on creating a safe space to explore sex and sexuality that centers the voices of women of color, trans* and gender non-conforming folks, sex workers, queer people, and differently-abled individuals.

The World Professional Organization for Transgender Health (WPATH)

www.wpath.org

Professional and educational organization focused on transgender health, opportunities for networking, offers an annual conference.

Woodhull Freedom Foundation

www.woodhullfoundation.org/

Human rights organization that works full-time to affirm and protect sexual freedom as a fundamental human right, hosts an annual conference.

Boundaries

For erotically marginalized sex therapists working with erotically marginalized clients, there is an additional challenge or need to clarify the separation between personal and professional boundaries and it is even more critical to make choices that support both your clients and yourself. Working within your community is like working in a small town. Some therapists who live in small towns decide to commute to the next town over, which can be an empowering decision to make. When you are working within your own marginalized community, you sometimes lack the opportunity to opt out, which can be quite challenging and also bring incredible rewards. We encourage therapists to consider the choice carefully and clarify for themselves their rationale for working with clients who are in their own community.

Vignette

Howard stated that he had found me online and wanted to talk about providing sex therapy to clients involved in BDSM in his area. Specifically, he participated in the BDSM community and was thinking ahead about potential dual relationships with clients and how to navigate them. Howard had a successful private practice that he had grown over the last ten years, but he had never specifically worked with clients involved in BDSM. I was curious about what had shifted for Howard to want to include this population in his professional work. During our first supervision session Howard discussed his participation in BDSM and how it felt both exciting and fulfilling. Although it was something he had thought about for a long time, he was new to his local BDSM community and had only recently began participating in events. As I learned more about his personal life, professional work, and his concerns about dual relationships, I became curious about why he wanted to make this professional change. Howard explained that there were few therapists who were BDSM and kink competent in his area and he wanted to provide a needed service. He also was excited to work with a clientele that he felt connected to. We talked about other professional/personal dual relationships in his life and learned that there were very few. Howard began to muse out loud about what had drawn him to want to begin to work with clients involved in BDSM and what it might be like to have dual relationships that connected his participation in BDSM community and his clinical practice. During our conversation he decided that for now it felt more comfortable to keep the two worlds separate and that he would revisit his decision in a year after having more of his own personal experiences in the BDSM community. We also talked about what he could do instead to fulfill his wish for more people participating in BDSM to have competent sex therapy available to them and he decided to reach out to other therapist in his area to develop a more robust referral list of sex therapists he knew were kink and BDSM competent.

Supervision

Based on best practices (Brashears, 1995; Saari, 2012) and our personal experience we encourage all sex therapists, regardless of the length of time that they have spent in the field, to engage regularly in supervision with one or more other clinicians. In their discussion about becoming a kink-aware sexuality professional Pillai-Friedman, Pollitt, and Castaldo (2014) outline a three-prong approach that includes didactic training, Sexual Attitude Reassment (SAR) training, and supervision to help clients navigate a path that may include, "still-taboo subculture that delves into intense physical sensations and emotionally powerful role play" (2014, p. 206). The authors note that supervision provides clinicians competence to work with BDSM practicing clients including "countertransference issues, and ethical concerns about professional competence" (p. 205) that go beyond just learning terminology or interventions. We have found supervision to have the added component of community building among colleagues and avoiding professional isolation that may parallel the isolation our clients often feel.

In the preface of this book we talked about how forming a community together has supported our work with erotically marginalized communities. Through this process it was clear to us the creating a community of colleagues is not just about self-care or an additional task to be dealt with after we have seen all of our clients. We believe that it is foundational to work as sex therapists with erotically marginalized clients. The connections that we form with other therapists and providers support all of the other work that we do. Whether you are a seasoned therapist or just starting out we encourage you to prioritize forming your own community of colleagues as we all continue to learn and grow from each other and our work.

Beginnings

This final principle brings us to the conclusion of this work, as it simultaneously reminds us of our beginnings, that we, the editors, are three therapists working individually, but in connection with one another, to our case contributors and to the larger national and international network of therapists working with erotically marginalized clients. We hope that these principles are ultimately a beginning, a starting out point, to encourage you to think deeply about the clients you serve and the work you are invested in and how to work with erotically marginalized clients with humility, confidence and openness. Throughout the process of writing this book, the language around serving erotically marginalized clients has grown and shifted, new articles and books have been published and we have had the opportunity to engage in many exciting and inspiring conversations that push the limits of our understanding and stretch our capacities to do this work. We hope that you, the reader, find inspiration and new ideas in these principles and cases, that you are fed and challenged, and that you also fill in the gaps in this work with your own ideas and experiences as we build together a rich landscape of resources to support erotically marginalized communities.

Key Clinical Points

- It is critical for therapists working with erotically marginalized clients to seek out an extended network of therapists working with the same population to reduce isolation and gain more support and affirmation.
- Therapists can also build an extensive referral network of interdisciplinary providers who work competently and ethically with erotically marginalized people.
- Get to know local, (inter)national and online organizations that support work with erotically marginalized clients.

References

Brashears, F. (1995). Supervision as social work practice: A reconceptualization. *National Association of Social Workers, 40*(5), 692–699.

Saari, C. (2012). The process of learning in clinical social work. *Smith College Studies in Social Work, 60*(1), 35–49. doi: 10.1080/00377317.2012.693027

Pillai-Friedman, S., Pollitt, J. L., & Castaldo, A. (2014). Becoming kink-aware – a necessity for sexuality professionals. *Sexual and Relationship Therapy, 30*(2), 196–210. doi: 10.1080/14681994.2014.975681

GLOSSARY

Defining Erotically Marginalized Identities

Ellie K. Lipton

Holding that language is culture and context dependent, this glossary attempts to convey that language around erotically marginalized identities can have powerful cultural, communal, and personal meanings. These meanings shift over time, largely depending on who has power to create and use language. Language, specifically around identity, has the power to both liberate and oppress. As Ritchie and Barker (2006) note, "Discursive possibilities thus construct but also *constrain* meaning" (p. 584). While it would be a fallacy to expect any of these definitions to neatly encapsulate every person's lived experience who uses this particular language, or to expect these definitions to remain fixed throughout time, this glossary aims to encourage ongoing humility, curiosity, and critical thought around language impacting erotically marginalized clients.

Biological and Designated Sex

Biological sex

Biological sex "refers to one's body – the physiological and anatomical characteristics of maleness and femaleness with which a person is born or that develop with physical maturity" (Shlasko, 2014, p. 28). The markers of biological sex include chromosomes, secondary sex characteristics, genitalia, and hormone levels (Hock, 2012, Singh & Dickey, 2017, Shlasko, 2014). A dangerous yet prevailing Western assumption is that the gender we are assigned at birth is reflective of our biological sex, which in turn should match our gender identity (Nanda, 2000).

Designated sex at birth/sex assigned at birth

At birth, each of us is assigned to a sex category based on genitalia. This is almost exclusively female or male, and is designated on our birth certificate. As we understand biological sex to be more complex than simply one's genitalia (including chromosomes, hormone levels, and secondary sex characteristics), we can see that this immediate sex designation does not capture the broader picture of a person's biological sex, as it excludes intersex identities. Further, sex assigned at birth does not equate with gender identity, which is a felt sense and internal identity. While some people's gender identity matches their sex assigned at birth, this is not always the case. Individuals designated/assigned female at birth often use the acronyms of DFAB or AFAB, while individuals designated/assigned male at birth often use the acronyms of DMAB or AMAB.

Intersex

Intersex is a broad term encompassing a variety of conditions describing sexual anatomy that does not fit Western definitions of female or male (Hird, 2008). An estimated 1.7% of humans are intersex, around the same number as have red hair (Hilda, 2015). Only around half of the intersex conditions that are known are detectable by looking at a person's genitalia (American Psychological Association, 2006). Examples of the conditions include adrenal hyperplasia, androgen insensitivity syndrome, Klinefelter syndrome, and progestin induced virilization (Hird, 2008). Intersex conditions may show up at, or after, birth, and have historically been medicalized and pathologized in the West. Kafer (2013) describes how "Children born intersexed or with 'ambiguous' genitalia have faced all kinds of surgical interventions intended to normalize them without regard to their pain, sense of self, or relation to their bodies" (p. 197). Sex therapists need to first be aware of intersex as a sex category, as well as work to understand how dominant discourses around sex and identity impact intersex individuals. Intersex individuals overwhelmingly face pathologization; as Lindahl (2018, para. 1) writes, "To be born intersex is to experience violence at the hands of a medical system determined to erase you, literally cutting your intersex parts away for the sake of 'normalcy.'" Sex therapists should use intersex-inclusive language, which includes eschewing gendered language for body parts.

Gender Identity and Expression

Gender identity

Gender identity is an individual's "felt sense of themselves in terms of their gender" (Singh & Dickey, 2017, p. 5). It is a psychological experience that is deeply personal and unobservable from looking at someone. Gender identity can change over time (Shlasko, 2014) and is influenced by structural and cultural forces (binaohan, 2014; Nanda, 2000). Gender identity cannot be understood "without locating the identity in a larger global context" (binaohan, 2014, p. 3).

Gender expression

Gender expression refers to the way an individual expresses, or performs, their gender identity. It can include physical appearance such as attire, hairstyle, body modifications as well as mannerisms and communication patterns (Singh & Dickey, 2017, Shlasko, 2014). Expression is also linked to feelings of safety. How someone expresses their gender is impacted by intersecting identities, and how safe or unsafe authentic expression may be. In particular, for people who identify as feminine and were assigned male at birth, safety concerns can significantly impact gender expression.

Transgender (sometimes shortened to Trans)

Transgender is broadly understood to encompass "anyone whose *gender identity* and/or *gender expression* differs significantly from what is expected of them in their culture based on their *sex assigned at birth*" (Shlasko, 2014, p. 1). Trans identities have been highly pathologized in the West, and the history of pathologization can be traced to colonization (binahoah, 2014; Zevallos, 2013). Some western narratives attempt to essentialize a singular trans experience. This is dangerous, erasive, and highly problematic. There is not a singular trans experience; as Sanger (2008, p. 84) writes,

> *Not all trans people are driven by a desire to conform to the other side of the gender binary, with increasing numbers of people problematizing the confines of current understandings of gender and sexuality and attempting to carve out a space for themselves beyond restrictive boundaries.*

Sex therapists can harm trans people by making these same assumptions, and thinking that there is a singular trans narrative.

Cisgender

"Cis" is a Latin prefix meaning "in line with." To be cisgender is to have one's gender identity match one's designated sex at birth (Singh & Dickey, 2017; Tilsen, 2013). Cisgender can also be understood as not transgender (Shlasko, 2014; Tilsen, 2013). Naming cisgender identities, rather than only naming transgender or nonbinary identities, is an important part of challenging "the dominant practice of naming only identities that occupy marginalized positions" (Tilsen, 2013, p. 18). Not naming dominantly held identities (e.g. whiteness, heterosexuality, able-bodieness) perpetuates dangerous assumptions and externalizable messages that these dominant identities are normal or preferable to all other identities. It is important that sex therapists are considering the experience of gender for all individuals – including cisgender individuals. This "makes visible the experience of gender for everyone" (Tilsen, 2013, p. 18).

Nonbinary (sometimes written as non-binary or non binary)

A nonbinary identity is a gender that is outside of, or encompasses more than, the female-male or woman-man gender binary. Nonbinary individuals often use pronouns such as they/them/theirs, xe/xem/xyrs, ze/hir/hirs, or other gender inclusive pronouns. Nonbinary identities are not new:

> *It is important to recognize that the existence of nonbinary identities is not a new, modern, or solely Western phenomenon. Reducing gender into two binary categories is an act of colonization and is firmly rooted in a history of racial oppression and erasure of indigenous people and/or people of color.*
> *(Sand, Singh, & Rossman, 2017, p. 21).*

Gender neutral

Gender neutral is a gender identity used by people who do not identify as male or female, and experience their gender as neutral (Ehrensaft, 2011).

Agender

Agender is a gender identity used by individuals who don't experience themselves as having a gender. Agender is occasionally used interchangeably with null-gender, non-genders, or genderless (Sand, Singh, & Rossman, 2017).

Genderqueer

Genderqueer is a gender identity that has been used since the mid 1990s, that typically describes a gender that is not woman or man (Moon, 2008; Shlasko, 2014). An individual's gender identity might be simply genderqueer, or might be genderqueer and trans, genderqueer and nonbinary, genderqueer and femme, etc. A 2012 study of 292 individuals who self-identified under the umbrella of transgender found that the majority of participants identified as genderqueer (Kuper, Nussbaum, & Mustanski, 2012). While this study speaks to the prevalence of genderqueer identities, the sample was relatively homogenous with 86.6% of respondents identifying as white.

Gender nonconforming (GNC)

Gender nonconforming is a broad term that typically describes a person whose gender identity and/or expression falls outside of what is typically expected of them, based on their sex assigned at birth and cultural context. For some GNC folks, it also includes a sense that their gender identity does not fully match their sex assigned at birth (Sand, Singh, & Rossman, 2017). Some people who identify as GNC also identify as transgender; other folks who identify as GNC identify as cisgender, some as neither trans or cis. Cisgender and GNC identified folks sometimes have additional queered identities "related to this variance in gender expression (e.g., boi, butch, femme, stud)" (Sand, Singh, & Rossman, 2017, p. 22).

Third Gender

Third gender is a gender identity that is claimed by some individuals who experience their gender as existing outside of the binary of "woman and man" or "female and male" (Namaste, 2000; Sand, Singh, & Rossman, 2017). As Sand, Singh, and Rossman explain, "people who identify as third gender do not usually view themselves as being on the same continuum or spectrum as men and women, but rather as a separate, distinct point" (p. 22).

Two spirit

Two spirit is a gender identity that is a part of Native American culture and history. Two spirit describes a Native American or Indigenous identifying individual who is neither woman or man, but "a transcendence of the two" (Redmiles, 2016, para. 4). It is important to recognize that gender is understood and experienced more fluidly, and as more connected to spirituality in Native American culture and tradition than in dominant American culture (Zevallos, 2013). It is additionally crucial to understand the role of colonization in the erasure of Native gender orientations and identities; "Before the colonization of this land, there were as many as six traditional gender orientation roles among numerous tribes" (Singer, p. 6). It is widely considered to be culturally appropriative for a non-Native individual to claim a two-spirit identity (binaohan, 2014; Redmiles, 2016).

Masculine of center (Masc/MOC)

Masculine of center is a term that describes a connection to the more masculine side of the spectrum between femininity and masculinity (Cole, 2011). It is often, but not exclusively, used by people designated female at birth. This term has become increasingly popular in recent years, particularly amongst people of color (Sand, Singh, & Rossman, 2017). "Some people who identify as MOC also identify as transgender or under the TGNC umbrella, while others consider themselves simply as gender nonconforming (without a TGNC identity)" (Sand, Singh, & Rossman, 2017, p. 23). There are many different ways of identifying and being masculine of center, including stud, boi, tom, and more (Cole, 2011).

Femme

Femme can be experienced as a gender expression and/or a gender identity. Femme refers to the more feminine side of the spectrum of feminine-masculine energies. For many femmes, femme includes a fierceness, reclaiming of feminine power, mixed with softness (Mayor, 2011). While femme can be a gender identity on its own, many folks identify as femme in addition to another gender identity (cisgender, transgender, nonbinary, etc.). Femme invisibility is the idea that others, both inside and outside of the LGBTQ+ communities, often assume heterosexuality of femmes who present along lines of traditional femininity. There is both privilege and oppression in femme invisibility; while being invisible may protect from violence or homophobia in certain spaces, it can also be invalidating and distressing (Dark, 2011). It is important for sex therapists to understand that femmes are also prone to be sexualized in a particular way; "Femmes are the hot object-of-the-masculine gaze lesbians, the female lesbians, and now we bear the burden of those identities rather than the burden of full invisibility" (Dark, 2011, p. 34).

Butch

The word butch is typically used as an adjective to describe a masculine gender expression. The butch label originated in lesbian communities, however people of any sexual orientation may identify as butch. Some people use butch as a noun that describes their gender identities. Butch-identified folks face particular types of oppression stemming from structural cis-heteropatriarchal heteronormativity, that expects women to look, present, and behave in particular feminized ways. As Gomez (2011) writes, a butch's presence says, "'I don't follow your 'women rules,' and 'my life is my own.' That's an immediately dangerous space to occupy" (p. 70). Folks steeped in heteronormativity often expect lesbian or queer-women couples to present in a butch-femme dichotomy, however this is not the reality of the types of partners all butch or all femme folks are attracted to.

Androgyny

Androgyny is a term used by individuals who experience their gender identity as neither, or both, masculine and feminine (Sand, Singh, & Rossman, 2017).

Sexual Orientation and Expression

Categories of sexual orientation change over time and across cultures (Foucault, 1977; Middleton, 2002). Today in the West we generally understand sexual orientation as the romantic and/or sexual attraction that a person has (Shlasko, 2014). While sexual orientation is understood in terms of gender, sexual orientation is different from gender identity and gender expression.

Lesbian

The term lesbian generally connotes a female identified individual who is sexually and romantically attracted to other women. A lesbian sexual orientation may suggest that an individual identifies as a woman (cis or trans), but not exclusively.

Gay

The term gay generally refers to male identified individuals who are sexually and romantically attracted to other men. It is also sometimes used as an umbrella term for anyone who is not straight.

Bisexual

Bisexual (sometimes referred to as "bi") is most commonly used to describe someone who identifies as either female or male, who is attracted to people who identify as both female and male.

Pansexual

The Latin prefix "pan" means "all." Pansexual (sometimes called pan) is a sexual orientation that describes attraction to people of all genders, including people who identify as nonbinary, on the trans spectrum, intersex, cisgender, and all other possible ways of identifying sex/gender.

Queer

Many queer scholars and queer-identified people (Halberstam, 2005; Hodges, 2008; Sand, Singh, & Rossman, 2017) cite the reclaiming of the word "queer," once used as a weapon against those whose sexual practices and gender presentations were outside of a very strict heteronormative gender binary, as an act of opposition and a reclaiming of identity and power. Queer is a refusal to accept binaries and a refusal to be put into boxes. Queer is a transcending of oppressive categories of identity, presentation, and behavior based on race, class, culture, gender, and sexuality. Although "queer" is often used "as an umbrella term for LGBT" (Tilsen, 2013, p. 21), it is important to remember that queer identified individuals often have deeply personal experiences of their queerness. As such, one person's queerness may mean something different than another person's queerness.

Ace-spectrum

Ace-spectrum describes a continuum of identities in which individuals either do not have, or have very limited, sexual and/or romantic attractions and desires. Examples of ace-spectrum identities include gray-asexual and aromantic (O'Brink, 2014).

Asexual

Asexual, sometimes called "ace" or "ase" for short, is an ace-spectrum identity that is perhaps the most visible in popular culture. It describes a sexual orientation in which an individual lacks sexual attraction (O'Brink, 2014).

Demisexual

Demisexual is an ace-spectrum sexual orientation in which a person does not experience sexual attraction to another unless/until forming a strong emotional connection with that person (O'Brink, 2014).

Heteroromantic

Heteroromantic is an identity/orientation that falls within the broader category of asexual and ACE identities. It typically refers to a person who is romantically attracted to someone of, what that person considers to be, the opposite sex or gender (O'Brink, 2014).

Language around Oppression

Microaggressions

Microaggressions are "subtle, yet pervasive experiences of bias" (Sand, Singh, & Rossman, 2017, p. 27) that are expressed through "verbal, nonverbal, and environmental slights, snubs or insults" (Sue, 2010, para. 2). Microaggressions can be enacted both intentionally and unintentionally. Unintentional microaggressions, in which the aggressor is unaware that they have caused harm, are just as harmful as intentional slights. It is critical that sex therapists understand the impacts of microaggressions and keenly attend to their own biases and countertransferential reactions around erotically marginalized clients to minimize the risk of enacting microaggressions in the therapy space. This involves intentional and critical thought about differential identity and power dynamics between client and clinician.

Gatekeeping

Gatekeeping is the process by which individuals and/or communities are kept out of spaces. Gatekeeping is an enactment of structural oppression that can manifest as both horizontal oppression and intersectional discrimination.

Gatekeeping can manifest in a multitude of ways including denying individuals of particular identities entrance to spaces and/or conversations, policing what voices and perspectives are allowed to speak and be heard, and invalidating individual identity expressions. In a therapeutic context, gatekeeping is most often understood as a therapist's power to provide a client access to gender affirming healthcare, such as gender affirming hormones or gender confirming surgeries, by means of writing letters of support.

Gaslighting

Gaslighting is a form of abuse that can occur within romantic relationships, family systems, and organizations. Gaslighting makes a victim question their experiences and realities. It can manifest as blatant lie telling, denying facts, incongruence between words and behaviors, creating intentional confusion, and generally denying another's reality. Calef and Weinshel (1981) reflect that, from a psychodynamic perspective, gaslighting can be understood as an "interjective defense" (p. 64) where a "victimizer" externalizes and projects psychic conflict onto a "victim," who internalizes the messages.

Erotophobia

Erotophobia refers to a range of phobias related to sex, as well as a general fear of sex. Erotophobia includes specific fears such as intimacy, sexual contact, vulnerability, nudity, kissing, etc. and may be experienced as a confluence of multiple fears. Erotophobia can be understood as "a basic underpinning of the culture of the United States" (founded by Puritans, lest we forget) (Gomez, 2011, p. 74).

Transphobia

Transphobia "relates to negative reactions that people have toward TGNC people related to their gender identity" (Singh & Dickey, 2017, p. 6).

Cissexism

Cissexism is the belief that being cisgender is "normal" and any other gender experience is "abnormal" and to be pathologized. Cissexism encompasses cissexual assumption, the assumptions held by many cisgender individuals that everyone they meet is also cisgender. Ethical practice with erotically marginalized individuals requires a decentralization of cissexism.

Homophobia

Homophobia is traditionally defined as the dislike, disgust, and/or fear of people who identify as lesbian, gay, or bisexual. We can also understand homophobia as the dislike and/or fear of individuals whose sexual identities fall outside of heterosexual – i.e. homophobia can be expressed towards queer identified individuals. Homophobia manifests as oppression when it is expressed in derogatory, aggressive, threatening, and/or microaggressive ways.

Heterosexism

Heterosexism is the belief that heterosexuality is "a normal, natural, or superior state of human sexual orientation, and the system of oppression based on that belief" (Russo, 2014, para. 1). Similar to cissexism, it is crucial that heterosexism be decentralized in a therapeutic context.

Chronic illness

A chronic illness is defined by the U.S. National Center for Health Statistics as a disease or illness lasting three or more months. While some chronic illnesses have clear treatment trajectories, other chronic illness have additional layers of complexity that can make it difficult for others to understand the realities and effects of these illnesses. As Morales (2013) describes,

> *People with the chronic illnesses that affect many systems . . . don't usually know exactly what is causing us to be sick the same symptoms can have difference causes, and how sick we are can vary a lot. Healthy people find this confusing. They think that "real" sickness is consistent. If the symptoms change from day to day, they can't be real.*
>
> *(p. 70).*

Some examples of chronic illness that people often experience oppression around are fibromyalgia, chronic fatigue, and Lyme's disease.

Invisible disability

Invisibility disabilities are disabilities of any kind that are not immediately visible to others. Examples of invisible disabilities include chronic pain, sleep disorders, HIV/Aids, fibromyalgia, and mental illnesses.

Visible disability

Visible disabilities are disabilities that are in some way visible to others. Examples of cues for visible disabilities include wheelchair and other mobility assistance use and signs of hearing impairment.

System

A system is a group of dissociated self-states, also called "parts" or "alters," that exist within one body ("Systems and Subsystems," 2016). The term is most commonly associated with Dissociative Identity Disorder, but can be relevant for clients with a range of dissociative experiences and diagnoses. Different parts "front" at different times. This means that different self-states, which have their own ages, genders, needs, perspectives on the world, and trauma experiences, alternate operating the body's executive functioning and interacting with the outside world ("Alters," 2016; Parry, Lloyd, & Simpson, 2017). Systems can consist of as few as two alters, or as many as hundreds ("Alters"). The concept of systems should be considered from trauma and family systems lenses. In a system, one part may have experienced trauma while other parts may have been shielded from that trauma (Parry, Lloyd, & Simpson). If multiple parts are trying to participate in therapy, there can be a significant amount of coded language used by different parts to protect other parts.

Relationship Orientations

Relationship orientations refers to the structure of romantic and sexual relationships that a person enters into. For some people, their relationship orientation is an important part of their identity. Although monogamy is socially constructed "as the dominant model for relationships in Western Society" (Chatara-Middleton, 2012, p. 116), many individuals engage in other structures of relationships.

Monogamy

Monogamy is a relational structure consisting of two people who are romantic and/or sexual only with each other, and romantic or sexual interaction with others outside of that dyad is forbidden. Monogamy is socially constructed "as the dominant model for relationships in Western Society" (Chatara-Middleton, 2012, p. 116).

Nonmonogamy

Nonmonogamy is a broad term that describes a range of relational structuring that are not monogamous, i.e., that are not limited to an exclusive dyadic partnership. U.S. based therapists have historically pathologized non-monogamous behaviors (Finn et al., 2012). In the early-1970s, when literature was being produced that showed individuals' positive experiences with non-monogamy, therapists largely condemned these relationship structures and held "a preference for clients to adopt a 'healthier' form of coupledom" (p. 206). Therapists made "assumptions about feared intimacy, unhealthy attachment styles, and unfulfilling marriages" (p. 206), which appear to be based in clinician bias. This pervasive belief in the superiority of monogamy, and the pathology of non-monogamy, began to shift slightly in the 1980s when social work literature saw "several positive or poly-friendly accounts of open non-monogamies" (p. 206). This literature, however, was limited to largely considering gay, cisgender male open relationships. Without an understanding of the meanings of non-monogamy for individual clients, sex therapists are at risk for misunderstanding their clients, projecting their personal beliefs about healthy relationship structures onto clients, and pathologizing clients.

Polyamory

Polyamory, sometimes shortened to "poly," is a form of non-monogamy, and is the ideology and practice of being in multiple romantic relationships at the time same, with full knowledge and consent of all parties. Polyamory is based on the belief that individuals have the capacity to love more than one person at a time, and can do so in an ethical way. There are many ways that polyamorous relationships can be structured; two polyamorous people may practice polyamory differently, with different understandings, values, and expectations in their relationships (Benson, 2016; Burdo, 2016; Ritchie & Barker, 2006). People who practice polyamory often identify as "polyamorous." For some people this identity label is an important part of their identity; "Many polyamorous people talk of polyamory as something they *are* rather than something they *do*" (Ritchie & Barker, 2006, p. 590).

Open relationship

An open relationship is typically defined as a dyadic romantic partnership in which both partners are allowed, by the structure of the relationship, to have sexual and/or romantic relations with others outside of the dyad.

Relationship anarchy

Relationship anarchy (RA) as a concept stems from political anarchy, and can be understood as an application of anarchistic political principles in interpersonal relationships. It is a way of living that rejects social hierarchy, including a distinction in importance between friends and romantic or sexual partners. RA differs from polyamory in that, whereas many polyamorous practices rely on fixed rules and boundaries, RA focuses more on the freedom of those involved and resists relational contracts.

Monogamish

Monogamish is a relational structuring that is primarily, but not exclusively, monogamous.

Triad

A triad is a romantic and/or sexual relational structure consisting of three people.

Compersion

Compersion is a term created by and for non-monogamous individuals that refers to a feeling of joy, pleasure, and/or arousal in response to a romantic or sexual partner taking pleasure from another relationship (Burdo, 2016; Ritchie & Barker, 2006).

Sexual Practices

BDSM

The acronym BDSM can be broken into these components:

-B/D, bondage and discipline

-S/m, sadomasochism or sadism and masochism

-D/s, dominance and submission or Dominant/submissive.

BDSM is a broad term that includes a variety of activities and dynamics which "generally involve the exchange of some form of power or pain, often but not exclusively, in a sexual context" (Barker, Iantaffi, & Gupta, 2008, p. 107). BDSM activities are framed as "play" (Barker, Iantaffi, & Gupta, 2008) and can involve "pain play, tying people up, taking dominant and submissive roles, and the erotic exchange of power" (Moon, 2008, p. 141). BDSM involves negotiation, consent, safewords, and aftercare. It is important to understand that pain and power play within BDSM is explicitly negotiated and consensual. BSDM play is very different from non-consensual sexual sadism. For example, in many BDSM dynamics the "bottom" or "submissive/sub" is understood as actually having the most power as they are "choosing to topped . . . they are the one in the position of power" (Barker, Iantaffi, & Gupta, 2008, p. 111). For some people BDSM activities are understood as activities they practice; for others BDSM is experienced as an important part of sexual identity. BDSM practices have been historically pathologized in popular culture and within a therapeutic context.

Negotiation, Consent, Safewords, and Aftercare

BDSM is commonly understood as having four pillars:

- *Negotiation* is connected to ideas of communication and consent. Each BDSM scene or act involves an initial negotiation process with clear discussion of each participant's desires, wants, needs, boundaries/limits, worries, and fantasies before beginning any play (Taormino, 2014).
- *Consent* is "explicit, informed verbal approval after negotiation" (Taormino, 2014, p. 28). "When you ask for consent, you clearly speak

your part in the exchange: I need to know you've agreed to this before we begin" (p. 28).

- *Safewords* are pre-determined words that a partner can use to end a scene or a sexual act if it no longer works for them (Moon, 2008).
- *Aftercare* is "the period after a BDSM scene when the top looks after the bottom, bringing them up from any submissive headspace and often praising them in general and in relation to the scene they have endured" (Moon, 2008, p. 141).

Dominant

Dominant, "domme," or "dom" comes from Dominant/submissive dynamics, which is a component of BDSM and a practice within the BDSM community. Dominant describes the person in a Dominant/submissive (D/s) dynamic that takes erotic and/or psychological control of the submissive. Some folks play with D/s dynamics exclusively in a sexual context, others incorporate D/s dynamics into their relational structures.

Submissive

Submissive or "sub" can be used as a noun ("I am a sub/submissive"), a verb ("I want to sub"), or an adjective ("I want to be submissive"). Submission is part of a Dominant/submissive (D/s) dynamic, in which the submissive partner gives up erotic and/or sexual control to the Dominant/Domme/Dom. Submissive is different than bottom in that, while bottom describes being controlled physically, submissive includes an element of psychological control given to the Dominant partner. Some folks play with D/s dynamics exclusively in a sexual context, others incorporate D/s dynamics into their relational structures.

Dominatrix

A dominatrix, sometimes called a "Domme," is an individual who plays a dominating role in a sadomasochistic relationship. Professional dominatrixes are a type of sex worker who work with clients, also known as submissives, and enable fantasies and desires of humiliation and domination in exchange for money. Dominatrixes may, or may not, engage in sexual relationships with submissives. The relationship is categorized by consensual dominating and/or humiliating dynamics. Anne O Nomis, author of *The History & Arts of the Dominatrix*, is quoted (Amo, 2014, para. 9) as describing dominatrix practice as a form of art,

> *There is a visual aesthetic, as well as aspects of performance, practices with props and equipment which is as specialized as any field of occupational profession. The practices are paired with intricate knowledge, passed on like a batten of erotic wisdom from senior Mistress practitioners to apprentices.*

Top

Top is a casual term for someone who enjoys being in control physically while engaging in sexual and/or BDSM play. Top can be used as both a noun ("I am a top") and a verb ("They topped me last night") (Moon, 2008; Taormino, 2014).

Bottom

Bottom is a slang term used to describe someone who takes pleasure from being controlled physically. Bottoms typically follow the lead or directions of a top and receive stimulation from the top. Bottom can be used as both a noun ("I want to be a bottom") and a verb "(It felt good when I bottomed") (Moon, 2008; Taormino, 2014). In BDSM circles "bottoms are often perceived as having more control" than tops (Barker, Iantaffi, & Gupta, 2008, p. 115).

Switch

A switch is a person who enjoys playing in both top and bottom roles. Switches may want to be a top in one scene and a bottom in the next; they may want to top in certain activities or types of play and bottom in others (Moon, 2008; Taormino, 2014).

Kink

Kink is an umbrella term for sexual desires, fantasies, and/or practices that are outside of culturally prescribed and socially constructed ideas of "normal sex." Kink includes, but is not limited to, BDSM, erotic role playing, fantasies, fetishes, and group sex (Taormino, 2014).

Safe, Sane, and Consensual (SSC)

BDSM is often framed as SSC – Safe, Sane, and Consensual. This "BDSM slogan . . . explicitly counters popular taken-for-granted assumptions that BSDM activities are dangerous, mentally unhealthy and abusive" (Barker, Iantaffi, & Gupta, 2008, p. 111).

Risk-aware Consensual Kink (RACK)

Some folks who practice BDSM and/or kink prefer the framing of Risk-aware Consensual Kink (RACK) to the framing of Safe, Sane, and Consensual. The RACK framework emphasizes informed choice and consent around possible risks of sexual/power play activities, as well as harm reduction strategies (Barker, Iantaffi, & Gupta, 2008). For individuals and communities who feel that the SSC framing puts an "unrealistic commitment to safety over risk-taking," (p. 111) they may see the RACK framework as allowing for more complexity as well as behaviors that have a higher level of perceived risk.

Bareback intercourse

The term bareback intercourse became popularized in the mid-1990, initially referring to anal intercourse without a condom, particularly among HIV positive gay men (Carballo-Diéguez, et al., 2009). Today individuals of different sexual orientations and HIV statuses may use the term to connote sexual penetration without the use of a condom.

Sex worker

A sex worker is someone who exchanges sexual services for money and/or goods. The sexual services a sex worker provides ranges and may or may not include live physical sexual contact.

Full service sex worker

Full service sex worker is a term that typically refers to a sex worker whose sexual services include penetrative sexual intercourse.

References

Alters. (2016, July 15). Retrieved from www.did-research.org.

American Psychological Association. (2006). *Answers to your questions about individuals with intersex conditions*. Retrieved from https://www.apa.org/topics/lgbt/intersex.pdf.

Amo, C. T. (2014, October 14). *The history & arts of the dominatrix: An interview with Anne O Nomis*. Retrieved from www.slutist.com.

Barker, M., Iantaffi, A., & Gupta C. (2008). Kinky clients, kinky counseling? The challenges and potentials of BDSM. In Moon. L (Ed.), *Feeling queer or queer feelings: Radical approaches to counseling sex, sexualities and gender* (pp.106–124). London: Routledge.

Benson, K. L. (2016). Tensions of subjectivity: The instability of queer polyamorous identity and community. *Sexualities*, *20*(1–2), 24–40. doi:10.1177/1363460716642154

binaohan, b. (2014). Decolonizing trans/gender 101. Retrieved from: http://publishbiyuti.org/decolonizingtransgender101/.

Burdo, K. (2016, November 21). 7 Poly terms everyone should know, whether you're new to polyamory or monogamous. Retrieved from www.bustle.com/articles/161962-7-poly-terms-everyone-should-know-whether-youre-new-to-polyamory-or-monogamous.

Calef, V. and Weinshel, E. M. (1981). Some clinical consequences of introjection: gaslighting. *Psychoanalytic Quarterly*, *50*, 44–46.

Carballo-Diéguez, A., Ventuneac, A., Bauermeister, J., Dowsett, G. W., Dolezal, C., Remien, R. H., Rowe, M. (2009). Is "bareback" a useful construct in primary HIV-prevention? Definitions, identity, and research. *Culture, Health & Sexuality*, *11*(1), 51–65. http://doi.org/10.1080/13691050802419467

Chatara-Middleton, A. (2012). Working wth non-monogamy: Dance/movement therapists' experience of working with individuals in non-monogamous relationships. *American Journal of Dance Therapy*, *34*(2), 114–128. doi:10.1007/s10465-012-9138-6

Cole, B. (2011). Masculine of centre, seeks her refined femme. In *Persistence: All ways butch and femme* (pp. 127–136). Vancouver: Arsenal Pulp Press.

Dark, K. (2011). My first lover was not a lesbian. In *Persistence: All ways butch and femme* (pp. 31–36). Vancouver: Arsenal Pulp Press.

Ehrensaft, D. (2011). *Gender born, gender made: Raising healthy gender-conforming children*. New York: The Experiment.

Finn, M. D., Tunariu, A. D., & Lee, K. C. (2012). A critical analysis of affirmative therapeutic engagements with consensual non-monogamy. *Sexual and Relationship Therapy, 27*(3), 205–216. doi:10.1080/14681994.2012.702893

Foucault, M. (1977). *The history of sexuality, Vol. I*. London: Routledge.

Gomez, J. (2011). Femme butch feminist. In Coyote, I. E. & Sherman, Z., *Persistence: All ways butch and femme* (pp. 67–78). Vancouver: Arsenal Pulp Press.

Halberstam, J. (2005). *In a queer time and place: Transgender bodies, subcultural lives*. New York: New York University Press.

Hilda. (2015, April 1). How common is intersex? An explanation of the stats. Retrieved from www.intersexequality.com.

Hird, M. J. (2008). Queer(y)ing intersex: Reflections on counselling people with intersex conditions. In Moon, L., *Feeling queer or queer feelings? Radical approaches to counselling sex, sexualities and genders* (pp. 54–71). New York: Routledge.

Hock, R. R. (2012). *Human sexuality* (3rd ed.). Boston, MA: Pearson.

Hodges, I. (2008). Queer dilemmas: The problem of power in psychotherapeutic and counselling practice. In Moon. L (Ed.), *Feeling queer or queer feelings: Radical approaches to counseling sex, sexualities and gender* (pp. 7–22). London: Routledge.

Kafer, A. (2013). *Feminist queer crip*. Bloomington, IN: Indiana University Press.

Kuper, L. E., Nussbaum, R., & Mustanski, B. (2012). Exploring the diversity of gender and sexual orientation identities in an online sample of transgender individuals. *Journal of Sex Research, 49*, 244–254.

Lindahl, H. (2018, June 2). We need to end intersex erasure in queer community. Retrieved from www.them.us.

Mayor, C. (2011). Me, Simone, and Dot. In Coyote, I. E. & Sarman, Z., *Persistence: All ways butch and femme* (pp. 154–165). Vancouver: Arsenal Pulp Press.

Middleton, D. R. (2002). *Exotics and erotics: Human cultural and sexual diversity*. Long Grove, IL: Waveland Press.

Morales, A. L. (2013). *Kindling: Writings on the body*. Cambridge, MA: Palabrea Press.

Moon, L. (2008). Glossary. In Moon, L, *Feeling queer or queer feelings? Radical approaches to counselling sex, sexualities and genders* (pp. 72–88). New York: Routledge.

Namaste, V. K. (2000). *Invisible Lives: The erasure of trans-sexual and trans-gendered people*. Chicago, IL: University of Chicago Press.

Nanda, S. (2000). *Gender diversity: Crosscultural variations*. Long Grove, IL: Waveland Press.

O'Brink, S. (2014). *Asexual and aromantic vocabulary*. Retrieved from www.mathews place.com.

Parry, S., Lloyd, M, & Simpson, J. (2017). "It's not like you have PSTD with a touch of dissociation": Understanding dissociative identity disorder through first person accounts. *European Journal of Trauma & Dissociation, 2*(1), pp. 31–38. Retrieved from https://doi.org/10.1016/j.ejtd.2017.08.002.

Redmiles, K. (2016, February 23). Life in the between: The beauty and importance of the Two-Spirit people. Retrieved from http://www.kosmosjournal.org/.

Ritchie, A., & Barker, M. (2006)."“There aren't words for what we do or how we feel so we have to make them up”: Constructing polyamorous languages in a culture of compulsory monogamy. *Sexualities, 9*(5), 584–601. doi:10.1177/1363460706069987
Russo, J. (2014). Definition of “heterosexism” [Blog post]. Retrieved from http://queerdictionary.blogspot.com/2014/09/definition-of-heterosexism.html.
Sand, C., Singh, A., & Rossman, K. (2017). Gender and sexual orientation diversity within the TGNC community. In Singh, A. & Dickey, L., *Affirmative counseling and psychological practice with transgender and gender nonconforming clients* (pp. 19–40). Washington, DC: American Psychological Association.
Sanger, T. (2008). Queer(y)ing gender and sexuality: Transpeople's lived experiences and intimate partnerships. In *Feeling queer or queer feelings? Radical approaches to counselling sex, sexualities and genders* (pp. 72–88). New York: Routledge.
Shlasko, D. (2014). *Trans* ally workbook: Getting pronouns right & what it teaches us about gender.* Madison, WI: Think Again Training & Consulting.
Singer, Phoenix A. (nd). “Colonialism, Two-Spirit identity, and the logics of white supremacy.” Retrieved from www.academia.edu/2259929/Colonialism_Two-Spirit_Identity_and_the_Logics_of_White_Supremacy. Accessed May 7, 2017.
Singh, A. A., & Dickey, L. M. (2017). *Affirmative counseling and psychological practice with transgender and gender nonconforming clients.* Washington, DC: American Psychological Association.
Sue, D. W. (2010, November 17). Microaggressions: More than just race. *Psychology Today.* Retrieved from www.psychologytoday.com/us/blog/microaggressions-in-everyday-life/201011/microaggressions-more-just-race.
Systems and Subsystems. (2016, March 3). Retrieved from www.did-research.org.
Taormino, T. (2014). *50 shades of kink: An introduction to BDSM.* Jersey City, NJ: Cleis Press.
Tilsen, J. B. (2013). *Therapeutic conversations with queer youth: Transcending homonormativity and constructing preferred identities.* Lanham, MD: Jason Aronson.
Zevallos, Z. (2013, September 9). Rethinking gender and sexuality: Case study of the Native American “Two Spirit” people. Retrieved from https://othersociologist.com/.

Appendix A

INSTITUTION/AGENCY AFFILIATION (IF ANY)

Clinician Name
Office Address
Clinician Email address
Clinician Phone Number

Date:
Name of Client (nee: legal name is different than name used):
Address:
Phone:
Email:
To Whom It May Concern:

My name is (Clinician Name); I am an independently licensed gender and sexuality psychotherapist at ____________________. I am also the founder of ____________, an advocacy, education, and training organization that works with institutions, agencies, and groups to increase awareness for trans and/or gender nonconforming identities. I am writing this letter of referral for (client name), who is a __-year-old (D.O.B. here) trans/nonbinary person living in ____________. At (client name)'s request, I have evaluated him over the course of the last three months and have established that he is properly informed and prepared for gender affirming chest reconstruction surgery.

I have been meeting weekly with ________ over the last two years, which was when he began his transition. ________ is currently taking Danazol, a synthetic androgen, to halt the menstrual cycle and lower estrogen in his system. After almost a year taking Danazol, which ________ is taking instead of testosterone for decreased estrogen in his system, ________ feels that he is ready to move forward with gender affirming surgical chest reconstruction and he intends to stay in therapy through the process of his medical/surgical transition. ________ is using Danazol as a way to help with gender dysphoria related to menstruation and to help with mood levels. ________ clearly meets the DSM-5 diagnosis for Gender Dysphoria and has been out as trans in all areas of his life, including his work places. His gender identification is affirmed by his support system and he has consolidated a trans identity through support from his jobs, at ______. ______ has an active lifestyle and healthy eating habits; he also lives with two roommates, who share his values about life, health, and nutrition.

Over the course of the last five months ______ has explored his gender history and how his identity has impacted his life, starting from family of origin and moving through to present day. He has been properly informed of the short and long term effects of transition and chest reconstruction and feels he is ready to move forward with his medical transition. ______ states, "At the minimum, not having to bind every day will have a huge impact on my physical and emotional well-being. Day-to-day I anticipate being able to stand taller, and breathe deeper. When I look in the mirror after a shower I will see the chest that I imagine. When my partner touches my chest, I won't be afraid that she'll accidently touch it in the wrong way. When I exercise I'll be able to expand and contract my back, stomach, and chest without feeling the tension of an elastic band holding me back from growing in the direction I desire." ______'s support systems include his partner of four years, his mother, and a handful of extremely close friends. He intends to continue individual therapy for added support, and I am available to coordinate care with all of his providers.

These are the treatment recommendations that I am making at this time:

- First name/Last name should continue on an appropriate dose of Danazol.
- First name/Last name should be cleared for chest reconstructive surgery.
- First name/Last name should continue weekly/bi-weekly psychotherapy as a clinical support component of his gender affirming treatment and transition.

First name/Last name meets the DSM-5 criteria for Gender Dysphoria, and the WPATH standards for eligibility and readiness, as well as the criteria for medical necessity, and it is my recommendation that he should be cleared for gender affirming chest reconstruction as the next step in his transition process.

Sincerely,
Clinician name, Credentials

Appendix B

Shannon L. Sennott, LICSW

TRANSLATE GENDER, INC.
CENTER FOR PSYCHOTHERAPY AND SOCIAL JUSTICE
EMAIL: SHANNON.SENNOTT@GMAIL.COM

Self-Determined Gender Psychosocial Form

**The Gender Psychosocial Form was originally created by Arlene Lev, LCSW-R, CASAC, CST. The Self-Determined Gender Psychosocial Form is an adapted version.*

Name and address and years lived there (Please include email telephone and email information):
Age: ___________
Birth date: _______________
Country of Residence (do you hold dual citizenship?): ___________________
Ethnic/Racial/National identity (i.e., where are your ancestors from, how you identify your cultural background; please be specific, and make note of ways that this identification is important to you.):

In your own words, state your reasons for wanting to begin gender affirming medical treatments.

What medical treatments are you preparing for at this time?

Why are you seeking treatment at this point and not at another time in your life?

How do you think that the gender affirming medical treatment you are seeking will impact you? What are your greatest hopes and fears about this treatment?

Please share some details about your family of origin. Describe your parents, the quality of their connection, and any other significant relationships for them. What is the health status of your parents?

Siblings (Names, ages (include yourself in the birth order)), partnership status, children, and relationship to you:

Using 3–5 words, describe each of your parents and siblings:

Using 3–5 words, describe your relationship to each of your parents and siblings:

How did your family understand your gender identity growing up?

Describe your current home environment:

Are there any specific issues about your family that would be helpful for us to know about? Events that happened when you were young (i.e., divorces, deaths, abuse, mental health concerns) that affected your childhood development?

How do you think your family and/or parent/s will feel about your choice to seek gender affirming treatments? Have you told them about your decision? If not, do you intend to? If you do how do you plan to share this with them?

If you are currently in any relationships, please discuss your relationship(s) below. Describe how you met, how long you've been together, if you live together, and if possible, try to describe the quality of your connection(s).

Please list 5 words to describe your partner(s):

Please list 5 words to describe yours and your partner(s)'s relationship(s):

Please discuss your communication patterns. How do you argue? How do you resolve your disagreements?

What do you enjoy doing together with your partner(s)?

Has there ever been any violence in your relationship(s)? If so, please describe, if you are comfortable doing so:

Please list any significant previous relationships below:

Do you have children? Please list your children's names and ages:

How do you anticipate them navigating your gender affirming treatments? Have you told them? If not, how do you plan to do so?

Please list your educational background, schooling completed and where, degrees earned, current pursuits:

Please write your current job title, place of employment, number of years at this job, and job satisfaction:

Please write about any history of medical or psychological concerns you've struggled with in the past, or are currently still addressing. This can include physical health concerns, physical disabilities, and any mental health concerns. Also, please include any criminal history, if pertinent to your intentions around gender affirming treatments:

Are you taking any medications? Please list the name, dosages, prescribing physician, and reasons for use:

Do you use alcohol? If yes, please state what you drink and how often:

Do you use any other substances for recreation or relaxation? If yes, please state what you use and how often:

Have you ever been treated for alcoholism and/or substance abuse? If yes, please state when, where, and current relationship to your recovery and/or your current use:

Have you ever been treated for a mental health concern, or been hospitalized for any mental health concerns? If yes, please state when, where, and how the issue was resolved or treated?

Are you currently engaging in any mental health treatment (psychotherapy, group therapy, couple counseling)? If yes, would you be open to signing a release of information to facilitate collaborative conversation if we think that could be beneficial? Please list name of practitioner below. (Note: you are under NO obligation to sign a release for consultation as part of the process of treatment or acquiring a letter for gender affirming treatments.):

How do you cope with stress and crisis? Give an example of a crisis you have faced and how you addressed it:

Describe how you first learned about trans and/or nonbinary identity development. Please describe your relationship to the process of understanding your own identity development?

When did you first begin to realize that your relationship to your sex/gender was different than others that you knew?

Describe your feelings and behaviors from childhood through adolescence regarding your gender identity:

If you could change your feelings about your gender, would you? If so, why?

Describe your current support systems:

Do you feel you have a community of people with similar gender identities/expressions to you? Are you connected to support groups with others who are navigating gender affirming medical treatments?

Do you have any concerns about starting gender affirming medical treatments at this time?

Appendix C

A.P.M.: THE ALLYSHIP PRACTICE MODEL FOR THE TRANSFEMINIST THERAPEUTIC APPROACH

Transfeminist therapists DO. . .

- Understand that everyone, regardless of their gender identity or expression, can be an activist and ally in the movement resisting gender oppression;
- Recognize the intersections of trans/gender justice with reproductive justice, the women's movement, and other justice movements;
- Recognize the intersections of gender with other systems of oppression (including, but not limited to: racism, classism, sexism, ageism, ableism, cissexism, heterosexism, misogyny, homophobia, transphobia);
- Acknowledge how gender privilege and oppression have and continue to operate in their own lives;
- Recognize that trans and/or gender non-conforming people need allies, just as all oppressed and marginalized people need allies;
- Provide space for people to self-identify their gender and provide space for people to self-identify the pronouns they use to describe or identify themselves;
- Use gender inclusive/all-gender language until the pronouns a person uses are established. This sometimes means asking what pronoun(s) and/or name a person uses (e.g. "What name do you use?" or, "What pronouns do you use?"). It is also important to receive consent to use this name/pronoun in some, or all, settings and to respect this confidentiality. Some people might prefer you use a certain pronoun in session, but not when talking to them on the phone when they are home, etc;
- Mirror back language, especially self-identification;
- Expect to make some mistakes – but never use this as an excuse for not acting;

- Acknowledge having made a mistake (e.g. mis-pronouning someone), apologize, correct themselves, and move on;
- Ask questions respectfully, and understand when someone elects not to respond if the question makes them feel uncomfortable.
- Work to create inclusive non-discrimination policies in their institutions, organizations, agencies and communities;
- Challenge oppressive language and behaviors in themselves and those around them;
- Avoid and challenge gender assumptions and stereotyping;
- Work to create and maintain accountable spaces (e.g. encourage transparent communication, obtain consent, take ownership of personal actions);

Transfeminist therapists DON'T. . .

- Believe that resisting oppression only benefits targets of oppression;
- Accept the status quo (e.g. the gender binary);
- Believe themselves to be experts on any person's identity other than their own;
- Assume an individual's sex, sexuality, or gender based upon the individual's appearance and/or presentation;
- "Out" a trans and/or gender nonconforming (or lesbian, gay, bisexual, queer, intersex, or questioning) person without their explicit consent;
- Place the name, pronouns, or self-identification of a trans and/or gender non-conforming person in quotation marks;
- Ask people about their bodies, genitalia, or sex lives;
- Assume that there are no trans and/or gender nonconforming people present;
- Assume that anyone knows what a trans and/or gender nonconforming person "looks like";
- Question a trans and/or gender nonconforming person's assessment of their identity or experience;
- Question anyone's assessment of whether an incident was transphobic;
- Deny their privilege;
- Assume that everyone has equal rights;
- Ignore acts of discrimination and oppression without taking action;
- Show pity and sympathy for targets of oppression;
- Use guilt – for one's personal and/or a group's actions, past or present – as a reason not to act.

Appendix D

Eve N. Bogdanove, LICSW

486 Main Street/PO Box 1011 ~ Greenfield, MA 01302
Telephone 413-992-6591

Note from the document author: This document has been developed over time in consultation with several colleagues from the ASSECT ALTsex listserv, in particular Dominic Davies and David Shannon.

Professional Ethics Statement: Policy on Dual Relationships

This document supplements my Practice Policies, including HIPPA laws, and addresses my practice policies as they relate specifically to dual relationships. Please read it to understand how I conduct myself as a mental health professional in my communities (geographic, cultural, recreational and social) and how you can expect me to respond to interactions that may occur between us should we share space in any community.

If you have a question about anything within this document, I encourage you to bring them up when we meet. Additionally, when new issues arise, there may be times when I need to update this policy. If I do so, I will notify you in writing of any policy changes and make sure you have a copy of the updated policy.

******

Providing psychotherapy services to people in the queer, kink and/or leather communities is similar to providing psychotherapy services in a small town, which makes clear separation between personal and professional life less possible. By choosing to provide psychotherapy services within my own communities, it is possible that I may know of and/or interact with clients, their friends or family (chosen or biological) before, during and after treatment.

Dual roles can raise questions about professional boundaries and ethics and for this reason it is important to me both professional and personally to maintain clear and transparent practice policies that are in alignment with the NASW Code of Ethics, Massachusetts state licensing board and laws and good clinical practice. My intention and practice is to protect your confidentiality, develop and maintain a effective therapeutic alliance, empower you to identify, process and communicate your feelings and needs as they related to any situation in or outside of a therapy session and respond to those feelings and needs in a reasonable and professional manner consistent with the specific therapeutic relationship we will or have develop(ed).

I have worked to build a positive professional reputation and am committed an ethical and thoughtful practice. I refer to the work of Ofer Zur, PhD (www.zurinstitute.com/DualRelationships2.pdf) as a guide for discussions with potential clients as it relates to the impact of and clinical considerations related to dual relationships in my work. For additional safeguards, I will seeking out case consultation as needed, collaborating with other professionals in the field on current best practices related to sharing community space, and routinely talking with clients pro-actively with whom I may share community space (in person and/or online) about any potential impacts (positive or negative) to their treatment.

Clients can expect direct conversation about these issues. If I have not raised the issue of dual relationships with you or possible contact outside of session in a shared community, then I am either unaware of the issue, or have decided it is most appropriate or clinically contraindicated to not discuss it until you, the client, brings it into the room. That being said, it is fair, appropriate and necessary for clients to raise ANY concern and know that I will not disclose information from/ about another client in responding to those concerns. The legal burden to protect client's confidentiality belongs to the professional not the client. I encourage clients to speak freely with me so that I can be aware of the complicated social networking. I will always err on the side of caution as it relates to confidentiality, so if there is ANY concern and clients do not raise it with me, I am not able to respond. If there is a concern raised and I am not able to respond to the specifics, I will communicate that directly.

1. As a general rule, I will not approach clients outside of session, or interact directly online unless we have discussed it previously in treatment. If we meet unexpectedly outside of session, I will always take my cue from the client and err on the side of caution to protect your confidentiality and emotional safety. I will never initiate direct communication or signal to others that I know you. If you choose to talk with me or introduce me to others, I will not disclose any information about our professional relationship.
2. Current clients: When it comes to my attention in or out of session, that I share community space with clients, I will talk with them about their needs and preferences as they related to any contact. Client should always let me know if they are planning on attending an event, so that if I am also

attending, we can talk about it before and negotiate how to share space within that community. If either of us have not anticipated an interaction and we do see each other, clients can expect that I will redirect my attention elsewhere up to and including leaving a shared event and that I will raise it at the next session for discussion to process what, if any, effect it had on you and potentially our therapy work together.

3. Potential clients: For those with whom I have had limited social/community relationships, it may be appropriate to work together as therapist and client, but only after I have an initial discussion by phone about the potential benefits or harm to you before agreeing to schedule an initial Intake. In the range between good friends and casual acquaintances, there is significant gray area and requires discussion of how the transition to a defined professional relationship may or may not work.

    3.1. If we already know each other well, and if either of us considers the other a good friend, or immediately connected to another close friend (e.g. current lover of an ex-lover), I will not take you on as a client. In some cases, I will be glad to talk with you personally and refer you to colleagues with similar practices with whom you do not share intimate proximity.
    3.2. If we are acquaintances or friends on social media with a limited real time relationship, and decide to work together, we will discuss the implications of any prior interaction and knowledge of each other in the phone intake or initial session as well as how working together might impact any future social connections. If we decide to continue work together, I will "unfriend" and block the you, the client, on any shared social media sites to protect the therapeutic alliance. Having information about each other that is not discussed in real time, could negatively impact your treatment.

4. Virtual communities: I utilize all available privacy settings and do not share any of my social media profiles with anyone who is not a real-time friend or aquaintence. If you have already seen any of my social media profiles either directly or through a friend, we will need to discuss what, if any, effect that had on you, and potentially on our therapy work together. If during our work together you become privy to personal information about me from any source, I encourage you to raise it in session, so we can discuss what, if any, effect it had on you and potentially our therapy work together.
5. As detailed in my Practice Policies/Social Media Policy, I do not accept friend requests from clients. In addition, I will not search clients online, but if/when I become aware of your online presence, I will block you so that you cannot intentionally view my personal profile.
6. Lastly, if any concern arises during the course of our work together, I hope you will raise any questions and concerns you may have, whether covered

here or not. I want to be able to help you, and others in shared communities, in a safe, ethical and comfortable way. It is often the case that clients come to me for issues and problems that are not all that related to what kind of sex they like; but they do not want to hide, translate or modify your/their presentation. In fact, this kind of censoring oneself in treatment is very difficult to do especially when one has strong feelings. I will always encourage clients to be open and share and let me do my job of protecting your and other client's confidentiality. If ever a question comes up that you are not sure if you should raise it, remember that it is likely clinically relevant and talking about it could be a helpful part of treatment.

By signing below, I acknowledge that I understand and accept the Policy & Procedure on Dual Relationships.

______________________________ ______/______/______

signature date

____

printed name

INDEX

For Product Safety Concerns and Information please contact our EU
representative GPSR@taylorandfrancis.com
Taylor & Francis Verlag GmbH, Kaufingerstraße 24, 80331 München, Germany

www.ingramcontent.com/pod-product-compliance
Ingram Content Group UK Ltd.
Pitfield, Milton Keynes, MK11 3LW, UK
UKHW022204190926
475702UK00003B/200
* 9 7 8 1 1 3 8 6 7 1 8 0 5 *